Wife, Mother and Mystic

(Blessed Anna-Maria Taigi)

Wife, Mother and Mystic

(Blessed Anna-Maria Taigi)

by

ALBERT BESSIÈRES, S.J.

translated by

REV. STEPHEN RIGBY

edited by

DOUGLAS NEWTON

TAN BOOKS AND PUBLISHERS, INC.
Rockford, Illinois 61105

Nihil Obstat: CAROLUS DAVIS, S.T.L.
Censor deputatus

Imprimatur: E. MORROGH BERNARD
Vic. Gen.

Westmonasterii, die Februarii, 1952

Originally published by Sands & Co. (Publishers), Ltd., 3 Trebeck St., London, W1, England, in 1952.

Reprinted by TAN Books and Publishers, Inc. in 1970, 1978, and 1982.

ISBN: 0-89555-058-X.

Printed and bound in the United States of America.

TAN BOOKS AND PUBLISHERS, INC.
P.O. Box 424
Rockford, Illinois 61105
1970

CONTENTS

5

INTRODUCTION

IN 1860 the Parisian Catholic newspaper *Univers* was suppressed by imperial authority for publishing an Encyclical of Pope Pius IX. Its Editor, the brilliant and incisive Louis Veuillot, who had made it a powerful weapon for championing the Church against the growing forces of atheistic materialism, took refuge in Rome. He arrived there at the moment that the Pope was considering the beatification of Anna-Maria Taigi. She had been dead no more than twenty-three years, yet the greatness of her soul had so impressed his mind that Louis Veuillot wrote to Pope Pius IX on March 6th of that year, begging him to introduce her cause. Not content with this, he consecrated to Anna-Maria Taigi a chapter of his book, *The Fragrance of Rome*.

Under the heading "Anna-Maria, Servant of God", he wrote:

"In the decree that introduces the process for the beatification of Anna-Maria it is said that she was chosen by God to draw souls to Him, to be a victim of expiation, to avert great catastrophies, all by the power of her prayers. . . .

"To the opened floodgates of iniquity God opposed a simple woman.

"She whose unknown name was thus announced to the world twenty-five years after her death, was, as far as social status counts, something even less than a 'simple woman'. She was the impoverished wife of a serving man at the palace of the Chigi.

7

"Thirty years before one could have met her in the streets, an old, infirm woman on her way to visit Our Lord, either sacramentally in a church or mystically at a sick bed. The dignity of her poverty, a certain air of majesty, the interested looks that passers-by turned on her attracted the attention of strangers. Sometimes with awe, sometimes in derision would be heard, 'There goes the saint!'

"In Rome, as everywhere, saints encounter a twofold trial—praise and calumny. They fear praise and love calumny. Poor Anna-Maria could not escape becoming one of the great personalities of Rome. She possessed the gift of miracles. She spread about her, with a large munificence, cures, consolation and light. For herself she asked only to obey, to love and to suffer. She lived by the labour of her hands.

"Numerous witnesses have testified to the splendour of this noble life. She was a Teresa, a contemplative . . . but without a cell. She had a husband to serve, a rough though good and upright man; she had many children, a thousand cares, frequent illnesses, enemies and detractors.

"She had been beautiful and attractive, but she did not wait till the flower of her beauty and grace had faded; she surrendered herself generously the moment her call came.

"Her intellectual gifts were altogether overshadowed by an unexampled miracle. Shortly after she had entered on the way of perfection there began to appear to her a golden globe which became as a sun of matchless light; in this all things were revealed to her.

"Past and future were to her an open book.

"She knew with certainty the fate of the dead.

Her gaze travelled to the ends of the earth and discovered there people on whom she had never set eyes, reading them to the depth of their souls. One glance sufficed; upon whatever she focused her thoughts, it was revealed to her and her understanding. She saw the whole world as we see the front of a building. It was the same with nations as with individuals; she saw the cause of their distresses and the remedies that would heal them.

"By means of this permanent and prodigious miracle, the poor wife of Domenico Taigi became a theologian, a teacher and a prophet. The miracle lasted forty-seven years. Until her death the humble woman was able to read this mysterious sun as an ever-open book. Until her death she looked into it solely for the glory of God; that is, when charity suggested or obedience demanded it. Should things for which she had not looked, or which she did not understand, appear she refrained from asking explanations.

"The poor, the great of the world, the princes of the Church came to her for advice or help. They found her in the midst of her household cares and often suffering from illness. She refused neither her last crust of bread nor the most precious moment of her time, yet she would accept neither presents nor praise.

"Her most powerful friends could not induce her to allow them to favour her children beyond the conditions in which they were born. When she was at the end of her resources she told God about it, and God sent what was necessary.

"She thought it good to live from day to day, like the birds. A refugee queen in Rome wished to give her money. 'Madame,' she said, 'how simple you are. I serve God, and He is richer than you.'

"She touched the sick, and they were cured; she warned others of their approaching end, and they died holy deaths. She endured great austerities for the souls in Purgatory, and the souls, once set free, came to thank her. . . . She suffered in body and soul. . . . She realised that her rôle was to expiate the sins of others, that Jesus was associating her with His sacrifice, and that she was a victim in His company. The pains of Divine Love have an intoxication no words can explain. After Holy Communion there were times when she sank down as though smitten by a prostrating stroke. To tell the truth, her state of ecstasy was continual because her sense of the presence of God was continual. . . . All pain was sweet to her. . . . She went her way, her feet all bloody; with shining eyes she followed the Royal Way.

"Behold, then, the spectacle God raised to men's sight in Rome during that long tempestuous period which began at the time the humble Anna-Maria took to the way of saints. Pius VI dies at Valence; Pius VII is a prisoner at Fontainebleau; the Revolution will reappear before Gregory XVI reigns. Men are saying that the day of the Popes is over, that Christ's law and Christ Himself are on the wane, that science will soon have relegated this so-called Son of God to the realm of dreams. . . . He will work no more miracles.

"But at precisely this time God raised up this woman to cure the sick. . . . He gives her knowledge of the past, present and future. She declares that Pius VII will return. . . . She sees even beyond the reign of Pius IX. . . . She is God's answer to the challenge of unbelief."

§

The pages which Louis Veuillot wrote in his little retreat at the Trinita dei Monti received the commendation of Pius IX; they are, in fact, a prophetic summary of the Decree of Beatification promulgated by Benedict XV, 30th May 1920. They were remembered with additional force in 1937, when the Church celebrated the centenary of the death of the Blessed Anna-Maria Taigi, the great lady of Rome—"the Patron of Rome", as Cardinal Salotti, her definitive biographer, calls her.

They are, furthermore, a fitting introduction to this volume. Blessed Anna-Maria Taigi was (and indeed is becoming more and more) "the answer of God" to a rationalism triumphant but restive and in search of the unknown God. The dedication of this book: "To those who are in search of God", and the quotations from Bergson and Louis Bertrand given in that dedication, bear emphatic witness to this questing restiveness. To them might be added the words of William James: "It is a question of finding out whether mystic states are not windows opening out on a new world", as well as those of Father Leonce de Grandmaison, S.J.: "These high experiences are signed and sealed like documents of their journeyings brought by explorers from inaccessible lands."

Therein is defined the object of this book. I have passed over nothing from a historical point of view, but the readers for whom I write would seem to be different from those for whom the early biographers of the saint wrote. I do not write primarily for believers already long established in the peace of the faith (although the book may perhaps serve their purpose as well), but for that throng whom St. Paul addressed from the steps of the Areopagus: the pilgrims in search of the unknown God, the God for whom they were groping, who was yet not far from them.

Now the reasonings of St. Paul would have only been partly effective if he had not been able to add, with the eloquence of an eye-witness: "This God, I have seen Him with my eyes, and heard Him with my ears. It is He who has transformed my life."

Pius XI speaks of "souls naturally Christian who have the faith, as it were a fire beneath the ashes", and so are predisposed to the light by "admirable natural virtues". To such souls this book would say: "Behold the answer of the Lord; behold news from the other world." Finally, for those who realise that "there are more things in heaven and earth than are dreamed of in our philosophy", these pages present a vast subject of meditation.

§

"Here below," said Napoleon at Fontanes, "there are only two powers, the sword and the spirit, but sooner or later the spirit conquers the sword." He did not know how truly he spoke. Documents of so detailed a nature that they cannot be ignored show the existence of an invisible duel organised by God, a duel to which the Decree cited at the beginning of the present work bears witness, between the Revolution and Anna Taigi; between him who was the victor over, and the soldier of, the Revolution, the helper and then the tormentor of the Papacy, Napoleon I, and this humble Roman matron. In this duel the Papacy, its liberty, its system of doctrine and morals stands for the "spirit", and is represented by an illiterate woman who shall have the last word. The Blessed Taigi shall conquer

Napoleon; and yet, by a divine vengeance, she shall console and shall guide in their exile the aged mother of the fallen Emperor, Letizia, and the brother of the Empress, Cardinal Fesch.

§

What I have just said must not make us overlook other aspects of this life. The mission of the saint, according to the Decree of Introduction and the Decree of Beatification, is manifold.

It is firstly a unique model for the family, for wives and mothers. It concerns a soul quite different from the virgins, nuns and widows canonised by the Church. The Blessed Taigi alone presents to our eyes the holiness of the mother of many children, of the wife who until death abides subject to a husband, "god-fearing and upright, but unpolished, rough and turbulent". She is a model for all wives, but especially for those who gain their bread in the sweat of their brow; Blessed Anna Taigi was poor. In her the Church will canonise the common life, the ideal of Nazareth.

Secondly, in this common life Anna Taigi is a victim of expiation; she atones for the sins of the shepherds and the sheep. On the heart of this poor woman the justice of God smites as on an anvil. . . . She is the lightning-conductor of the Papacy and of the world . . . at once, "the lightning-conductor and the lighthouse" in the revolutionary epoch. Thus do the Popes say, thus do they repeat.

It was an apocalyptic period in which thrones fell and people threw off restraints. Anna Taigi, in voluntary poverty, athirst for self-effacement, constitutes "the condemnation of this century wherein materialism, lies and pride predominate"—as Pius IX himself, the personified defence of the spiritual, said on 4th March 1874. Voltairian philosophy became a craze. Science, drunk with discovery of steam and electricity, had given its marching orders to the supernatural. God raises up an insignificant little woman to "cast down the pomp of the world, to oppose like a rock the waters of iniquity, raging to ruin the foundations of the Church and civil society. He makes of her a victim of expiation and a "bulwark of defence"*. The frontiers between the visible and invisible worlds are levelled to the ground, and God walks among men.

* Decree of Introduction.

PART I

THE PREPARATION

I

HER ORIGIN – THE GIANNETTI FAMILY – BIRTH – DISASTER – ROME – AT SCHOOL – ST. BENEDICT LABRE

ANNA-MARIA was born at Siena on 29th May 1769. She opened her eyes to a world in chaos, very like our own. In France the Court of Louis XV, sunk in debauchery, intrigues and factions, prepared the way for its own ruin and that of Christianity. The Minister Choiseul rejoiced to see the Press flood France with literature that scoffed at traditional beliefs. *The Encyclopædia*, for a while suppressed, thrived anew, and Voltaire was in the ascendant. As an old man of seventy-five he inundated the world with his "encyclicals".

The vitality of all things was sapped at the root—the Church, morals, royalty. Jeering displaced discussion. Vice was brazen and shameless. Louis XV, at sixty, put the finishing touch to his royal disgrace. The libertines, to dissuade him from a new marriage which might have reclaimed him, threw him a woman taken from the gutter, by the name of du Barry. The price of bread rose, the national deficit touched seventy-four millions, the people murmured; the young prince whose inclement destiny it was to become Louis XVI married an Austrian archduchess, the unfortunate Maria-Antoinette. Magnificent celebrations were sullied by the presence of Mme du Barry and by the blood of

1,200 Parisians whom the firework display threw into a panic.

At Rome reigns Clement XIV, who is about to suppress the Jesuits at the instigation of the Bourbons. The most Catholic nations are dragged into this whirlpool: Spain, Italy, Poland. The nobility of the last were second to none in godlessness; even the king sold his motherland. A Masonic Temple was installed at Warsaw on 7th July 1770, and the nuncio reported 250 carriages drawn up at its gate and the flower of the nobility thronging into it. The very princesses craved the honour of Masonic affiliation, following the example of the Princess de Lamballe. The Duke of Orleans (Philip Égalité) was to be President of French Freemasonry.

§

At Siena, the home of Anna-Maria, the Jesuits, driven from their college, had to live as seculars.

The "Beata" sprang from an honourable family. Her grandfather, Peter Giannetti (the name is spelt with one "n" or two, indifferently) kept a chemist's shop in Siena; his son Louis, taught the same trade, married a good Catholic of lowly fortune, Mary Santa Masi, who bore him, on 29th May 1769, a girl child, the future Beata. Two and a half months later, on the Feast on the Assumption, on the Island of Corsica, facing this Tuscan territory, Napoleon I was born. Like Anna, he was of Italian and Tuscan blood. Like her, he was of a middle-class but impoverished family. Thirty years later their souls were to encounter each other before the Chair of Peter—he, the conqueror of the world, striving to overthrow that Chair; she, the poor wife of a porter, defending it like a second Catherine of Siena, who in the fourteenth century had been "the bulwark of the Papacy". Again the weak thing was to have the last word.

Although in all probability Napoleon and Annette never saw one another, nevertheless "history", as Cardinal Salotti writes, "must unite these two names when it speaks of the misfortunes of Pius VII, dragged from one prison to another by the all-powerful Emperor, yet inwardly sustained by the tears and prayers of this holy woman". Pius VII regains his liberty: the Emperor is shut up in Elba. "The prayer of the Beata had more power than the might of the Imperial armies. History, which concerns itself with the study of human, social and political events, takes no account of a poor woman's influence on the fall of Napoleon. But what the historian does not see are the mysterious ways of God, who, at the prayer of a simple soul, decrees the destruction of the mighty and the humiliation of the proud."

Anna was baptised the day after her birth, in the Church of St. John Baptist at Siena. She received the names of Anna Maria Antonia Gesualda. Cared for by her mother, she passed her child-life playing among the olives and cypresses, the trellised vines and roses that crown the high plateau that dominates, with its red walls, the sandy plains of Tuscany. It was the landscape that had been familiar to Catherine, the twenty-third child of Benincasa, the dyer, and the despotic Lappa, who at the age of six, in 1352, saw the Christ appear above the church of the Dominicans, dressed in pontificals and crowned with the tiara, calling her to the salvage of the "little bark" of Peter, and who thereafter took upon herself the burdens of the church until she died at the age of thirty-three.

At six, Anna's life also underwent a portentous

change. She and her family left Siena for Rome.
Luigi Giannetti's business had failed, either because
his debts were too heavy and those who owed him
money too neglectful, or because of his lack of
business sense and his extravagance. His collapse
was complete and was to embitter his life. Yet he
remained an honourable man, making no attempt to
evade what he owed, though it meant selling all he
had. Still, shame at his fall was strong upon him,
and he and his wife and Anna stole from Siena in
the early morning when few eyes could see their
going. In poor clothes and carrying the remnants of
their belongings in packages, they set out to seek a
new fortune. It was ordained that it should be misfortune, for it was necessary to God's plan that in
Rome the daughter of Luigi and Santa should live
the life of the poor.

It was the year 1775. Pius VI, who had recently
been elected, had proclaimed it a Holy Year—he
was to die, after a reign of twenty-four years, a
prisoner at Valence. It is possible that the little
group joined one of the pilgrim parties going to
Rome. The journey was made in short stages to save
the child Annette from fatigue, the nights being
passed in the houses of hospitable farmers on the
road. In Rome they were able to take advantage of
the arrangements the Pope had made for the reception of the crowds.

§

The three pilgrims of involuntary poverty found a
home in the crowded dei Monti quarter, where lived
that pilgrim of voluntary poverty, St. Benedict
Labre. Here, until the death of the saint eight years
later (1783), the Giannetti lived under a humble
roof in the street dei Vergini. There can be no

doubt they often met the holy young man, whose features recalled Robespierre's, at the Church of Our Lady dei Monti, at the foot of the miraculous statue of the Virgin, which was the witness of his ecstasies and the guardian of his tomb. On "Spy-Wednesday" 1783 this unique beggar fell dying on the steps of a church. He was carried into a butcher's house in the Via dei Serpenti, and died there at eight o'clock at night, his age being thirty-five years.

The children—Annette no doubt among them; she was then fourteen—went about the town crying, "The saint is dead!" Rome was going to give triumphal obsequies to a lousy mendicant.* Santa, Annette's mother, being "used to performing such acts of charity," helped wash the body and put it in its shroud. This would ever after be a precious memory in the family. Santa always carried a picture of the saint, invoking him and drawing from this souvenir the grace "to understand the poor",† passing it on to her daughter.

The Giannetti reached the City of the Seven Hills just as Pius VI had been elected after a long and difficult conclave. The city was *en fête*, life was easy. Luigi, always wayward and grandiose in his ideas and his "siesta" attitude towards life, eventually found a position as a domestic. Meanwhile he lived on his wife's earnings from charing. Though Santa had her faults she was at least pious, sensible and valiant: everything depended on her.

Each morning Annette carried her dinner in a wicker basket to the free school of the "Good Mistresses", as they were called, founded early in the eighteenth century by Lucia Filippini. In this

---

* The word is correct. St. Joseph Benedict Labre had lice.
† "Blessed is he that understandeth concerning the poor and the needy; the Lord shall deliver him in the evil day." Ps. XI. I. Trs. note.

school, in the Via Graziosa, Annette's comely appearance, refined manners, keen wits and solid piety gave joy to the mistresses. The excellent education included household instruction as well as religion, writing and arithmetic. Not only did Annette master the tributaries of the Tiber, but what was of more value to her, how to make a dress or prepare soup, to wind silk and fix it in the bobbins.

At seven she went to confession. At eleven she was confirmed in St. John Lateran, "the Mother and Head of All Churches". At thirteen she made her first Communion in the parish church of St. Francis de Paul. Pious imaginations have run riot over these last two events.

The good Domenico, husband of the Beata, giving his testimony, as on old man of ninety, to the virtues of his wife said simply: "Her parents were good Catholics. I am sure they saw to it that their daughter received an excellent education and that she attended the sacraments in due course; I do not know precisely the time . . . but I do know for certain that they used to take her to church very early in the morning to Holy Mass. She went to confession often—at least I suppose so."

Domenico's simplicity is delightful.

We are told, and it may be true, that the good women of the district used to pause at their work, brooms in hand, to watch her as she passed on her way to school with a red kerchief on her head, telling each other: "What a pretty child! Give her a white skirt with a golden fringe and she'd be like the daughter of a king."

Father Calixtus, following Mgr. Natali, assures us that she did not fail to say her prayers with her parents morning and night. Over and above that there was the recitation of the Rosary, Annette giving out the mysteries. She helped her mother with the household work in the early part of the day. On Sunday, after dinner, she went to the parish church for Catechism. Life was not without its clouds, but change of fortune did not disturb the ardent nature of the little girl from Siena, who accepted it with the ease of childhood. Yet it did embitter her father and mother. As dismal and trying days succeeded one another, far from becoming accustomed to their lot, they found the wound increasingly envenomed. Luigi, though primarily responsible for their position, far from beating his own breast, vented his ill humour on the child, ill-treating her without reason.

They never understood, as Annette came to understand as she grew older; meanwhile she bowed her head: God was moulding her. Apparently she remained scarcely more than two years with the "Good Mistresses". An epidemic of smallpox, which left its traces on her face without actually disfiguring it, cut short her schooling, and subsequently she had to help her mother in the house. She never returned to school. She had learned to read but no more. She, about whom volumes were to be written, knew not how to write; in fact, scarcely knew how to sign her name. The wonderful accounts we have from her of what was revealed to her and what she discovered in her state of mystic prayer, were all dictated. God worked a miracle to teach St. Catherine of Siena to write; to confute the century of self-styled "enlightenment", he did not deign to do so in the case of Anna Maria.

§

This fact gave the Promoter of the Faith (the future Cardinal Verde) material for vigorous opposition to her cause, but her advocates replied with justice that the voluminous memoirs committed to paper by Mgr. Natali, her priest-secretary, were no more to be considered the work of the Beata than the life of Catherine of Siena by Raymund of Capua was to be considered the work of Catherine. Granted that all that Mgr. Natali relates is of an edifying character and of value to biographers, nevertheless (as he himself said), only his juridicial depositions taken under oath must be held as authentic in the strict sense of the term.

Apart from this, we must admit at the outset that very few saints' lives are as closely documented as that of Anna Taigi. Over and above the memoirs of Father Louis-Philip, her confessor, and the memoirs of Mgr. Natali, her confidential priest (these last are full of vexatious erasures and annotations made by hagiographers who used them), which would make two large volumes, we possess a document of matchless value—the deposition, amounting to one thousand pages, of Cardinal Pedicini.

Of a noble family of Beneventum, the Marquis Pedicini on becoming a priest consented to be the secretary of the humble working woman. For thirty years he noted down day by day the facts collected in his long deposition. Created Cardinal by Pius VII, Prefect of the Congregation of Immunity by Leo XII, Prefect of the Congregation of Rites by Pius VIII, Prefect of Propaganda and Vice-Chancellor of Holy Church by Gregory XVI, he did not die till six years after the Beata, after having given his testimony without hurry and in juridical form. It is a document of exceptional historical value, and is moreover confirmed by the depositions of some twenty witnesses, consisting of members of the family of the Beata, of princes of the Church, of ordinary men and women, and of the Roman aristocracy.

Anna, then, did not know how to write, or at the most made tortuous efforts at her signature. But that did not prevent her from knowing her catechism perfectly—in fact, "as well as a parish priest", as her daughter Sophie deposed—or from reciting the Book of Psalms or amazing theologians by the certainty of her knowledge. True these things were a free gift from God but they were also the beneficial effect of her early Catholic education.

Her early trials were the means of saving her from pride, the first of her dangers. Poor she may have been, but the gifts she inherited gave her a certain superiority among the poor of which she was not ignorant. For the rest she was a good and obedient child. Grandma Santa would later on hold her up as an example to her grandchildren: "Anna-Maria, your mother did not behave like *that*. . . ."

I I

ANNETTE AT HOME AND AT WORK 1781 – THE MORAL CRISIS 1782–1788 – AS A MAID

ANNA-MARIA has reached her thirteenth year. The world buzzed with Necker's sensational experiments in finance, and with battles. Louis XVI opened his reign in a cloud of wars.

France and America fight England, winning the recognition of American independence: monarchical arms founded a republic. New ideas triumph. The passion of Rome and France is for Diderot, d'Alembert, the *Contrat Social*, and balloons. "Man has conquered the skies and beaten the gods," was the cry. Mesmerism becomes a religion for the fashionable. Beaumarchais produces *The Marriage of Figaro*: the King himself joins the applauding mob at theatrical shows that mock at lords and royalty, religion and morals.

Anna Taigi winds silk and cuts out dresses in a shop run by two old ladies, who show her a mother's love and reward her, at rare intervals, with a crown piece for her work as an apprentice. Returning home, she washes the clothes, cooks the meals and does her best to bring smiles to the faces of Luigi and Santa, now irretrievably servants, but unable to resign themselves to their destiny.

§

This twilight existence had its reactions on the young Anna. Her first biographer, Mgr. Luquet, a Frenchman and Bishop of Hesebon, postulator of her cause and friend and confidant of the Taigi family, speaks of certain "tempestuous years" that preceded her attainment to grace. He indicates rather than states. The world, he says, smiled on her. She had youth's natural desire to taste its joys, and an innocence of the dangers that her own charms and ardent temperament might bring. He speaks of an "occasion", though he does not tell us what it was, which opened her eyes to future risks: "She decided to shelter her virtue by giving it the safeguard of a chaste marriage."

Mgr. Luquet had lived a hard and trying life, which had ended in great austerity. He was a suppliant of the Beata, to whom he owed many graces, and wrote much to glorify her; and the unedited documents he left to the great Seminary of Langres have provided a great source of information.

Other biographers think he was over-severe. For instance Father Bouffier, S.J., does not emphasise the "tempestuous youth" of Anna, neither does he explain it away: "She knew the fascination of trifles," he says. Against this Father Calixtus, the Trinitarian, says: "It is true that she accused herself of grave faults, but we claim that it is impossible to discover in those alleged faults so much as a venial sin." An unsupported statement. Cardinal Salotti sums up by saying that her vanity exposed her to numerous dangers, but that, as a matter of fact, she did not fall.

Work as a silk winder offered few opportunities for vanity, so she sought them otherwise. She was encouraged by her mother, who retained just one remnant of her more prosperous days, Anna herself, the young beauty of the neighbourhood, to whom she said more often than she should: "You are my own daughter, and how beautiful you are!" In any case, it would have been something of a miracle if the young girl from Siena did not realise that she had a pretty figure, a pretty face, a cultured accent, and that her glass necklace took on the gleam of pearls in the eyes of local youth. There was no crime in that in an Italian girl of sixteen who hoped to have a home of her own, nor in the sentimental novels she delighted in, or the dances she loved. With all this, the parish priest assures us, pretty Annette is faithful to her prayers and her Sunday Communion, and sometimes can even be seen at daily Mass.

§

In March 1782 the parish priest announced that Pius VI was leaving Rome for Vienna, and that all must pray that the young Emperor Franz Joseph and his minister, Kaunitz, both under the spell of the philosophers, would listen to him. They wanted to reform the Church by submitting it to the State control, a plan that would place the Faith in the hands of infidel ministers. It was then, declares Father Calixtus, that a sudden interior light showed

Anna that she must offer herself as a victim to God in order that the Papacy might triumph.

When Pius VI returned she was among the enthusiastic crowd, and knew by the anxiety in his face that great tribulations were about to begin. Joseph II, "The Sacristan", had made promises and broken them. Josephism and philosophy gone mad were about to undermine the Altar and the Throne. Aristocratic Vienna was as intoxicated as Paris by the success of *The Marriage of Figaro* with its call "Behold what alone distinguishes us from the other beasts, to drink for the sake of drinking and to make love all the year round."

> *Here a king, a beggar there;*
> *Birth uneven grants its lot;*
> *Chance in blindness sets them far,*
> *All is changed if will prevails.*
> *Twenty kings—incense them all;*
> *Death their altar overturns;*
> *But immortal is Voltaire; immortal is Voltaire!*

The crowd in its insensate folly took up the refrain:

> *"Everything finishes in song. Everything finishes in song."*

And, we may add—in blood.

In 1787 Anna-Maria left her workplace seeking a better post. Luigi, her father, had now found service in the Mutti or Maccarani palace. His mistress, Maria Serra, being in need of a lady's maid, he suggested Annette. The idea so pleased Madame Serra that she offered employment to the girl's mother also. The Giannetti took themselves and their modest possessions to the palace. A great blessing. They could all work together, and Santa need no more go from house to house charing.

Madame Serra is an enigma. She was in her thirtieth year and was married, but sometimes she calls herself by her married name, Serra, at others by her maiden name, Marini. She has a well-found establishment, her meals are brought to her from the neighbouring palace of the Chigi, and she is separated from her husband. Father Calixtus is dubious about her character. The Cardinal says she was separated from her husband, and that she was bound to the house of Chigi by ties of friendship. Her household was hardly a school of austerity. Indeed, she made much of Annette, praising her charms, so that the girl began to notice how many eyes looked at her with interest, and took to spending more time before her mirror. But she did not forget God. Also, as Father Calixtus suggests, the Beata, who could not have been entirely ignorant of her mistress's character, was grateful for her affection and presumably rewarded it by obtaining for her the grace of repentance, since Madame Serra enjoyed a reputation for virtue and well-doing, when she died at an advanced age.

Meanwhile Annette's coquetry developed and waxed strong. She did not notice the "sparrow-hawks that prowl around the dove". "The beautiful young girl," says the Decree of Beatification, "early encountered the dangers that imperil chastity." Someone shocked her by indelicate talk; her conscience awoke; she sought a protector who would allow her to remain—well, yes, a little of a coquette still, but without danger to her virtue.

III

THE BETROTHAL AND MARRIAGE OF ANNA TAIGI

ANNETTE had been nearly three years in the service of Madame Serra when Providence sent the worthy Domenico Taigi across her path.

She seems to have been considering the possibilities of a vocation for some time: the cloister or the world? Her confessor advised marriage, since the thought of a religious vocation had not come to her with any real force. Her mother thought the same, but she dreamed of a fairy prince who, won by the charms of Annette, would give them back the lost joys and position of their Siena days. Alas! God sent a porter, an under-serving man, the worthy Dominico.

It is true that Father Balzofiore, the Augustinian, in a Life of the Beata, devotes an appendix to prove the noble ancestry of the Taigi, or Taeggi, as it should be spelt. "Taigi" was the invention of the Good Mistresses, who entered the Beata and her daughters thus on the school books; the mistake was copied and spread by Mgr. Luquet and was finally canonised, so to speak, by the Decree of Beatification. Domenico's name, Taeggi, is entered correctly on the servants' roll of the Chigi Palace. It had been a name almost as illustrious as the Chigi. Before misfortune overtook them the Taeggi of the Taeggia Valley had been loaded with honours by kings and dukes of the fifteenth century. Count Palatine Taeggi founded and gave his name to a college at Milan in the seventeenth century.

If Santa knew these details, doubtless they consoled her and made her more favourable to Domenico. He was born in 1761, and he too came to

Rome to improve his prospects. The descendant of the Counts Palatine became a porter in the service of Prince Chigi's cook, carrying sacks of vegetables, loads of wood, piles of plates, an occupation which made him somewhat stooped. All the same, Domenico whom his comrades called "the handsome little angel", was a good-looking youth with black curly hair, of medium height and robust constitution. His morals were without stain, his piety solid, but as the Decree of Beatification puts it, "his manners were rough and uncultured and his temperament unamiable". Thus his character was a perfect contrast to that of the Beata: he was slow in understanding, pig-headed and turbulent; she was sensitive, pliant and gentle, born in "the most civilised town of the Peninsular"; thus was made a perfect household.

The Chigi palace occupies the whole of the north of the Colonna Square, and one of its façades gives on to the Corso; hither once or twice a day Domenico brought food to Madame Serra. Mussolini, before taking up his quarters at the Palace of Venice, considered the Chigi palace fit to be the headquarters of the Fascist regime.

The palace "of the three hundred windows", like the majority of old Roman palaces, makes one think both of a fortress and of a convent. It has thick cast-iron gratings in the lower storeys, brick-coloured walls; at a corner, a statue of Our Lady, before which burns a watch-lamp. To gather some notion of the pomp and display of these princely dwellings you must go inside, mount the spacious staircases of white marble, and go through the suites of rooms thronged with statues, pictures, tapestries, beneath the lofty gilt ceilings with their sunken panels, also of gilt, whereon sprawl the bodies of bewinged and gilded cupids.

Yet it was in this palace, where everything spoke of the pride of living, that a great part of a life whose expiatory sufferings are terrifying to think of, was to be spent. All one can say is that palaces are not palaces for *all* who dwell in them. The Taigi inhabited the servants' quarters, two rooms opposite the Colonna Square, giving on to the narrow alley called "Sdrucciolo" (the Slope), hemmed in between lofty façades that allowed no sun to penetrate. The slope has been widened recently in the direction of the Parliament Palace, and has, moreover, been cemented, but an inscription on marble bearing the date 28th August 1790 gives a hint of the veritable sewer it must have been. Under severest penalties, the municipal authorities forbade evil-smelling offal to be thrown there. Later on the Beata was to have a similar dwelling at the Fiorelli Palace, in the square of St. Ignatius, near the narrow Via del Burro, and was to work there in darkness sixteen or twenty hours a day. No wonder that as a result she nearly went blind.

§

The Chigi family, one of the noblest and most praiseworthy in the city, was, like the family of Anna, of Sienese origin, and had given birth to many who were to become Popes.

Granted that Domenico played a humble part in the household of this Prince, the Prince none the less had a high opinion of him. He showed it by entrusting him with the delicate matter of his pensionary, Madame Serra. He showed it in a more striking manner when, in his capacity of Marshal of the Holy Roman Church and Perpetual Guardian of the Conclave (an hereditary dignity bestowed in 1712 by Clement XI), he chose the worthy Domenico for his companion at the conclaves. The porter thus took part in three Papal conclaves, and at the election of Pius IX, though in retirement, he was again invited to accompany the Prince, but excused himself on the ground of the infirmities of age. He did not die, however, till seven years later, in his ninety-third year, being thus able to give his unhurried deposition at the official enquiry.

His long deposition, which one delights to read, shows a robust common sense and a piety inexpressive but solid. It casts a light upon the comment attributed to Prince Chigi as he slapped his good servant genially upon the shoulder: "Domenico, I am certain you will enter Paradise carrying the whole Chigi family on your back."

Meanwhile Domenico used to carry dinner to Madame Serra, have a bit of a chat with Luigi and Santa Giannetti and take the usual glass of wine in the servants' pantry. Nothing more was needed to link them all in ties of friendship or to allow Domenico to take notice of Annette. She was in her twentieth year, he in his twenty-eighth. She was on the look-out for a good Catholic on whom to lean in a moral sense, who would at the same time be able to support her in a temporal sense; he for an agreeable and brisk companion blessed with good health. Humble folk do not go in for long-winded diplomacy, and Domenico made a shrewd guess that his suit would be acceptable. Mgr. Luquet and the daughter of the Beata put the matter with delightful brevity: "Domenico found favour in the girl's eyes, and the girl in his." Both sides made careful enquiries about the other. Prince Chigi promised to continue Domenico in his service. As to the differences of temperament, the poor give but a second place to considerations of that kind. All the world knows that no one is perfect and that the cross has to be borne, and then hard work has no time for sentimental theorisings.

This was Domenico's subsequent account of the great event to the Court of the Ordinary Process: "When I had thoughts of getting married, I made enquiries about the servant of God and her family, and finding that everybody spoke of her in terms of the highest praise, I made up my mind to marry her. She was about eighteen years old and was a maid to one Madame Serra. As I took the dinner every day to this lady, who lived at the Maccarani Palace, I completed the marriage arrangements within a month. After obtaining a promise from the young girl that she would marry me, I asked for her hand of her mother and of her father. I knew that she asked God for light to see His will, and I did the same. I still remember how modestly and tastefully she was dressed."

The Promoter of the Faith ("the Devil's Advocate") raised difficulty over the marriage being settled in a month; surely an indication of frivolity. Sophie, the daughter of the Beata, replied with a touch of humour: "My mother told me that if she arranged everything within forty days it was because she did not want to be for ever at home 'warming the seat', but to get on with it once she was assured of a good and honourable future; delay could only bring boredom and danger. She never regretted her action. My father was a rough character, and anyone but my mother would certainly have repented of marrying such a man, but although he tried her patience sorely, she was always glad that she had married him."

The betrothal arrangements being concluded in November 1789, Annette, her mother and Madame

Serra set about gathering the trousseau, and the marriage was solemnised by the parish priest of St. Marcel in the Corso on 7th January 1790, the morning after the Epiphany: everybody concerned went to Holy Communion.

There was an excellent dinner; there was singing and dancing and plenty of high spirits, though the pious authors who have turned this homely marriage into a gloomy taking of the veil will scarcely forgive me for saying so.

In this candid gaiety and in their faith, Annette and Domenico found the courage not to feel too keenly the incompatibilities that divided them. These came later in the strain and clash of life. It was the marriage of a wolf and a lamb, but the lamb softened the wolf. "It is false," said Pius IX, 30th April 1876, to some pilgrims from Toulouse, "to say that diversity of character is necessarily an obstacle to the union of husband and wife. Recall to your minds the chariot which Ezechiel saw drawn by four animals. The ferocity of the lion united in accord with the wisdom of man, the speed of the eagle and the slowness of the ox. Natures so diverse did not prevent all working together in peace. The chariot moved rhythmically because it was directed by the one same Spirit of God. Make a generous sacrifice of your own inclinations to God and God will inspire you with His counsels."

Therein lay the whole secret of the Blessed Taigi, model of wives: self-renunciation. The wolf will rage, but a smile and a still tongue will appease his wrath.

Prince Chigi put two rooms on the ground floor, looking out on to the alley, at the disposal of the simple couple. Domenico offered one to his mother-in-law in ignorance of her trying ways, but his father-in-law continued to lodge at Madame Serra's.

§

The honeymoon! A damp and dark lodging, made elegant by the cunning fingers of Annette, in time became gay with six cradles. All the children except the seventh were born there. Domenico was very proud of his wife, and thought only of making her an object of admiration.

The Decree of Beatification refers discreetly to what in reality was a second crisis: "In the first years of marriage, which was celebrated in the flower of her youth at the age of twenty, Anna-Maria, to please her husband, sacrificed a little to the vanities of the world and avoided neither coquetry in dress, nor care to her hair." But do not let us be too solemn about this. If the good Domenico saved up to buy a red silk dress for his darling, ear-rings and a necklace of pearls in place of that of coral and gold given by Madame Serra, it was surely fit that she should wear them!

Father Bouffier, discerning of eye, even if a trifle solemn, writes: "Born in Siena, brought up at Rome, Anna-Maria was Italian by blood, race and warmth of temperament; ever ready for distraction, ever quick to gaiety, ever eager to indulge in laughter and song, and delighting in making the most that her lowly state permitted of the fresh beauty of her twenty years. If the memories of her maidenhood recalled the presentiments of danger, now that she had a protector she was, under his shadow, sheltered from every fear, and in the innocence of her heart she gave herself a free hand. She was not apprehensive about her salvation, since she gave without fail due measure to the duties and practices of religion."

Father Calixtus takes the Jesuit father severely to

task for these sentences: "All the so-called great
faults of Anna-Maria," he says, "may be reduced to
this: She was given to vanity and loved pretty
clothes." Her other biographers also stress this
human weakness.

Soon, on that mountain of Horeb where God is
about to lead her, Annette will discover the immense
misery we call humanity in all its appeal for compassion. Providence bides His time, and Teresa of
Avila took longer to come to herself than Anna-
Maria.

§

We are in the year 1790–1791. The storm that is to
purify the world has broken, but God has not opened
the eyes of this expiatress. A young woman like the
rest, she hears her heart crying: "You are twenty,
and you are pretty."

The momentum of the Revolution gathers
violence. At Paris the National Assembly convoked
by Louis XVI calls itself the Constituent Assembly
and proclaims the "Rights of Man", forgetting the
rights of God. The secularisation of Church goods
is the first example of contempt of the rights of men
necessarily involved in the contempt of the rights of
God; then the civil constitution of the clergy
attacked the rights of conscience after the attack on
the right of property; there followed the suppression
of chapters, abbeys, convents; religious were expelled, churches desecrated; the nomination of
priests and bishops rested upon the votes of the
people; the fifty thousand priests who refused to take
the oath to the civil constitution were hunted, put
in prison, massacred. Pius VI is punished for having
condemned the heretical Constitution by the confiscation of Avignon and the county of Venaissin;

monarchs, either trembling for their thrones or won over to philosophism, remain deaf to the warnings of the Pontiff, not seeing that this first violation of rights would beget others that would sweep away those very thrones for which they trembled. Louis XVI ascended the scaffold on 21st January 1793, and Pius VI, with courage, spoke the praises of the ill-starred king, condemning over again the acts of the regicide Assembly. The Assembly turned upon him in its wrath and decreed the end of the Papacy and the Church.

These events were to convulse Rome, but Anna-Maria smiled into her mirror and frequented the Corso and the play.

We have now reached the last crisis on Anna's road to Damascus. There was for some time a misapprehension of its nature. Mgr. Luquet devotes many pages to it in his unedited MSS. at Langres. As the postulator of her cause, he took the gravest view of it, and in his short biography of 1849 declares that she was pursued by a man of position, who used every device such men know in order to break down her resistance, and that in her young and heedless vanity she fell. He published, and indeed emphasised, the heinousness of her fall to show how sin, even of the gravest kind, can be made good through repentance, and to demonstrate the remorse, suffering and burning desire to expiate her fault at work on Anna's soul.

Other biographers of the Beata, her daughters and Domenico her husband, protested against this reading, which had been spread throughout the world through many translations of Mgr. Luquet's book, but it was not until 1854, three or four years before his death, that Mgr. Luquet discovered his mistake. Possibly due to confession of the guilty party, filled with remorse on his death-bed for the calumny so long attached to the memory of the Beata, Mgr. Luquet admitted that he had been wrong, that he had been deceived by lying reports, the apparent frivolity of Anna's behaviour, and finally by her own description of herself as "a great sinner", an accusation she used as frequently as St. Teresa of Avila.

Now he declared that, though in her vanity and her zest for life she had travelled a road which had ended for many others in the abyss, she, in point of fact, was able to resist the most perilous temptations. He described in full the pursuit of the libertine and ended: "It is certain that the grace of God caused her to triumph." She found in this another motive for thanksgiving and love for her Good Master who knew how to save her from dangers like this. Not that she was irreproachable. "Chaste in morals, attached to her wifely duties, Anna-Maria yet lived more for the world than for God. In this perhaps she tried to distract herself from the remorse which had been aroused by the experience in her sensitive nature, and which was to deepen as time went on, so that she was for ever calling herself 'a great sinner'."*

IV

THE CALL

An increasing sense of spiritual disturbance began to mingle with Anna's frivolities. One day she went to the Basilica of St. Peter's. There was a great throng. She was leaning on the arm of her husband, all radiant and decked with her prettiest

* Cardinal Salotti submits the story to critical analysis and exonerates the Beata conclusively.

necklaces. They were in the piazza, surrounded by
Bernini's colonnade. The jostling of the crowd
threw her against one Father Angelo, a Servite. He
had never seen the young woman before, but he
heard an interior voice say: "Notice that woman, for
I will one day confide her to your care and you shall
work for her transformation. She shall sanctify herself, for I have chosen her to become a saint."

Anna noted the closeness of the priest's regard,
but did not understand; all she knew was that
remorse weighed yet heavier on her spirits. It would
seem she laid these anxieties before her confessor,
who reassured her, saying: "Be content with obeying
your husband and being faithful to him. . . ."
"That is not sufficient," was the peremptory re-
joinder of the interior voice, as she prayed in the
basilica. She went later to another confessor, but the
days passed and in the meantime life had to be lived.

On Sunday evenings Domenico, tired by his
week's work, claimed his recreation—a stroll in the
Corso, where you applauded the parades of mum-
mers, the cavalcades, the carriages made into travelling gardens with bowers of irises, arums and gladi-
olas. Anna had to make herself attractive for his sake;
she was his only glory. She beautified herself,
standing in front of her mirror, putting a few pome-
granate flowers into her luxuriant black tresses,
clasping the golden chain and the pearl necklace
round her throat.

But Domenico, catching the expression of sadness
in her eyes, would growl angrily: "I see you are
coming against your will," and Annette, checking
her tears, would smile and parry the question. 'We
are going to church for the 'Angelus', aren't we,
Domenico?" Her gentleness disarmed the blustering
porter. Nevertheless, the problem remained, how to

reconcile the call to perfection with the duties of a young wife. Eventually Annette made up her mind to make good the resolution taken at St. Peter's. She went to a neighbouring church, seeking in confession the solution of all her problems. She chose a confessional surrounded by numerous penitents, but on entering it in her turn tears overcame her, and she cries: "Father, you have at your feet a great sinner." The priest wondered for a moment who the unknown might be, and then said brusquely: "Go away; you are not one of my penitents." However, he consented to hear a hasty recital. Yet discovering nothing to justify her passionate outburst, he gave her absolution and curtly slammed back the slide, leaving the unfortunate woman more troubled than ever.

There followed a period of discouragement. In a soul of poorer calibre the matter might have had a tragic ending; in truth it had an ending as fortunate as for St. Teresa, so misunderstood and mishandled by one confessor after another.

After having savoured this humiliation, Anna returned to pray in the church of St. Marcellus, where she had been married. Entering one of the confessionals in trepidation, she found herself in the presence of the curate, a religious of the Servite Order, Father Angelo Verandi. It was he who in the piazza in front of St. Peter's had heard the interior voice say to him: "Take notice of that woman. . . . I am calling her to sanctity." The same mentor enabled him to recognise her: "So you have come at last, my daughter," he said. "Our Lord loves you and wants you to be wholly His;" and he told her of the message he had received before St. Peter's. Anna had spent three years in vain triflings, and now a new life was to begin.

§

Who was this Father Angelo? He left at the monastery of the Servites a venerated memory for his sincere zeal and enlightened love of God. He needed it to undertake a task so infinitely delicate. For Anna Taigi was neither a Carmelite nor a devout widow, but the young wife of Domenico, by whom she was to have seven children in a dozen years. There lay her essential duty. Everything else: penances, prayers, miracles, ecstasies, could play their part only in so far as the obligations of her state would allow. Consequently it was no good for Father Angelo just to re-read St. Teresa; he had to have, together with mystical learning, a robust common sense and a profound humility, for often he had to be content with a merely external co-operation with the interior action of the Master.

The first demand of the Master was purification: to that end he gave Anna a keen conscience of her own misery. St. Catherine of Genoa describes the terrible exactions of the divine power by saying: "He finds fault with everything." This spirit of penance, so far as the Beata was concerned, dated from the moment of her confession at St. Marcellus, and was never to leave her. Upon returning to the Chigi palace she prostrated herself before the little altar in her room, gave herself a pitiless scourging and beat her head severely many times on the floor till the blood came. Father Angelo soon had to check this thirst for austerities and to remind her she was a wife.

The ever-present difficulty was that Domenico was no St. Joseph. The first of Anna's miracles was to get him to consent to forgo all those luxuries in which he led the way. Finished now the walks in the Corso;

finished the Carnival days; finished the Sunday
visits to the theatres and puppet-shows of which
Domenico was so fond; finished the adornments
which made him hold his head high with pleasure
when a friend at work congratulated him on his
wife's necklaces.

Wonderful to say, he was resigned: "About a
year after our marriage," he says in his deposition,
"the Servant of God, while yet in the flower of her
youth, gave up for the love of God, all the jewellery
she used to wear—rings, ear-rings, necklaces, and
so on, and took to wearing the plainest possible
clothes. She asked my permission for this, and I gave
it to her with all my heart, for I saw she was entirely
given to the love of God." This miracle moves me
more than the cure of incurables, of which we are
yet to hear, but it was a miracle that had to be several
times repeated.

V

THIRD ORDER OF THE HOLY TRINITY – HUMILITY
– ECSTASY – THE MIRACULOUS SUN

"I HAVE chosen her. . . . I call her to sanctity."
Such was the message heard by Father Angelo.
God had decreed that this woman of twenty-one
years, who was suckling a new-born baby, was to be
a Saint and a bulwark of the Church.

We should only waste our time trying to analyse
the miracle of vocation which changed the profligate
officer Charles de Foucauld into Father de Foucauld,
the astounding ascetic of Tamanrasset; or that of
the great Sienese, St. Catherine, whose body lies
under the altar of the Minerva near Saint Marcellus.
"A young woman of lowly birth and no learning,

who at twenty filled the thoughts of the most famous of her time; at twenty-five is the soul of Italy; at twenty-eight inspires Popes and kings and dominates Rome and Europe; at thirty-two dies in a sort of apotheosis." "God willed it," as he willed the sanctity of Anna Taigi, the coquette of yesterday. This sanctity never faltered. God willed it. He called upon her for constant collaboration, but it was always His Almighty Power that set the stage.

§

It is towards the end of 1790; Anna and Napoleon are both twenty-one. Napoleon will be a general at twenty-four, Commander-in-Chief of the the Army of Italy at twenty-six. The career of the two adversaries is about to develop with a bewildering rapidity, but the development of the Beata will be a thousand times more rapid. While Napoleon still considers which way lies success and hovers between revolution and reaction, Annette, fixed in the Eternal, lives a life that is one long miracle.

Annette told Father Angelo that God was calling her "to be a victim of expiation for the sins of the world". To help her in this vocation he recommended her to become a Tertiary of the Order of the Trinity. An Order founded by St. John de Matha and St. Felix de Valois, its Third Order counted a great number of Popes, kings and queens who, like Anna Taigi, were proud to carry its white scapular with its red and blue cross. It was not Father Angelo, but a Trinitarian, Father Ferdinand, who brought the matter to a happy issue. Domenico consented. He says in his deposition:

"She was devoted to the Holy Mysteries, especially to that of the Most Holy Trinity. She asked my permission to take the habit of the Tertiaries of this Order, and I willingly gave my consent. Father Ferdinand of the monastery of St. Carlino received her, but only on the condition that she should always fulfil her duties as wife and mother, for a married woman is no longer mistress of herself, but is subject to the man. Such were the conditions; she ever observed them with a prompt obedience and whole-hearted fidelity."

Well said, Domenico! But there arose a complication. "When she took the habit of a Tertiary," he continues, "Father Ferdinand advised her to live with me as with a brother. I do not know whether the suggestion came from the priest himself or from the desire of my wife. I emphatically refused, for in this case my wife ought to have become a religious and not to have married."

Domenico had the makings of a theologian, and Father Ferdinand would give him other occasions of proving it. Did he not tell Anna to wear her Trinitarian habit, even in the open street? Anna obeyed. When examining her cause the Promoter of the Faith protested that this indicated imprudence both in her confessor and in Anna. So difficult can it be at times to do one's duty or even to get to know what one's duty is! But Domenico protested before him, especially during the pregnancies of his wife, and Anna and Our Lord agreed, for she decided to change her confessor.

It was only in 1808 that Father Ferdinand gave Anna the holy habit, but not without difficulty. Anna, carried away by one of her customary ecstasies, burst into sobs, and the ceremony was threatened. Father Ferdinand checked her by a sign, and Anna obeyed; then and always she was docile, even when her directors made mistakes. Our Lord made up for what was wanting in her directors. "I shall Myself be your guide in the way of perfection," He told her, and kept His promise by an uninterrupted converse with her.

§

We know the general lines of this converse from the memoirs of the confidants to whom Anna was told to reveal all. The first of these was the eminent prelate of whom we have already spoken, the future Cardinal Pedicini. He played his indispensable part for nearly thirty years and supplied, as we shall see, what was wanting in sundry confessors as they took their turn. A man of great and patient intellect, he was as large of heart, and altogether priestly in virtue. In the inevitable obstacles that the wonder-worker was to meet, and in face of jeering or wrathful sceptics, he was ever her providential champion. After him came Mgr. Natali, whose qualities we shall speak of later.

Anna was at times disquieted. Was it the good or the evil spirit that spoke to her? "You must know," said Jesus to her, "that when I speak to you I produce in you tenderness, peace, compunction; above all, humility. Know well, my daughter, that no matter how much he desires to love me, if a man enter not the straight path of humility he will keep on stumbling. Man has within himself a dust that settles round his heart; it is called self-love. . . . Man is full of pride, and I have nothing to do with the proud."

"Only the humble find favour in My sight."

"He who wishes to taste My delights must despise the world, and expect to be despised by it in turn."

"I make My abode in humble souls that are full of simplicity. The more lowly and uncultured they are, the more I take pleasure in them. As to these wise and learned professors whose heads are full of the fumes of pride, I put them down from their seats, and you yourself shall soon learn where I send them. Thus ends their false wisdom and self-advertisement."

"O My daughter, I exalt those who humble themselves. They merit My Kingdom, and to these I unfold all My secrets."

"Love, then, to meet with contempt, for love of contempt is the true foundation of virtue."

Like all the souls whose uplifting is described by St. John of the Cross, Anna experienced depressions and disgusts after her transports. Jesus rebuked her: "Daughter, when the soul is fervent it ought to humble itself and not be so self-sure, for otherwise it makes hasty promises, and then, when coolness returns, it becomes timid and full of fears. Every soul starting on the spiritual life should pray in this way: 'O God, who art so great and powerful, do with Thy servant what Thou wishest, provided he does Thy will. I am determined to endure all Thou wishest me to suffer, but remember, none the less, that I am good for nothing. Souls who seek perfection should never for a moment forget that Peter, my Beloved Apostle, made promises in a moment of great fervour and then, when the moment of trial came, he forgot My love. Remember, daughter, what I have so often told you, namely, that men are like the weathercocks that spin on the house-tops. If my grace did not preserve them they would turn with every change of the wind."

As Annette was not living exactly in a desert, her devotions soon provoked criticism. Priests gave the example, devout people were not slow to follow their lead. Anna was upset about it: "You are in too much of a hurry, My daughter! Repress this natural impetuosity of yours, live in peace, and roll the world under your feet. Remember that if a soul tries to fly from the cross I have given him I promptly load him with a much heavier one. What, My daughter, you who are so thirsty for suffering let yourself be so quickly overwhelmed with sadness! But you know well and understand that you shall suffer unto the end."

Anna took to the road again. A new crisis came. . . . Her husband and her mother began making scenes. Bread became scarce; jealous housewives began to chatter. Sadness grew afresh. . . . The Unseen Master was there to encourage and stimulate.

"Ah! ungrateful daughter, over and over again have I given you a wealth of good instruction and you do not take the trouble to recall it to mind; you allow yourself to be overcome by sadness and discouragement. A wise and prudent person, in whatever distressing set of circumstances he finds himself, always says: 'I have thoroughly deserved it; in fact, it is nothing to what I deserve.' He does not become anxious interiorly. I have told you many, many times that to become possessed of My peace and calm one must lay aside one's own judgment, bow the head, and be filled with My holy humility."

As she was praying one day in the church of St. Andrew della Valle, before the crucifix of St. Lawrence in Damaso, she heard this question from the lips of the Crucified: "What is your wish? To follow Jesus poor and naked and stripped of all, or to follow Him in His triumph and glory? Which do you choose?" "I embrace the Cross of my Jesus," she answered. "I will carry it, like Him, in pain and ignominy. I await at His Hands triumph and glory in the hereafter."

§

It was in 1790, the very year of her call, that the Beata was the object of a most remarkable favour.

The Decree of the Beatification thus refers to it: "Among other gifts the most remarkable was that for a space of forty-seven years she saw a kind of sun in whose light she descried things at hand and things afar off, foresaw future events, scrutinised the secrets of hearts and the most hidden and most inward impulses." Suddenly, then, in her little back street of the Sdrucciolo, Anna saw a little above her head, as it were, a blazing sun crowned by a circle of thorns; two long thorns clasped it round; in the centre was the Eternal Wisdom (presumably), represented by a young woman seated in contemplation. Films of cloud dimmed the dazzling light, but an interior voice told her that the clouds would disappear according to the increasing measure of her purification. In this light she was to see, until her death, not only everything that might conduce to her perfection, but also everything that could win confidence in others for her life's work, and allow her to succour the Church militant or suffering.

Cardinal Pedicini, whose position in the great Roman congregations argues a man little given to credulity or wild assertion, speaks with emphasis and at great length in his juridicial deposition on this prodigious gift. "For forty-seven years, day and night, at home, at church, in the street, she saw in this sun, which became increasingly brilliant, all things on this earth both physical and moral; she penetrated to the depths and rose up to heaven, where she saw the eternal lot of the dead. She saw the most secret thoughts of persons nearby or far off; events and personages of bygone days. . . . She had only to think of a thing and it presented itself in a clear and complete manner. . . . A mere glance at this mystic sun and she entered at will into the most secret council-rooms of kings. She saw the people who handled affairs, the places concerned, the opinions held, the sincerity or guile of the ministers, all the back-door diplomacy of our era, as also the decrees of God for the confusion of these mighty ones. She saw the plottings and the dark fore-gatherings of various sects; the members of these societies, their ranks, their ceremonies—all in the minutest detail and in all parts of the world—all as if it were all happening in her room. . . . We may say that this gift was one of omniscience, for it was the knowing of all things in God so far as the intelligence is capable of such knowledge in this life. . . . She saw on distant seas ships being wrecked and heard the cries of the shipwrecked; she penetrated into the prisons of China and Arabia . . . where confessors of the faith, slaves and prisoners languished in agony. . . . In this way did she exercise an un-bounded apostolate, won souls to grace in every part of the globe, and prepared the way for missionaries; the entire world was the theatre of her labours. . . . Nor let any one think I am exaggerating, for, on the contrary, I find myself incapable of describing the wonders of which I was for thirty years the witness." The Cardinal adds that if obedience compelled the holy woman to hide nothing from him, she took extreme pains to remain hidden herself from people whom she benefited by means of the lights God gave her. Above all, she was most anxious to receive no gifts from them.

Mgr. Natali and her confessor give further details about this sun in their respective depositions.

A seer at twenty-one years old! For nearly half a

century, right up to her death, she was to live in a sort of perpetual ecstasy, with the great book of the world ever open before her eyes. Never did she find any self-satisfaction in it; in fact, at the beginning she feared it as a diabolical prodigy, and her directors had to reassure her. The scenes which followed one another before her eyes, as in a film, taught her, above all, new motives for humility and expiation, and directed her in her task as "rampart of the Church". Jesus described her mission: "I destine you to convert sinners, to console people of all sorts and conditions—priests, prelates, My very Vicar himself. All who listen to your words will be granted signal graces at My hands. . . . But you will also meet with false and treacherous people; you will be submitted to ridicule, scorn and calumny, but you will endure it all for love of Me." This frightened her. "My God, whom are You choosing for this task? I am a creature unworthy to tread the earth." "I see that also," answered the Voice. "It is I who will guide you by the hand, as a lamb is led by the shepherd, to the altar of sacrifice."

Princes of the Church, kings, queens, Popes and saints came to ask this humble woman to teach them the secrets of heaven. She enlightened them to the extent demanded by obedience, putting far from her all spirit of curiosity, not even asking an explanation of those things she failed to understand.

"A prodigy unique" in the annals of sanctity is the way the Decree of Beatification speaks of it, and it is to be explained by the unique circumstances in which the world and the Papacy then were. A crumbling world threatened to involve the Church and the Papacy in its own ruin. St. Gregory the Great tells of a similar manifestation, but one far from equalling this in importance. "One night," he says, "on going to the window, St. Benedict addressed a fervent prayer to God. Suddenly the shadows of night fell away and he saw a brilliant light so splendid that the light of day itself would have paled before it. . . . He saw the entire world concentrated before his eyes in this one light. As he watched, marvelling in the shining of this ray, he saw the blessed soul of Germain, Bishop of Capua, in a globe of fire, being transported by the angels to heaven." But Domenico's wife did not live in the solitude of Monte Casino. She made soup, darned socks, suckled babies. The great lesson of this life is not in these gratuitous gifts of God, but in the striving after holiness, which is itself the guarantee that they are genuine and unfeigned.

They are also guaranteed by innumerable facts that can be tested and by the prolific abundance and solid agreement of the witnesses whose depositions are recorded in the 7,200 pages of the process. Is there a similar wealth of documents for the life of a St. Catherine of Siena, a St. Francis of Assisi, a St. Teresa?

PART II
STEPS OF THE SOUL'S ASCENT

I

CHILD – WIFE – MOTHER-IN-LAW – DON RAFAËLE

WE are forced to take things out of their historical sequence for the moment, in order to follow the sequence of interior vitues in the Decree of Beatification. We shall accordingly be guilty of a few repetitions.

The first appeal Anna-Maria heard was "Penitence", but within the lines marked out by the duties of her state of life.

The interior guide insisted upon this. "Remember these three things that constitute the substance of perfection: A love pure and unblemished by any natural affection, a constant fidelity to the inspirations of My grace and a perfect abandonment to the hands of My Providence. . . . The greatest merit consists in being in the midst of the world and yet holding the world under one's feet."

The Blessed Virgin was even more precise: "Know well, My dear daughter, that here below you will have for every one good day a hundred bad ones, because you must be like My Son Jesus. You must be devoted above all to doing His will and submitting your own constantly to His in the state of life to which it has pleased Him to call you; therein lies your special vocation. Later on, when people come to examine your conduct closely, every individual must be able to convince himself that it is possible to serve God in all states and conditions of

life without the performance of great exterior
penances, provided only one fights vigorously
against one's passions and conforms oneself in all
things to the holy will of God. Remember it is far
more meritorious to renounce one's own will and
submit oneself entirely to the will of God than to
perform the greatest bodily mortifications."

Once when Maria was having a conversation with
one of her disciples Our Lord appeared to them and
said: "Virtue consists above all in the mortification
of one's own will. It consists of concealing, as far as
possible, from the eyes of men the works that you
do. The true servant of God is content to know that
his services are known to the Heavenly Father. You
must prepare yourselves to receive all things, evil
as well as good, with an equal resignation and even
with gaiety of heart. Be good, therefore, and charitable to your neighbour; be humble and patient in
yourselves."

§

Anna had to exercise this virtue of patience for
forty-eight years with reference to her husband.

"What St. Augustine tells us" (we are quoting
the Decree of Beatification) "of St. Monica is true
of Anna-Maria; namely, that in modesty and mortification she obeyed her husband as the representative
of the Lord, and did all she could to win him to God."
Domenico in his deposition spoke as follows:

"For love of God she used to abstain from drink,
but I used to say to her: 'Marianne, take something
to drink', or 'You have had nothing to drink'. She
would then smile and would obey me. I found her
always as docile and tractable as a lamb. She had
given up all the pleasures of the world, even the
most innocent, but I sometimes said to her:

'Marianne, let us go to such and such a place', and she met my wishes with a charming readiness, as, for instance, when I wanted to go and see the puppet show; but when eventually I noticed that she went rather in obedience than for the pleasure of the thing, and that for her it was a penance, I left her in peace.

"I can assert in very truth that from the beginning of our marriage she never refused my rights, but never asserted her own. She contracted no debts, because she always guided her outlay by her income. If any of us fell ill she lavished every attention on us, to the extent of omitting when necessary her Mass and her devotions. As for me, I have always thought in the past and say now that God took this excellent servant from me because I was not worthy to have her. . . . I have always thought her a soul of lofty virtue, but I did not know and did not even suspect a host of things that I have learned since her death. I believe the Lord took her to Paradise immediately after her passing because of her great goodness and eminent virtues, and I hope that she prays for me and all my family."

This panegyric of Domenico's is worth a dozen eloquent discourses. This rough and turbulent soul, far from becoming estranged from his wife when she turned towards perfection, did but increase his admiration and love for her.

Still, God knows it was difficult to keep the peace in Domenico's home. On one side there was a husband in a perpetual state of ferment, threatening every minute a volcanic outburst; on the other a queer crab-grained mother-in-law, ever on the watch for a chance to cross her son-in-law. Anna went from one to the other recommending patience.

"I depose," said Domenico, "that she had ever the most tender affection for her parents and lavished all possible care upon them." And Domenico came to share that affection, for, being allowed to bring back the leavings from the table of Prince Chigi as a supplement to his meagre wages, and being asked by Anna in that disarming way of hers to give the best part of them to her mother, he consented. "God be praised," he said, "we have succeeded in contenting our mother." But Santa did not change; the older she grew the more cantankerous she became. Yet her daughter let her want for nothing; even gave her pocket-money. "The worst of it was," says Sophie, "that Grandma loved chattering about the one and the other with the lodgers." Annette respectfully suggested to her that a prayer at the church would be worth more than gossip. "Don't bother me," answered the old lady. "I'll do what I like. I don't need you to tell me to go to church." But Anna, by dint of persevering devotion, had the last word. She took care of her mother night and day when she fell ill and watched her die a most holy death in her arms at the age of seventy-three. As she prayed for her mother in her agony, the Master said to her: "Yet a few hours of suffering in this life wherewith to expiate the punishment due to her sins; then a purgatory short and not severe to purge away her faults."

§

The Beata had a yet more difficult time with her father.

At the death of his mistress, Madame Serra, Luigi, who could never set the Thames on fire, thought it better henceforth to do nothing at all, and squandered his slender pension roaming Italy. When he had spent his money, the former chemist returned to Rome and lived at his daughter's expense, but

refused to dwell under her roof. Annette ended by
making him accept a post as porter at an orphanage,
and then, when age and infirmity had made him
helpless, got him into the home of St. John Lateran,
where he eventually died. At the home he found
things irksome, complained of the regime, was for
ever coming to his son-in-law's house, but ever refused to enter. He used to sit complaining on the
last step of the stairs. Annette would hurry to him
begging him to come in. "I do not want to come
in, and if that does not suit you, so much the
worse!"

He shouted and made scenes like an ill-tempered
urchin. The Beata treated him as such, came and
sat down by his side on the stairway, cleansed the
repulsive scabs of the skin-disease with which he was
covered, washed him, combed his hair, mended his
clothes, gave him the choicest of the delicacies
brought home from the prince's table, and slipped
him a few white pieces with which to buy himself
tobacco or the morsels he fancied. The meals at the
hostel were never to his taste, and that explains
why he never thanked his daughter after eating the
dainties she gave him. . . .

"This poor old man," deposed Domenico, "never
showed the slightest gratitude towards his daughter
for all her care of him. He accepted everything as
if it was his due and never said 'Thank you'." Less
patient than his wife, Domenico at first complained
of such ingratitude but ended by entering into the
charitable plot. When the old man could no longer
leave the hostel, Anna, in spite of her own infirmities,
made the long journey nearly every day to visit him
and bring him dainties. His last years were frightful.
"My father-in-law," says Domenico, "was smitten
with a horrible leprosy." Anna staunched the dis-

charge and bathed the skin. She prepared him to die a good death, got him the last Sacraments and the suffrage of many prayers. "One would think" (such as Domenico's admirable conclusion) "that God gave the servant of God such parents simply to put her great virtue to a keener test."

It was certainly for the same reason that God inflicted such a husband on her. Anna transformed him into what she herself described as "a saint". He survived her by sixteen years and lived but in the recollection of her saintly memory. But what went before that consummation?

He says a golden thing when he says in his deposition: "I can say that her entire life was a continual and very painful exercise of patience."

Mgr. Natali, who saw him at close quarters, deposes that at the beginning he was "given to certain *vices*" and not merely to the "*faults*" of which he modestly admits he was corrected by Anna's influence. What are the vices in question? His insane fits of anger lead one to suppose that like many porters he had a pronounced taste for white wine! Then there were the rustic manners of this descendant of the Counts Palatine. It was impossible for instance, to make him wear a coat—it irritated him. Impossible to make him accept trousers that reached his ankles—they irritated him. Impossible to get a shirt on him—it irritated him. Annette faced with his obstinacy, smiled, kissed him, and all was over. Domenico was not a ' Red", but for reasons unknown this fallen patrician wanted to live and die as a porter. The Princess Chigi who, like her husband, thought highly of him, wished to promote him or at least to change his name from porter to commissionaire, but Domenico made an appalling fuss and insisted that he should be called porter—*facchino*. "I came to you as a porter; I intend to remain a porter; porter or nothing!"

When this fire-eater of a man came home everybody had to be at his beck and call. Anna knew it. She did not hesitate to dismiss the most illustrious persons in order to be all to her master.

Here is an excellent description of the good man by his daughter Sophie: "My father was as pious and earnest a man as one could desire, but of such a fiery, exacting, haughty and wild temperament as to amaze one. On coming home he would whistle or knock, and we had immediately to dash to open the door at the risk of breaking our necks. In fact, twice my sister Mariuccia fell down through rushing too quickly to meet him, and on one of these occasions she had one of my baby daughters of five months old in her arms. If everything was not just as he wanted it he came in furious, and would go so far as to snatch hold of the tablecloth, where the dinner was served, and throw everything to the four winds. Everything had to be prepared to the tick, the soup hot in the tureen, the chair in place. He was as exacting in the matter of his clothes and of everything else." He used the stick or worse to gain the children's obedience. One day one of the children, to escape a beating, fled into the street. Mad with rage, Domenico threw an armchair at him out of the window. Even this picture leaves out certain details given by Cardinal Pedicini. In his tempers Domenico forgot himself so much that he would make use of foul language in front of the children. Annette, the Cardinal tells us, succeeded in curing him of that also, but only by dint of a permanent self-sacrifice and a long voluntary martyrdom. Anna-Maria never lost her calmness of mind, but humbled herself to performing the lowliest attentions towards him; quitting the presence of a bishop to welcome her lord; washing his hands and paring his nails. Ever smiling, she brought home to him that one does not talk to children as if they were bears' cubs, and Domenico, the bear, bowed his head to her rebuke. Listen to him: "I wish to say this, for the glory of God, that I lived for forty-eight years or so with this saintly soul and never did I hear from her a word of impatience or discord. We lived in a perpetual peace as of Paradise. I used to go home often dead tired and a little distraught (euphemistic, Domenico, but who could blame you?) after my day's work and difficulties with my employers, and she would restore my serenity of mind." Never did a religious practise an obedience of higher merit.

In this obedience there was indeed a large proportion of virtue, but there was also a keenly just sense of Domenico's difficulties. He was not a hero, but needed to be to cope with the life he led. To extreme old age he had to struggle for the daily bread for his household, and that fact palliated many things, and Anna made allowances.

There are mortals for whom day begins with the stars and night begins with the sun. It has a different aspect for their servant. After the prince's dinner, Domenico had to sweep the rooms and wash the crockery, and that at midnight or one in the morning. The last to leave, he did not come home till "towards the dawn", and though he had served dinner for others, had not dined himself.

Anna, though wearier by her own long day, is still up and is waiting for him with a smile. For form's sake Domenico chides her:

"Why do you wait for me all this time? Why do you not go to sleep and not worry about me seeing you have to be on your feet all day long?"

"But, Domenico, who will look after you, if I am not here to do so? You must have your food properly in order to be able to begin work again in the morning? Eat your supper at ease, then we will go to our rest in the peace of the Lord."

Domenico is pleased; he eats with a good appetite; he makes jokes, and tells all that has happened during the day. By now it is three or four in the morning and the night's rest will be short, but Anna gives him holy water, and on her knees, surrounded by the cots of her little ones, says night prayers, which are sometimes lengthy.

But Domenico found them short, for listen to what he says:

"She prayed for the Holy Father, for the Cardinals, for the conversion of sinners, of heretics, for all the world, and for evil-tongued people; it all seemed to me a paradise."

There assuredly we face one of the triumphs of love, for the ferocious porter loves his Annette with a terrible and a jealous love and becomes a cavalier, or if you desire it, he reassumes the dignity of a Count Palatine. The prelates of the enquiry must have smiled, seeing the old man of ninety-one years draw himself up to say: "If I saw anyone annoying her I saw to it that it cost him dearly." Neither was this bravado. One feast-day he was going to church and Anna, who was with child, was leaning on his arm. A soldier whose duty it was to keep order pushed the young woman rudely. Domenico's blood rose instantly; he threw himself on the trooper, loaded him with abuse, took his carbine away from him and began to beat him to a jelly. He might have killed him if some of the passers-by and Anna herself had not intervened.

It was not the only occasion on which this wolf

of Gubbio needed pacifying: "Although she was at pains to do good to all and sundry, there were people with whispering tongues who gave her no rest, whether it was because they were jealous at seeing so many persons of distinction at our house, or because the devil induced them to beset her. But I could not be with her everywhere. Moreover, I saw that the Servant of God was pained when I took a hand in these matters, so in the end I said to her: 'Do what you like and as you like; if you wish people to throw stones at you and to suffer thus at their hands, you are free to do so'."

§

Domenico here touches on a subject that might have been a fruitful cause of domestic unhappiness—namely, the incessant file of people of all kinds, priests, princes of the Church, lords, ordinary folk, coming to consult the Saint, to ask her guidance as formerly the crowd of disciples thronged into the little room of their "Mamma", Catherine of Siena. In this lay a formidable danger of jealousy. "Sometimes, on coming home to change my clothes, I found the house full of people. Instantly my wife left everybody, lords and prelates, and hurrried to receive me, to brush me down and to wait on me, with the greatest charm for me and the greatest satisfaction to herself. You could see that what she did she did with all her heart down to settling my shoe laces. My house was frequented by many, many people, especially in the earlier years of our marriage, but I could be quite happy about it all and could close my eyes without any disturbing suspicion. I knew what sort of a woman my wife was, what her thoughts and actions were; so much so that I refrained even from questioning her. I knew that these people came simply to ask her prayers or advice." Is it not St. Francis of Sales who says that Alpine hares become white as snow by living amidst the snows and feeding from them?

It was like that with Domenico; but what prudence it required from Anna. "When she had a visitor she kept her mother or her daughters near her. If the subject were confidential she would withdraw into a corner of the room in which her mother was working, or, if she went into the next room, she left the door open, that she might have witnesses of her behaviour."

But even that did not suffice, as we shall see, to silence evil tongues, or even to reassure Domenico —at least at the beginning. The "devil's advocate" did not fail to point out that Domenico, jealous to the point of folly, stood on no ceremony, but sent many visitors about their business.

Our Lord had forewarned the Beata:" Remember that you must be prudent in everything. . . . The devil, My daughter, is a spirit of contradiction. He who is under the devil's influence cannot rest either day or night. My spirit, on the other hand, is a spirit of love and peace, full of condescension for everything that is not sin. Who possesses My peace, possesses all things. Many souls do severe penance in order to reach this great good. None can reach the peace of my elect unless he is at pains to become as simple as a child and to acquire from the start true charity. Who possesses charity, My daughter, possesses patience. Charity works with zeal and love. It speaks evil of no one, for it fears to lose the precious pearl of My friendship. It understands all, sees all, notices all, but it covers all with its mantle. It excuses the faults of its neighbours, and sympathises with his sorrows and says to itself: 'Alas!

my God, I should be still worse, if You did not come
to my aid'."

Tugged this way and that by these three impossible characters, her mother, her father and her
husband, Anna succeeded in reconciling opposites.
She is silent in the face of Domenico's blustering,
and he falters, becomes abashed and is ready to fall
on his knees: "Well, Annette, do in this matter what
you wish, for I know nothing about it."But Annette
does not try to score off him. "As for me, Domenico,
I should behave in this manner. Does that suit you?"
"Suit him?" Why, he would have gone to fetch the
obelisk from the square of St. Peter's if it would
have given pleasure to his little saint!

"It was owing to her supreme and gracious tact
that there was never any serious difference between
her and me. She could give advice charitably, and
I owe it to her that I was corrected of certain faults
(euphemistic again!). She corrected you with a
kindliness that cannot be described, for all her ways
so disarmed you that you were irresistibly obliged
always to do what was pleasing to her for the good
of the whole house."

It is indeed quite clear that the common good
alone and not the instinct for control directed all her
actions. Even Domenico, for all his mental myopia,
recognised this.

"If my wife saw anybody troubled or disquieted,
she said nothing, but waited for him to become
calm, and then with the greatest gentleness asked
him to reflect, giving him excellent counsels towards
patience and humility. For the rest, these disputes
were a rare occurrence; my poor wife was so prudent
that the moment she discerned any little difference
arising, be it a question of the old mother or of the
daughter-in-law, she made haste to stifle it with such

a meekness that peace and harmony were more secure afterwards than if no difference had arisen at all. . . . It often happened that I came home in a bad temper, but she had the gift of restoring my serenity. In one word, she knew how to be silent, but she knew still better how to talk when talk was necessary."

Domenico's deposition is golden, and he is never at a loss. Here are some details, yet more delightful, about his mother-in-law.

"My wife caused a reign of perpetual and heavenly peace in the home, although we were numerous and of different characters; her influence was specially felt when my son, Camillo, came to live with us in the first years of his marriage. My daughter-in-law was a difficult character, because she wanted to be the mistress, but the servant of God knew so well how to keep each person within her own sphere that anything I could say would be very inadequate."

That was the last thing needed to the glory of the Beata. Model of wives, model of mammas, at last see her model of mothers-in-law. Let the reader form an idea of what such a master achievement means: Anna imposing peace in this Noah's ark, where dwell cheek-by-jowl wives, husbands, parents-in-law, a daughter-in-law and two families of children, one family comprising seven, the other six. Domenico had good reason to voice his admiration.

Here are the words of strangers: "Often enough Domenico came home at night in a bad temper from wranglings with the other servants, but he always found in Anna-Maria a soothing influence. She was at pains to understand his likes, the better to satisfy them, his troubles in order to sweeten them. The moment he put his foot over the threshold she knew if he was upset, and said gently:

"You have had much to try you to-day, haven't you?" "I have indeed. I could stand no more." "Very well, sit down; take your ease, for all is well here." Domenico sometimes spoke ill of his fellow-servants and of his employer. Anna let him run on, then made excuses for them, and re-established them in his estimation, for his Milanese good humour soon reasserted itself. If he was bad-tempered enough to use evil language Anna accepted this (for to her it was a real injury) and buried it in the abyss of her charity. However, Mgr. Luquet tells us that if Anna's father forgot himself so far as to lay hands on her, Domenico, in spite of his frequent acts of physical violence, never used them against her.

§

But even now we have mentioned only a few of the members of her household. Among them was an habitual guest—Mgr. Rafaële Natali, whose name appears again and again in the process as that of priest-confidant or secretary. Born at Macerata in 1781, and thus twelve years younger than the Beata, he gave his age at the Ordinary Process as seventy-two and at the Apostolic Process as eighty-two. He lived till he was ninety. Curate of St. Victor's, secretary of the Blessed Mgr. Strambi, Bishop of Macerata and Tolentino, then secretary of Cardinal Barberini, then Master of the Chamber to Leo XII, and later "father" of the College of Pontifical Chaplains, he was thus a Roman prelate of importance. How did it come to pass that he was attached to the Beata and her family is such sort as to share for more than half a century their life of want?

In this way, Mgr. Strambi, a former director of Anna-Maria, sent Don Rafaële to Rome in 1815 to preach the clergy retreat; he suggested his seeing

Anna, but warned him to be careful of gossip. Mgr. Natali therefore asked the Beata to meet him in the crypt of St. Peter's. Anna, not keeping the appointment, the priest had to go to her home. Frank as always, the Beata, who had learnt of the subterfuge, welcomed him with a smile and said: "His lordship has allowed himself to be overcome by human respect because I am a poor woman. If I were a great lady he would not have behaved so. Tell him that I thank him." Saints love to be treated with frankness just as they are frank themselves, so Mgr. Strambi welcomed the comment humbly. Don Rafaële returned to see Anna several times.

He was deeply spiritual, and was won by her, but Anna was not won by him. She saw in him an instability of spirit, an affectation that would have induced her to keep him at arm's length. But Our Lord said to her: "Don Rafaële is a bird that flutters from bough to bough and needs to be put in a cage for his own good. . . . I confide the apostolate of his soul to you." From that moment their spiritual friendship began. The priest could not lodge in the cramped quarters in the Chigi palace, but boarded at the Beata's house, and after meals read and discussed with her spiritual books. Each morning he gave her Holy Communion in the chapel of the Pieta opposite the Chigi palace.

He was given a benefice at Macerata and was recalled by Mgr. Strambi to that town. "Go," said Anna to him simply, "but his lordship will send you back." And so it fell out, for Don Rafaële, reaching Macerata, went to confession to the Beatus without giving a hint of his desire to return to Rome, and Mgr. Strambi, on reflection, went back on his decision: "Return to Rome," he said, "and continue as before." The priest remained some days at

Macerata with members of his own family, but the Beatus insisted:" Go back to Rome as Anna-Maria wishes, and do not leave her."

Don Rafaële returned, and Mgr. Strambi following him later, on becoming secretary to Leo XII, made use of the priest to consult the Beata each day. In 1817, when the Taigi household took up more commodious quarters in the Corso, Don Rafaële went with them. For twenty years, that is to say, up to the death of the Beata, he continued to lodge with them. Anna's confessor entrusted to him the task of recording day by day, as Cardinal Pedicini had hitherto done, the revelations received by the Beata. She had been told that as she could not write, she was to tell everything to her secretary except what strictly concerned her confessor alone. Don Rafaële gave her advice, but above all received advice, and became a holy priest. He shared the severe poverty of the Taigi, even after the death of the Beata and became, as it were, necessary to Domenico in his old age and to his family, of whom he was the tutor and the procurator.

His unpublished letters to Mgr. Luquet, preserved at Langres, show that his was no sinecure. He asked for money for the process when it was nearing completion. Mgr. Luquet, who had already given much and had no more to give, makes a marginal note on the priest's letter: 'Answered on 29th April 1853 that I have never thought it right, as I have always made clear to him, to contract a debt for the cause of Anna-Maria." He also had to find money for the dowry of Luisa, granddaughter of the Beata, who wished to become a nun.

Two other letters tell Mgr. Luquet of the death of the aged Domenico. He died like a saint. In cruel pain from a disease of the bladder for which it was

impossible to operate, he received the Viaticum and
Extreme Unction from Mgr. Natali himself. During
the two days in his agony (an extremely distressing
one) he gave not the slightest sign of impatience,
but "manifested a constant resignation to the Divine
Will". Again the question (ever renewed) of
expenses arose. Mgr. Natali was in debt for the
funeral. He could not pay either priest or under-
taker. Everybody demanded payment. He had
nothing to sell but a garnet-bead rosary that had
belonged to Anna and was worth fifty crowns. But
who would buy it? On 13th August 1853 Mgr.
Luquet accepts the invitation and acquits himself of
it, and Mgr. Natali is effusive in his thanks.

With untiring devotion until his ninety-first year,
Don Rafaële classified his writings: the story of
Anna's life, the letters she dictated to him and the
daily revelations which he wrote down every night
at her dictation. But as to the last, we must remember
that he sometimes abbreviated them, sometimes even
wrote them down from memory, and that makes
them less valuable from the point of rigid authen-
ticity. From the opening of the process he occupied
himself, with the authorisation of the Cardinal
Vicar, in taking down the evidence of the principal
witnesses, and induced Mgr. Luquet to prepare a life
of the Beata. Eventually God granted him a long
enough life to make his deposition at the Ordinary
Process and the Apostolic Process. None merited
more than he at the Saint's hands.

II

THE PERFECT MOTHER

THE perfect mother! Domenico's deposition provides us with information very much to the point. "The servant of God, my wife, in spite of her love of austerities, took care during her times of pregnancy to take more food; she stopped fasting and refrained from over-exertion; in a word, she took every precaution that her condition demanded.

"Seven children were born of our marriage, four boys and three girls: Camillo, Alexandro, Luigi and Petro; Margarita, Sophie and Maria. Camillo died when he was forty-two; Alexandro at thirty-five, Luigi at eighteen months; Pietro at twenty-five months. All are dead except the youngest, the two girls, who live with me still. Maria is of marriageable age; Sophie is the widow of Paoli Micali, of Mantua, Chamberlain of His Eminence Cardinal Barberini. The servant of God suckled all these children at her own breast and took care to have them baptised almost as soon as they were born, and confirmed in due course."

Domenico made his deposition when he was ninety-one years old. His memory, usually faithful, seems to have failed him here. His daughter Sophie says he had three boys and not four, four girls and not three. Similarly the names differ a little, and the order in which the children were born and died, for the Beata assisted at the death of four out of the seven children. But Sophie is wrong also. The baptismal registers of the parish of Saint Marcellus, which are authoritative, do not agree entirely either with Domenico or Sophie. They contain the following entries, and let us observe in passing the quick sequence of the births: Anna, 1790; Camillo, 1793; Alessandro, 1795; Luigi, 1797; Sophie, 1802; Luisa, 1806; Maria, 1810. All were baptised either on the day of their birth or the day following.

Sophie adds some delightful details. "My mother brought up her children and at the age of six or seven years or so had them confirmed—earlier still, if they were ailing. Mariuccia was confirmed at the age of five, when the French invasion carried fears of the expulsion of the bishops. After a course of catechism there was first Communion at the age of twelve, then the customary age, Anna continuing the spiritual formation of the children. On rising in the morning, family prayers; after supper, the Rosary, on our knees, with a reading from the life of the Saint of the day. Sometimes we sang a hymn, then after receiving our parents' blessing we went to bed, the girls in one room, the boys in another; further privacy was gained by shutting off each bed with curtains. On Sunday and holidays we all went to Mass with a sermon, then Anna made the girls accompany her to the hospital to train them in the ways of charity. She never allowed the girls to go anywhere unless their mother, or grandmother, or Luigi (called "Little Luigi", the son of the Knight Antonini, a man of trustworthiness, education and piety) accompanied them. As to these outings Cardinal Pedicini makes a remark which, coming from a Roman, has its unconscious humour. Anna refused to visit the museums where Domenico wanted to take her and even the children. "She knew," says the Cardinal, "that galleries and museums contain indecent objects, even one must admit, in this city of Rome! The churches themselves are not free of such things. One of the allocutions which the servant of God heard had reference to

the representations of children in an indecently
naked condition. As the poor woman contemplated
the mystery of the Incarnation in front of a picture
in the church of St. Silvester in the Quirinal, Our
Lady complained of this abuse, which is at variance
alike with holy purity and the Gospel facts."

Here is a further deposition of Sophie: "Our
mother trained us to be always busy. It was a habit
which developed into a necessity." Even Mariuccia,
Domenico's darling, "could not remain idle a
minute; she was always at work either for some small
reward or out of pure charity. She used to say:
'Laziness is the mother of all the vices'."* Mamma
loved us all tenderly and with an equal love that had
no favourites. She used the stick, if necessary, but in
moderation, and preferred to make us go without
our dinner or to put us on dry bread." The method
was successful. The Decree of Beatification notes
that the children of Anna "will call her blessed".

All of them were good Catholics and lowly
working-folk, for the Beata never consented that
they should leave the class in which they were born,
although friends made numerous alluring offers.
They were not saints. Holiness is not hereditary,
like the cast of one's face or the colour of one's hair.

§

Camillo was apprenticed to a barber and Alessandro
to a hatter. Alessandro was the pet of Grandma
Santa. Given to card-playing, on feast days he played
ducks and drakes with the money he had and the

---

* The French quotation marks are perplexing. The punctuation itself seems
wrong, for Mariuccia as a child would scarcely have said: "Laziness is the mother
of all the vices." It seems better to read: "Mariuccia even, the spoilt child of
Domenico, could not rest idle a minute. Mamma was always employed, either in
what would win a small income, or for pure charity. She used to say: 'laziness,
etc.'."

money he had not. Grandma was there to pay his debts, and to that end would deprive herself of snuff. The Beata warned her she would go to Purgatory for this sin, and thus induced her to stop her misplaced charity. As a further precaution she asked the master-hatter to let her know whenever his apprentice was absent. So it came to pass that he was cured. He became in due time a small owner himself, was married, and died of phthisis at the age of fifty years.

Camillo was apprenticed to one Milani, model of barbers. Annette economised and advised him to buy a shop that would be his own establishment in the future. All was going well when calamity descended upon them. Camillo was twenty years when Napoleon, having occupied Rome and carried off Pius VII, pressed his recruiting sergeants to send new levies for the Russian campaign. A system of lots was employed. Those who drew high numbers were provisionally exempt, low numbers had to go. Camillo drew a favourable number that exempted him, but a crafty woman named Checca, who lived in the Chigi palace where her husband worked with Domenico, saw her son Nicholas draw an unfavourable number. She arranged matters with the recruiting sergeant, who pretended that Camillo had drawn the bad number and Nicholas the good. She was so pleased with her artifice that she boasted of it. Domenico threatened fire and slaughter. The Beata kept silent and, hastening to the barracks, hoped to take Camillo in her arms and advise him for his good. Unfortunately the troops had been hurried off, and her child was already far away. Annette came back weeping and went into her little oratory to pray, and Our Lord consoled her. Her son was not to go into the firing-line, but to return safe and

sound. The colonel of the regiment needed a barber
and naturally chose Camillo for his orderly. After
the debacle of Napoleon's Russian campaign, Camillo
came home unexpectedly. The imperial armies,
though not exactly a school for sanctity, had not
spoiled him, and Annette found him a place as a
servant in the household of Mgr. Mastai, uncle of
the Giovanni Mastai, who was to become Pius IX.

Fresh trouble was not long in coming. Camillo,
earning but twelve crowns, fell in love with a girl
called Antonia Pari, whose entire dowry amounted
to thirty crowns—enough to buy her a dress.
Annette suggested time for reflection and prayer,
pointing out that they would have a hard life of it,
but eventually she agreed that they should marry
at the end of four months. The marriage took place
and the young couple, with neither hearth nor home
of their own, took up their abode under the Beata's
roof, remaining there for two years. The daughter-in-
law gave a moving testimony of her mother-in-law's
holiness at the time of the Ordinary Process, but
Domenico added that the said daughter-in-law was
the occasion of a great increase in that sanctity. She
was a difficult character who attempted to control
everything in a home which was so far from belong-
ing to her that she was received into it out of charity.

Alessandro was a fresh source of worry. Domenico
narrates how "he was put in prison for some trifling
offence, and my poor wife was distressed about it,
but kept her peace of mind in silence." It was during
the French occupation, and he had, it seems,
foolishly gone to play on forbidden ground. A
zealous police officer told him it was more dangerous
to walk on the grass than to jostle one's companions
in the path, and forthwith put him in gaol, but
thinking better of it, set him free the following day.

Like Camillo, Allessandro fell in love with a young girl of very lowly origin and very poor. The Beata, who had a better plan in her mind, was chagrined, but did not insist when she saw her son was obstinate.

The marriage was celebrated. The Taigi household surrendered its quarters in the Chigi palace to the young couple and established themselves as tenants in the Corso, for the Chigi quarters were altogether too restricted. In spite of this, Alessandro could not make both ends meet, and Anna had to send him some of the leavings from the prince's table. Above all, she unobtrusively mentioned work to her daughter-in-law, who having brought but poverty as dowry to an already poor husband yet wanted to live like a duchess. The Beata thus taught her two daughters-in law how to be thrifty and handy. The very pearl of mothers-in-law, she sent little gifts of money or food to them on feast-days in order to gladden their table. Camillo was to die in the flower of his age of a malady of the chest. Ill herself, Anna-Maria had herself carried to his bedside. Her daughter-in-law demanded a miracle, saying that her mother-in-law could work as many of them as she wished, but the Beata took her into her arms, telling her her husband's place was ready for him in heaven. "Let us, too," she said, "go in that direction; soon we shall find him again in Paradise."

§

Sophie, whose depositions are of equal interest with her father, Domenico's, is a very engaging character. The Beata put her in the care of her old teachers, "the Good Mistresses", first near the Gesu, later at the school of St. Denis, where she remained for three years as a day-pupil. She showed rare talent for singing, and her mistresses proposed teaching her

music free of charge, but the Beata refused, fearing
that this artistic accomplishment might turn her
head and set her thoughts towards the theatre. She
asked the ladies to teach her housekeeping that
would equip her for marriage and motherhood.
When she left school Sophie went into a silk-worker's
shop, whose owner was a splendid type of Catholic.
On returning home she was her mother's joy and
eventually married a young man of good family,
called Paolo Micali.

Paolo was excellent in every respect, but he had
no means of livelihood, and Maria-Louise, former
Queen of Etruria and friend of the Beata, promised
to obtain him a position, but died before she could
fulfil her promise, with the result that Anna was
charged with another household. The espoused
couple saw one another two or three times at
Annette's home, and, as with the other match-
makings, so with this—a family dinner-party, a good
bottle of sparkling Asti and the whole thing was
settled. Sophie was to have six children. The household was an ideal one. Her husband got two posi-
tions instead of one—as gentleman of honour to
Cardinal Barberini and major domo of Count Cini.
He died suddenly in 1835, and Sophie, her servant
and her six children fled for refuge to Annette, who
welcomed them with open arms.

Sophie was distressed, feeling herself a burden to
the poor home, but Anna rebuked her gently, saying:
"Why are you worrying, child? God will provide.
Never will you or your children lack food." And so
it proved. The Beata thought it would be a good
thing for the young widow to marry again, and a
desirable young man was forthcoming, but as Sophie
disliked the idea of this marriage, Anna-Maria did
not insist. In the manifold illness which was to

besiege her mother, Sophie was her nurse and her confidante. She died in 1867, thirty years after her mother, laboured for her glorification, and eventually lay in death at her side at the church of St. Chrysogonus.

Maria or Mariuccia did not begin so well as her sister, Sophie, yet according to her deposition, which was a long one, her mother left no stone unturned to give her a complete education. Anna-Maria taught her her catechism. There were morning and night prayers, the family rosary, school at "the Good Mistresses" till she was thirteen years old; a retreat followed at least three times during the carnival. What more could be done? Anna herself accompanied her to school, or at any rate confided her to the care of Luigi Antoni, that good man whom we must certainly not fail to mention. He was elderly, a little lame, charmingly simple, a disciple of Anna's by whom he had been miraculously cured, a faithful friend who delighted to do the odd jobs she gave him—to chaperon the children, to go shopping when Anna was too ill, to give alms, to visit the sick, to cure by proxy, through bringing them a wad of cotton-wool dipped in the oil of the votive or watch-lamp in her little oratory.

But to return to Mariuccia. The youngest of the children, and spoiled by Domenico, she was vain, coquettish and lazy, and yet her father adored her. To touch her with your little finger was to risk the most frightful scenes. The little vixen knew it and took advantage of it. The saint temporises, prays, expostulates now and then with all gentleness and succeeds in the end, for Mariuccia becomes a pretty girl, well-behaved and diligent, almost to equal Sophie. The devil's advocate blamed Anna-Maria for the childish vanities of her child and for her silk

dress, but Mariuccia herself was there to rebut the
charge, and yet with restraint. The said silk dress
was, after all, of black, which was a sober enough
colour; moreover, the silk was bought not by mother
but by Mariuccia; her vanity having got the better
of her idleness, she had worked to buy a remnant
out of which she made the dress herself. Mgr.
Natali adds his testimony: "The Beata adapted herself to the character of each; she cherished their good
qualities, mildly corrected their bad ones and thus
trained her children perfectly. Would that all
mothers and all superiors modelled themselves upon
her."

Mariuccia never married. She became the spinster
aunt at the service of a multitude of nephews and
nieces; a trifle given to grumbling, no doubt, for she
took after her father, but with a heart of gold. She
survived her mother by forty-eight years and died a
very holy death in 1885, a member of the Pious
Institute of the Sisters of Charity of St. Vincent de
Paul, which she had joined several years before the
death of the Beata. She was for ever telling her
nephews and nieces of the virtues of their grandmother, and they profited by her lessons. Sophie's
six children were worthy of their mother and their
grandmother. One of them, Marie-Louise, who was
eleven years old when the Beata died, entered religion as a Reformed Tertiary of Saint Francis and
died in 1863, leaving behind her a great reputation
of holy joy and of austerity.

§

These details about the children of the Beata have
made us forget the appalling labours which were the
price of their education. To feed this nest of at least
twelve mouths the Beata had to spend the six crowns

of Domenico's monthly wages (six crowns would amount to about two hundred to three hundred francs of present-day money*). This she supplemented with part of the leavings of the prince's table—"part" only because Domenico had naturally to share them at second-best with the chief cook.

This explains why Domenico found his wife still at work when he returned home at two or three o'clock in the morning, she was still striving to eke out the salary received in money and that received in kind; it was a distressing business.

In addition, the Beata, over a period of fourteen years, was frequently carrying or suckling a child and was herself the principal instructress of her little ones.

Domenico, as a matter of principle, left the training of the children to her, and indeed the less he had to do with it the better, for he knew only two methods—the stick or barley sugar.

The gentle watchfulness of Annette counteracted this mischievous policy. In the morning (so testify Sophie and Maria) the order was prayers, finishing touches to their appearance (for Annette believed in neatness), the journey to school, the return, grace before meals, dinner, and grace after meals. In the evening, rosary and other prayers (which Mariuccia found tedious) said on the knees and before supper. After supper a reading by Mgr. Natali from the *Lives of the Saints* or the *Annals of the Missions*, hymns, the blessing, and bed. Anna remained behind, working and praying till dawn.

To all this Domenico adds a wealth of detail. "She gave unceasing thanks to God for having caused her to be born in the Catholic Church, and she taught her children to praise Him for so great a favour.

* 1936.

When any priest came she rose in order to kiss his hand and made her children do the same. The girls went to the sacraments each week; the boys two or three times a month. She looked after the children like the gentlest of mothers and placed them eventually in workshops above reproach and kept herself informed of their conduct. When she could not do the shopping herself she sent, not the girls, but Antonini to do it. These precautions may seem exaggerated, but Anna, apart altogether from her own experience of the dangers to be run, could see at close quarters happenings frequent and serious enough to put her on her guard—and Domenico himself approved of the strictness she adopted. "When there was question," says Domenico, "of Sophie marrying Micali, my wife, in order to give the young couple opportunities of becoming acquainted, allowed the young man to frequent the house for a period of two months and to talk to Sophie, but she herself was always present." The marriage feast consisted simply of a family reunion at the table.

Domenico further gives us the picture of his wife going the round of the little white beds every night, tenderly bestowing here a word of counsel, there a work of reproach, and telling all to be loving and obedient to Daddy, who is always working for them all. Then, after a final kiss and a last sign of the Cross on their foreheads, she goes back to her work. "I shall save your children," said Our Lord to her one day, "for they are blood of your blood. Moreover, they are poor, and the poor are my friends. Yes, I shall save them, though they have many faults." "If they did not all become as good as she desired," remarked her confessor, "it was not her fault."

They *were* all good; indeed, heroic holiness apart, the most ordinary of them led a life of great Christian virtue. After all, neither the children of St. Louis nor of St. Jeanne de Chantal were saints.

One of the lessons with which the Beata strove to impress her children was that of doing their work in an orderly and systematic manner. Domenico abandoned to her not merely the children's education but the management of the home. "I let her," he said, "do the managing, for I saw well she could do it to perfection. Yet she desired my opinion before doing the slightest thing. She had hands of gold. I had nothing to worry about, she made my trousers and coats, everything." She worked regularly from two to three hours after midnight, yet was up at five for Mass and Communion. When she came back from church, about six, she put everything to rights and prepared breakfast. "When illness forced her to stay in bed she set herself to mending linen, and never remained idle."

§

In 1799, during the French invasion and the captivity of Pius VI, provisions became scarce and extremely dear; people formed queues outside the bakers, waiting for hours in the midst of the winter rains. Domenico was out of work. Anna heroically undertook to provide bread for all. She made bodices, petticoats, half-boots and socks, but refused to let anybody take her turn at waiting at the door of the bakeries.

"In one word," said Domenico, with feeling, "she was an incomparable woman. . . . I am an old man now, but if I were young and searched the world to find a woman like her, I should not succeed. I have lost a treasure of great price."

He never tires of adding attractive details. Anna loved neatness in her little apartment, which was very unassuming. You would have called it a sanctuary. On the walls there were some holy pictures, chaste in style and devotional of expression. At the end of the room was an oratory with a picture of St. Philomena and a painting of the Madonna, before which burnt the votive lamp whose oil performed numerous miracles; crowning all was a crucifix. On the shelves were four candlesticks and vases of flowers. Near the door the holy-water stoup was never dry, for Anna used holy water to sprinkle her children morning and night and every time they left or entered the house. All these pious relics are preserved to-day at St. Chrysogonus in a little museum near her tomb. The most touching mementos are the poor work-table at which Anna laboured day and night, and the miraculous picture of the Virgin Mother of Sorrows with the dead Jesus, which is wonderfully moving and before which the expiatress so often sobbed. It is a reproduction of the miraculous painting attributed to Guido Reni, above the altar in the "Pieta" chapel, two minutes walk away from the Chigi palace. Anna established the custom of saying, on entering the house: "Praised be Jesus and Mary!" It was her greeting morning and night, the while she bowed her head with reverence.

In all this there was nothing gloomy. She sometimes took the children for a walk. They visited some church or other and then had a little delicacy in the shape of chestnuts with a little wine, in which Anna shared in order to give them pleasure. When Domenico was free all went together to Benediction, and often at night to some church where the Forty Hours was in progress. Such were their relaxations.

§

If anyone objects that this was a life for monks and nuns, it may be asked if a daily turn at the cinema, or a joint visit to a cabaret is a better popular school of thrift and happiness. And Anna often said that thrift and foresight are the only qualifications that entitle one to count on Providence.

And how she needed to count on Providence! From 1797, the seventh year of her marriage, the Beata witnessed one public calamity after another. Bonaparte broke up the Legations and deprived the Pontifical government of its best resources, so that the Pope was obliged to raise his taxes. There was discontent and armed rebellion, led by some French officers. The Directory sent General Berthier to occupy Rome, and on 13th February 1798 the Republic was proclaimed and sacrileges and profanations followed. Pius VI, eighty-one and ill, was carried in the middle of the night to Siena, whence he was taken to Florence, then to Parma, Turin, Briançon, Grenoble and finally Valence. There he died, 29th August 1799, and the governor of the district wrote to the Directory: "The erstwhile Pope is dead; now for the end of superstition."

Anna foresaw these events in her sun day after day, followed the sorrowful Calvary of Pius VI, assisted at his death, and foretold the name and hour of election of his successor. Meanwhile the seven consuls in charge of Rome succeeded only in delivering the city to hunger and the depredations of robbers. Annette worked day and night, caused her children to pray and invoked St. Joseph, the patron of lost and hopeless causes.

Providence did not fail. In the midst of all the disturbances, of daily slaughter, neither Domenico, his children, nor Annette, who persevered in going to Mass every morning, were molested. Three months after the death of Pius VI the Conclave met at Venice, 1st December 1799. On 14th March 1800 Cardinal Chiaramenti was elected as Pius VII. On 3rd July 1800 the French left Rome, and the Pope made his entry into his ruined and blood-stained capital.

The Prince Chigi, who had brought Domenico to the Conclave, noticed that the lodging placed at his disposal in a little street of the Sdrucciolo, was certainly inadequate, with its two rooms for twelve people.

He gave him a dwelling more fit for human habitation near the palace in the Via del Giardino. They had again to break up the home in 1817 to go to No. 195 The Corso, where Mgr. Natali now came to instal himself as a lodger. In 1828 still more removals, but eventually they settled for a period of seven years opposite the church of St. Ignatius, at the Fiorelli Palace. They occupied the ground-floor, which had iron barred windows, facing the narrow street Dei Burro. In 1835 Sophie Micali and her six children came to occupy these narrow quarters, and so there was a seventh removal, this time to the Righetti Palace on the Corso, opposite the church Santa Maria, in Via Lata, at the corner of the little street of the Holy Apostles. Here it was that the Beata died in 1837, a hundred yards from the Bonaparte palace, where died the mother of the Emperor.

Truly Anna never had a lasting dwelling in this world. Domenico, his family and Mgr. Natali had to leave this house also after Anna's death and went to live in the Road of the Four Fountains.

§

Alas for the migratory existence of the poor! Why does not our devotion to the saints and to history induce us to respect the places where they passed by and suffered.

Those who have acquired the Bonaparte palace in the Corso have respected and consecrated the memory of Letizia, who lived and died there, and it is well that they should. But why, in the Chigi and Righetti palaces and other places where Anna lived, is there no memorial of her? Even in a church where the saint went morning after morning for long years, now rejoiced by wonderful ecstasies, now tried by great distresses, men have forgotten her; there is not even the tiniest picture of her. If you make enquiries, the name is known, but that is all.

Annette maintained her serenity through all these multiple uprootings and farewells to roof-trees that had seen cradles and coffins follow one another. "The soul," said our Lord to her, "that lives with the life of the Spirit cannot always have his chart in hand, for it is thus worldlings behave, who fear to feel their feet on uncertain ground. He that trusts in Me is richer than the kings of earth. . . . It is not in peace that one recognises the true soldier, for at that rate all the world could play soldiers. It is when keeping guard he sustains the want of food and drink and sleep, and fights faithfully for his king one finds his worth. . . ."

Domenico could hardly reach such heights, and he would have liked the saint to trade more on the esteem in which she was held. "Numbers of distinguished people came to see her at home, and I used to say to her, 'Why not drop a hint to such a one on behalf of the family?' She used to answer: 'Let us place our trust in God', or other expressions that closed my mouth. . . . Yet her confidence in God was so great that in fact we never did want for anything, not even in the most critical times, and for that may God be praised a thousand times.

"Also, while she besought God, she did not imagine that the raven would come from heaven without her doing anything for herself. To keep such a large family without ever being in want was a perpetual miracle. The friendship which the late Queen of Etruria had for her was alone sufficient to keep us out of grave need, but she resigned herself completely to Divine dispositions. In the most distressing situations she kept silence, contenting herself with the words: 'May the will of God be done.' When we lost our children, whom she loved very dearly, she placed them in the shroud with her own hands, as she had done for her old mother and for her father."

Four of her children died before her. "When our child Camillo was conscripted by an imposture she was unable to speak for a long time. She was grievously distressed, but remained resigned and complained of nobody, not even of her whom we had grave reason to think was the cause of the fraud."

When Sophie lost her husband and had no resources for herself or her children and was apt to complain, Annette remarked: "How little faith you have and how little confidence in God. Do not be anxious for your future. God will take thought for you."

§

God put His sign manual on this impregnable confidence by working miracles. One day, to the inconsolable grief of Sophie, her little Peppina tore the pupil of her eye while playing, and the doctor declared that the sight of the affected eye was lost, and that of the other in great danger. Annette made the sign of the Cross on the injured eye with some oil from her St. Philomena lamp (little St. Philomena was saddled with Annette's miracles as, later, with those of the Curé d'Ars) and the following day the child was able to go to school perfectly cured.

Domenico was stricken with an attack of apoplexy. Annette put him to bed and laid her hand on his head. When he woke up he was cured. Here is his own account:

"One winter's morning in the church of St. Marcel I felt suddenly very ill. Scarcely had I returned home when I lost consciousness and I was told afterwards that I had had (God preserve us from the like) an apoplectic convulsion, not to say a stroke. When I returned to consciousness I remembered nothing of it, but discovered at my bedside the priest and my wife, who had her hand on my brow and was pleading for me with the Most Holy Virgin. Her prayer was heard by God, for, without any human remedy, I recovered my health instantaneously, and there remained no injury and no trace of any kind on my head or elsewhere of the seizure I had sustained. I hold it for certain that it was the servant of God who obtained for me this astonishing and instantaneous cure. The parish priest, finding my pulse very feeble, had given me conditional absolution." Some time afterwards Domenico was afflicted with such headaches that he was unable to work and walked the streets like one demented. Annette made the sign of the Cross over him and he was delivered from the affliction for ever after.

It was Sophie's turn next. A malignant fever overtook her, and the doctor seeing no hope, recommended that the priest be called. Annette made the sign of the Cross over the patient with a relic she always carried, and though Sophie was in a state of coma, she awoke immediately, cured. Another alarm soon followed. Sophie began to have such violent pains near the stomach that she could not walk and could breathe only with difficulty. Whether it was cancer or something else, her mother prayed, touched with her hand the seat of the evil and it disappeared.

Anna wished her home to be a place where God came first, and God heard her prayer.

"She went to Mass every day and Communion, too, as I know for a fact, although I could not see her with my own eyes, except on feast days, when I went with her; then I saw her communicate and left her in the church after me. It was on feast days, if I had a little leisure, that we also went with the children to Benediction or the Rosary at the Minerva. Morning and night there were family prayers, from which no one was absent. At night, before supper, or as soon as possible after, we read, now the life of one saint, now the life of another, by way of recreation. My wife spoke of God and the things of God, but she was not a bore as some devotees are, who talk for ever of themselves and their piety, or make a parade of their devotions. She laughed at any witticisms made at the table, but knew how to turn the conversation imperceptibly towards holy things.

On week days she worked and washed and saw to the household generally with a vigour that would have tired four ordinary women, but on holy days and Sundays she abstained altogether from servile work. She employed her time in prayer, in having read to her works of piety, and in hearing several Masses. When the children came back from catechism she took them to hear a sermon, and assist at Benediction, and then for a walk. During the day she did only what was strictly necessary; that is to say, she made the beds and cooked the meals. Thus did she see to it that holy days were kept holy by all the members of the family." At night the family played hide-and-seek or blind-man's-buff, or Domenico, to Anna's great delight, would try blindfold to catch hold of tiny Peppina. "It was the peace of God," sighed Domenico.

III

THE ROYAL ROAD OF THE CROSS – THE LOVE OF ABASEMENT – PATIENCE – CONTINUOUS MORTIFICATION

THIS peace was bought by the Beata by a constant spirit of renunciation. Our Lord gave her this golden advice: "My daughter, spiritual profit consists neither in penance nor in the frequentation of the Sacraments, nay, not even in abiding sorrow for sin, but in the union of your will with Mine. Those who wish to follow My way must renounce their own will everywhere and in all things. Do what you do not wish to do; leave undone what you wish to do; one act of violence to oneself of this kind is much more pleasing to Me than an entire year of penances. You must not for the future use such language as: 'I want this; that is pleasant, that other thing unpleasant, and I would much rather not do it'—such is the language of the world." "She herself," comments Cardinal Pedicini, "interpreted the necessity of renunciation in the following words: 'To acquire the love of God one must always pull against the stream and never cease to resist one's own will'."

Every page of the process assures us that she carried out her instructions without, of course, advising us to regulate our conduct by hers. Every soul has its own way and graces to follow that way, and he is a fool who, without taking thought, would imitate Benedict Labre, for instance.

She made a formal pact that, so far as it rested with her own will, she would never allow herself any satisfaction of the senses, nor any pleasure—no sinful pleasure, obviously, and no pleasure that might lead to sin, but not even innocent pleasure. Someone may say that it was principles of this kind that led the Jansenists and Mother Angelica into folly, for of Mother Angelica it is said she was "proud as Lucifer" and imposed renunciation more on others than on herself. It was otherwise with Annette. She was humble, and made her severe laws for herself alone. She was charitable to all, but if she felt a spontaneous attraction towards anybody, she restrained herself, whereas if anybody had done her an injury she was lavish towards such a one. If she was inundated during prayer with divine consolation, she cut her prayers short; if she was desolate, she prolonged them. It was doubtless this spirit which cancelled the objection of the Devil's Advocate, who accused her of extravagance on the evidence of one good woman, who said: "Whenever I went to see her in the morning she always offered me a cup of coffee or chocolate. The Devil s Advocate may also have been influenced by the woman's added comment: "It is true that in doing so she was conforming to the Roman custom."

"Be humble, be patient!" she used often to say to her spiritual daughters. She once talked to Our Lord about a certain soul, and Our Lord said to her: "Tell her to be humble with everybody without exception; submissive to everybody without exception; obedient to everybody without exception." She obeyed this advice herself, for all her directors note that though she was gifted with extraordinary visions, her humility was so great she obeyed in every detail not only her confessors, but, so far as that was possible, all the members of her household.

Never did she lose sight of her own nothingness. "Whosoever lives in fear," said Our Lord to her more than once, "will never fall, but whosoever fears not has already fallen. If you love, you must fear, and yet your fear ought to be full of confidence. Let not your heart be afraid, for if the enemy sees that it is, he will speedily vanquish you. By humility will you find the middle path. He who wishes to be My disciple must walk in My footsteps, for he that bears humiliations with faith and love, he is My son. Suffer scorn and contempt with humility for My love's sake. Keep silence and bow your head saying: 'I deserve worse for my Spouse has suffered much more.' You must constantly desire humiliations, for it is by this way that you must sanctify yourself."

She would never play the foundress when little religious coteries begged her to take their head, and this horror she had of all ostentation resulted in some quaint episodes.

Marie-Louise de Bourbon, daughter of the King of Spain, one time Queen of Etruria and later Duchess de Lucques, owed many cures to Anna, had a fervent affection for her, and called her "Sister". If, in the streets of Rome, when walking with her entire retinue, she caught sight of the lowly working woman she would run to her and greet her kissing her hand. Annette, if she saw the royal cortège would slip down a side-street, or into a shop, or hide in the shadow of a gateway. Yet she never tried to evade one of those shrews who persecuted her.

"He that is humble is patient," Our Lord had told her; "the soul that suffers patiently the tribulations that come from creatures is greater than a penitent. My true disciple is he who, ever equable in himself, suffers interiorly and exteriorly without allowing himself the least complaint against anybody whatsoever. He that has patience enjoys all things here below, and is in expectation of a crown at last."

§

"To suffer and to deny oneself." Annette had not read the Stoics. Her strong point was not in elaborating theses, but in shouldering in practice the burdens she praised in words. From the beginning of her call, at the age of twenty-one, God gave her such a thirst for austerity and expiation, that one is terrified at its manifestations. In her mind was a Europe prostrate with misfortune, where yet no one was content with his lot. Debauchery gave place to murder. Think of the House of Orleans and the royal palace, asylum of profligates and notorious libertines, where wives were treated like harlots. The "Affair of the Necklace" raised but a corner of the veil which curtained a society rotten to the core. Think of Laclos, that depraved novel-writer, the companion in orgy of the Duke of Orleans, the pillar of the "Club of Frenzy"; Champert, Marmontel consign religion and all moral and social order to the pillory of abuse. In 1791 even their wishes were surpassed, and Marmontel in particular was so distraught by the amazing upheaval that he committed suicide—cutting his throat. This revolutionary of the Academy would have found in Annette's doctrines all that was necessary for the happiness of humanity about which he never ceased his affected lecturing.

Providence taught its lesson to the world in a way that left no escape—the way of suffering. Indeed, it was not only the philosophers that wanted the lesson. Ecclesiastical dignities were almost entirely the perquisite of the wealthy classes wherever the Bourbon authority held sway. It was not the custom to serve others, but rather to be served by others and to consider oneself superior to the code of morals that the "common" people were expected to keep. The unedited memoirs of Mgr. Luquet show that here and there existed monasteries where juniors were invested with clerical office almost as late as 1850, ten years after Anna's death. Sad survivals of an *ancien régime*, hotbeds of scandal for which Anna had to make reparation.

As to a spirit of penance, herein she equalled the greatest ascetics.

Our Lord appeared to her as when Pilate said, "Behold the Man," inviting her to share his sufferings. "Voluntary exterior penances," He said, "are sometimes the price one has to pay for the grace to bear, and not to faint under the involutary interior tribulations of heart and soul."

Her fasts were perpetual. "She ate like a sparrow," complained Domenico. In the morning, on returning from Mass, she had a little cup of coffee; at midday a few drops of soup and a morsel of meat. She did not sit down, but waited at table on the others, including the servants.

"The first and the best for the old mother, eh, Domenico?"

"Of course, the oldest must be first served, but

why not sit down; why not make yourself easy?"

"Well, Domenico, when the Prince takes his meal does not the servant stand, ready to serve him? Did I not become your servant from the day you took me to wife at St. Marcel?"

Domenico would be flattered and smile, and consequently failed to observe that if she poured out something to drink for him, or scraped cheese into the soup, she forgot to do the same for herself.

But he was not entirely unobservant. "My wife was very self-denying, especially on Fridays." We may add that she fasted specially also on Saturdays, when she was content with morning coffee and midday soup. On Wednesday, in honour of St. Joseph, it was the same. The Lenten Forty Days was not enough for her; she added other periods of Forty Days whenever there was some spectre of public misfortune to lay, or some soul to save; and, even what she ate she contrived to make a little penitential.

She would put aside for two or three days the meat she intended for herself, and if her daughters remarked that it stank, she said she preferred it like that.

She was naturally disposed to thirst, and in the sultry heat of Rome suffered continually, yet used it as a splendid opportunity for sacrifice. It was her absolute rule not to drink between meals, but, more than this, when at meal-time she had filled her glass, she would drink only in tiny sips, so as to mortify her thirst; then she would serve her children and not return to her glass till considerably later. Eventually Domenico noticed her devices: "What are you at? What is it all about? You are toying with your glass. Come! drink it up quickly." Anna smiled and drank half a glass of water. The youngest daughter also would call her father's attention saying: "Papa, mamma is not drinking." Domenico would then fill his wife's glass and bid her drink it in his presence, and this led her to rebuke the little spy: "It is not well, child, to notice at table who eats, who does not eat, who drinks and who does not drink; you must correct yourself of that bad habit."

If it were a question of delivering a soul from Purgatory she would go a whole day, two days— even (so we are assured) eight days without drinking anything at all, and that at the height of the terrible Roman heats. She admitted to the Mgr. Natali that her thirst on such occasions was enough to make her throw herself into the nearby fountain to quench the intolerable burning.

Domenico knew not to what saint to commend himself, torn as he was between affection and respect. "You eat nothing, Anna."

"But I do eat, even as you do, and in moving about to serve you I help myself to masticate and digest. Besides, you sleep deeply after eating lightly. Is it not said that the air here in Rome obliges one to keep a light stomach?" "There was no more to be said," comments Domenico.

Anna, like her mother, was very fond of sweets and would, naturally speaking, have become a glutton. Now Domenico brought back from the prince's table the leavings of sweets, ices and sherbets which formerly had been the favourites of his wife. She thanked him, praised the delicacies and touched them to her lips, but hastened immediately to distribute them to her mother and the children. "But at least take this ice," Domenico would say. She hurried to do so, but, making a face, would say, "Ugh! How cold it is! How cold it is!" Domenico would shrug his shoulders. "You are an idiot. Of

course it's cold! It is ice! That is exactly why I
brought it for you. You do not understand anything
about anything."

On the contrary, she understood everything quite
well, even gratitude, and so, handing that same ice
to the children she would say, "Taste how delicious
it is; taste the good things Dadda brings us." Stern
with herself, she was all mildness to others. The
servants and charwomen could easily have been
embarrassed by her austerity, but she herself served
them, giving large helpings and being delighted to
see them enjoy good meals. Domenico tells us how
his wife, during her illness, had a maid and another
woman attendant and would not be content unless
they ate in her presence, for she feared that otherwise they would be under-nourished. When she was
not confined to her bed she gave them a large
helping of everything; what she gave was more tha·
sufficient. She also instructed them in their religion
and frequently took them with her to Mass. It is still
Domenico that tells us (for he went from point to
point of the long questionnaire with patient docility):

"She kept careful custody of her senses, above all
of her eyes. In spite of her vivacity she saw nobody
but me, her husband. She never took a walk with
anybody but me. I never descried in her the slightest
departure from modesty. She never allowed herself
any caresses or kisses that savoured of sensuality. In
the midst of the roughest household duties she was as
modestly clothed as if in public. In her sufferings
she maintained the reserve and guard of a religious."

Her daughter tells us that her mother hardly slept
at all at night; even when she did she rose habitually
before dawn after a bare two hours sleep. She used
the time when the rest of us were enjoying the siesta
for prayer.

Other penances were known to none but her confessor—hair shirt, chain girdles bristling with points, scourges, a crown of thorns that she wore during her solitary vigils, yet without ceasing from work. She was, as Domenico asserts, docile to her confessor in the matter of exterior mortifications. It was only after her death that there were found on her the instruments of self-torture that she used.

Someone once wrote: "These are the habits of a fanatic savage." But stay! At this period the Revolution made heads fall as tiles fall from a roof in a gale. For thirty years from the Tiber to the Nile, along the Beresina, the shambles were multiplied, blood flowed in torrents—and many who are *not* shocked at this homicidal frenzy, or even sing its praises, *are* shocked at a lowly Christian woman who was willing and desirous by her voluntary sufferings to diminish the involuntary sufferings that were imposed by turbulent spirits who had no belief in the glory of God, but a besotted belief in the glory of men.

IV

"CONVERSATION IN HEAVEN"–HER FAITH, OBEDIENCE AND SPIRIT OF PRAYER–HER TEMPTATIONS AGAINST FAITH

FAITH! Never had its kingdom seemed nearer ruin. Man had made a lucky find that suited him admirably—for the authority of God, he substituted the authority of certain scholars of philosophy: Voltaire, Rousseau, Condorcet, La Reveillere Lepeaux.

Kant maintained that the postulates of revealed religion were inadmissible and warned mankind gravely that Christianity was in the death-throes. La Mettrie thought it was consolation to tell us man was—well, a machine, or a plant, or, at the most, a monkey. And this twaddle had a marvellous vogue. It was a twofold frenzy spreading from the intellectual to the people at large and consisting in blasphemy that took on the airs of morality. Never were people more level-headed in their own conceit; never were the words of morality and brotherly love so much on people's lips as in those days of systematic butcheries. The world was like a ship without a compass, and the Beata like a candle set upon a candlestick.

"For her," says Cardinal Pedicini, "the world was an open book consisting of one word, GOD. The slightest rustle of the wind, the song of a bird, the sight of an insect or a flower, was enough to carry her out of herself to God in an ecstasy. The simplest ditty of the poor blind folk who walk the streets of Rome smote her heart. She had to lean on her companion and enter a church as soon as possible. Her husband understood nothing of these gifts." Her life was the supernatural reduced to tangible and visible action, and that during a period of forty-seven years.

Faith, then, is no more? "There is nothing *but* Faith," the experience of this life tells us. Faith gives knowledge both of the next world and of this, and both worlds were the object of this lowly woman's contemplation in her mysterious sun. It was the reward of her heroic faith. That faith might triumph, she desired every possible martyrdom, and her ecstasies were one dolorous cry: "Hallowed be Thy Name; Thy Kingdom come."

Her unforgettable sign of the Cross was a sermon in itself; it humbled the most learned theologians, even as her knowledge of theology and her contempt for circumlocutions humbled them. "He who serves

God," she said, "must be humble and deferential, but frank and sincere." Her letters to the Queen of Etruria were of an admirable frankness.

§

Let us say a word about this princess who played an important part in her life. In 1801 the realm of Tuscany, having been converted into the realm of Etruria, was given to Prince Louis de Parme, who died in 1803. His widow, Marie-Louise de Bourbon, daughter of Charles IV, King of Spain, administered the realm in her son's name. She was forced to abdicate, and in 1808 her kingdom was absorbed into the French Empire. The unhappy princess almost lost her reason. She became afflicted with epilepsy and had to be confined in her palace in Rome. The Beata cured her, became her friend, her comforter, and showed her the hand of God in these scourges that wiped out a kingdom. Dukes and kings of Tuscany were among the Catholic princes whom the Church could put up with least, especially in their enactment of the infamous "Leopoldine laws", which were impregnated with the extreme of idiotic Josephism. The Beata was anxious not to flatter, but to cure. Her husband never caught upon her lips the slightest ambiguity or the "whitest" lie. Faith alone, as we shall see, inspired the austere counsels she gave to Letizia, the mother of the fallen Emperor.

Anna brought this same faith to the reception of the Sacraments. She had a great devotion to confession, and found therein physical comfort for her maladies. "She wished," says her confessor, "to go to confession always before Holy Communion, but I bade her receive every day and to confess every week." Her confessions were short. To those she directed she counselled short and frequent confession, the choice of a good confessor and fidelity to him once chosen. She rebuked those pious devotees who boasted of doing the round of confessionals where confessors of fame were hearing. She, like St. Teresa (whose distresses in this matter are well known) had to change her confessor frequently, but it was not through her own fault. Here are the facts; let everyone judge for himself.

We know who was the first director to whom Providence sent her—Father Angelo, the Servite. Humble and detached, Father Angelo speedily realised that the task of directing such a soul was beyond him and told her to go to Mgr. Strambi, who approved and admired the spirit of his holy penitent. He never abandoned her and never ceased to counsel her, but, above all, to be counselled by her. But overwhelmed by the occupations of his high offices, promoted to be Bishop of Macerata, he confided Anna to another Passionist. This was at the time when she was transported to the deep waters of ecstasy. The new confessor lost his head a little and concluded that the devil had a share in all these revelations. He thought that such favours were in keeping with a religious, but not a married woman. He told her to ask Our Lord, if it were indeed He, to hold His peace. Our Lord answered by saying that the confessor must not make laws for God, who can distribute His own gifts at His own choice. Moreover, it became impossible for the Beata, assailed as she was by numerous ailments, to reach the distant monastery of the Passionists. Domenico got angry. He found that his wife's absences were far too long, and she had to find a confessor nearer home. It was Father Philip Salvatori, who, formerly a Jesuit, continued his ministrations after the suppression of the society, in the church of St. Ignatius.

He was very zealous, the author of numerous works on the lives of the saints and about asceticism; he was a director of directors; but his labours did not allow him to follow at close quarters the Divine action in the soul of his extraordinary penitent, and, moreover, by a too loudly expressed admiration he drew a crowd of curiosity-seekers to the Taigi household. More demonstrations of anger on Domenico's part! Father Salvatori and Our Lord were agreed that another confessor must be sought.

The fifth one chosen was Father Ferdinand de St. Louis, discalced Trinitarian. He was a religious of rare worth, who occupied the situations of gravest responsibility in his order. During the first French invasion he suffered the worst possible distresses, hunger and daily threats of death. Taken before the Revolutionary Tribunal to swear the oath of agreement to the civil constitution of the clergy, he refused. He was well versed in mysticism and became the director, not only of Anna, but also of her friend (similarly endowed with sanctity and mystic graces), Elisabeth Canori-Mora, a mother of a family like Anna, but married to a scamp. Converted by the death of his wife, this scamp lived devoutly for eleven years in the habit of the Conventual Friars Minor.

Father Ferdinand was not content with enrolling Annette in his Third Order, but insisted upon her wearing its dress not only at home (to which Domenico did not object) but also in the streets. Now Domenico wanted to be accompanied by a woman dressed like everybody else, not like a religious. When Annette became pregnant with Mariuccia, the exacting demands of Father Ferdinand laid Dominico open to a thousand gibing remarks, and so he insisted upon a change of confessors. This change (the sixth) was, by the grace of God, to be a lasting one. Father Philip-Louis of St. Nicholas, discalced Carmelite, was Anna's director for thirty years, that is, up to her death. His juridical deposition, which makes a large volume, is a masterpiece; Raymund of Capua, director of St. Catherine of Siena, did not produce a greater. It is from this Father Philip, from Cardinal Pedicini and from the confidential priest, Mgr. Natali, that we get to know her interior life.

This "confidential priest," whose duty it was to note day by day the heavenly communications made to the Beata and who, consequently, lived in her home, necessarily attracted the attention of the Devil's Advocate. Time after time he returned to the charge, saying it was imprudent and involved peril of scandal. The answer to his charge was that the virtue and prudence of the priest removed all such danger. Moreover, Domenico, for all his susceptibility, always had the greatest veneration for him and desired to die in his arms. Father Philip-Louis says: "He is my penitent. I ordered him to make a note of all that happened to the servant of God, and I ordered the servant of God herself to keep nothing back from him." St. Teresa tells us that Our Lord instructed her to have her revelations controlled in a similar way. In addition to all this, Anna was occupied with the cares of a numerous family, was often ill, and could see her confessor but once a week, whereas every day of the week she received communications of interest to the Church. Cardinals, Princes, Popes consulted her. She could not confide the answers to their questions to Domenico, so that Mgr. Natali was her secretary and message-bearer, not by his own will, nor by the will of Anna, but by the will of her confessor and of the Blessed Mgr. Strambi, Mgr. Natali's bishop.

What a singular interplay of kinds of sanctity there is at all crises of the Church's history. At about the moment of Blessed Anna's death, he who was to be saint John Bosco, entered the seminary of Chieri; he was the friend of St. Joseph Cottolengo and was directed by the Blessed Joseph Cafasso. The Beata received her first call to detachment through the example of Blessed Joseph Labre; her first steps and her progress in holiness were directed by a man as outstanding for science and discretion as he was for holiness, the Blessed Mgr. Strambi. Mgr. Strambi, Passionist missionary, professor of theology, Rector of the mother-house of his order in Rome, provincial and definitor of his order also, and Bishop of Macerata, was in addition to all this a confessor of the Faith. He was exiled in 1808, but on the fall of the Empire, returned to his diocese and asked Pius VII to relieve him of the episcopate. The Pope refused, but Leo XII caused him to remain at the Vatican in an advisory capacity. Mgr. Strambi assisted the Pope in the serious illness with which His Holiness was smitten soon after, and offered his own life for that of the Pope. Leo recovered, and in a few days the Monsignor died. He was beatified in due course and, in 1925, the cause of his canonisation was resumed—that is one year before his client's cause was resumed, in 1926. Truly an interplay of saints!

§

When we come to the *obedience* which Blessed Anna-Maria showed to Blessed Strambi and her other directors, we come to a delightful chapter of a "Golden Legend". She not only gave up her fasts

at a word from a director, but heeded his orders
even at a distance. One day Mgr. Natali went with
the Duke Altemps on retreat to the monastery of
Saint Bonaventure on the Palatine. Blessed Anna was
ill in bed, but Mgr. Natali, being smitten with a
grave scruple of conscience, conceived the quaint
notion of bidding her (she was some two and a half
miles away) cure herself in order to be able to get
up and come to his relief! She came—out of breath
and saying with a smile: "Don't play any more of
these tricks on me. I am the mother of a family and
cannot lose time travelling so far." She then soothed
the priest and went her way.

The director's authority was for her God's
authority. When in an hour of great tribulations she
wanted to abstain from Holy Communion but to go
to Confession every day; "Communion every day
and Confession once a week," her confessor told her,
and she obeyed.

Cardinal Pedicini suggests in his deposition that
her confessors did not always know their business.
In the midst of the persecutions to which the Devil
submitted her, and of the terrible obsessions of
which we have yet to speak, her confessor "very
rarely consented to hear her. She presented herself
before him every week, but he dismissed her with a
simple blessing and without hearing her. At this
period I knew her probably better than her confessor,
and can attest to the heroism of her virtue". It is
well to remark that the eminent prelate was not
himself without heroism in remaining at that time
her secretary; for, as he himself admits, he had to do
constant violence to himself in order to scorn the
calumnies that this aroused.

When the voice of her confessor was at variance
with the voice within her, she obeyed the former,

even when she knew that the thing enjoined her
would certainly prove futile.

And what shall we say of her prayer? Domenico
says: "In the prayers we said together as a family
her faith was so lively, the tone of her prayer so
thrilling, that she spoke to God and the Blessed
Virgin as if she saw them with her bodily eyes."
Her daughter-in-law says: "She could talk of nothing
but God. She could scarcely open her mouth to talk of
the goodness of God without being wrapt in ecstasy."

This did not prevent the Devil's Advocate from
advancing other testimonies of those familiar with
Anna: that she laughed and talked like everybody
else and with the manner of ordinary folk of no
pretensions. But then we are not to imagine that
the saints live perpetually on a pedestal. The inhabi-
tants of Nazareth cannot have seen Our Lord
so, or else their amazement at "the Son of the
Carpenter" announcing the Kingdom of God would
be inexplicable.

§

Anna's faith was contagious enough to reconcile
the worst cases of incredulity, though sometimes
the reconciliation entailed protracted discussion.
Some theologians would have it that she was not fit
for such discussion, and decided to put the ecclesiastical authorities on their guard, but Mgr. Strambi,
as learned as these theologians and holier than they,
showed clearer discernment. He was once in despair
of converting a scamp of a Freemasonic dignitary,
and so betook himself to her.

Here is the story, and it reads like a novel: Mgr.
Natali's elder brother, Joseph, was the scamp in
question. He had been brought up well and piously,
but on losing his father, early in life, he threw over

his mother's control and sank himself in the worst
disorders. To give himself confidence he read
profligate books, took to playing with the pistol and
the knife, and went so far as to threaten the priest
who tried to stop him going forth in company with
a group of young gangsters. He returned from the
expedition wounded and the priest took care of him
and cured him. Meanwhile Pius VII was taken to
Savona, and the French occupied the Papal States.
Joseph gained the confidence of the new masters
and undertook well-paid missions for them. He
became a "carbonaro" of mark, but even in that
kind of company, scarcely exacting in its demands,
his profligacy caused consternation. He eventually
linked himself to a noble lady who was separated
from her husband. God did not leave him without
warnings. On one occasion, crossing a river on
horseback, the current caught him and he barely
escaped drowning; on another he was smoking a
cigarette at the window when lightning struck him,
knocked him down and made him lame; on yet
another, while crossing the plain of Arcoli, he
narrowly escaped highwaymen who in fact massacred
his companions. All these warnings were to no
purpose. The only good remaining to him was a
charitable heart. But now, with Napoleon banished
to St. Helena and the Papal States restored to their
master, the young carbonaro, head over ears in
debt, and workless, takes to his bed, stricken with
illness. The woman, missing his visits, goes to him,
calling with her a doctor and two servants. She
presents herself at his house, but suddenly drops to
the ground, smitten with apoplexy. She has but time
to cry: "Quick! Send for the priest!" but dies before
his arrival and is buried as one unabsolved. Joseph
thereupon decides to take his own life.

Mgr. Natali told of his brother's plight, left Macerata, crossed the snow-covered mountains and reached his brother, to find him getting the pistols ready. He prevailed over him, brought him back to Macerata to his devout mother, and confided him to the care of Mgr. Strambi. But Mgr. Strambi, with the Devil as counsel for the prosecution, only wasted his breath. Mgr. Natali, however, returned to Rome and spoke to Blessed Anna of Joseph, adding that Mgr. Strambi was anxious for her interest in him. She smiled and said: "If he comes to Rome I will take him in hand. Your brother will repent at the end of his life, as the fox changes his pelt, but God will deprive him of consciousness forthwith lest he fall back into sin. God will seize hold of him as it were by one hair of his head."

Joseph returned to Rome very sick. Anna prayed and gained his confidence by bringing him dainties. He got better for a while and returned the Beata's visit—at first somewhat haughtily on the defensive, but she, by no means put out, tells him with the directness of an eye-witness the ignoble story of his life, shatters his difficulties and overcomes him. He returned home and the devil took hold of him anew and suggested to him the idea of ruining the faith of his benefactress and perverting her. Her confessor tells us the young man made unbelievable efforts to break down her faith and destroy her convictions, but she on her side entered upon extraordinary fasts and woeful penances. The battle lasted three days, and the victory cost Anna dear. Out of that victory there came to her a mortal disease, and hell broke loose against her. On the night following the day on which the young man entered her house for the first time the devils hurled all manner of abuse at her and then tried to strangle her, so that Mgr. Natali spent the night in mortal fear at the sound of the infernal uproar.

When summer came Joseph, apparently unrepentant, returned—a broken man—to Macerata. His former friends received him as one stricken with the plague, and he fell into a new crisis of despair, but the prayers and counsels of the Beata bore him company. In the month of August 1818, seeing his end approach, he called for a priest, confessed his sins, abjured his errors and immediately fell into a coma and died. "God had seized him by a hair of his head."

§

On another occasion it was a priest who had gone over to Protestantism that consented to see her. He found her in her poor little room, clothed as our picture of her shows, in the Tertiary habit, that is to say, in a white woollen dress, with a white scapular adorned with a red and blue cross; over her shoulders a white shawl attached to her apron; her head bandaged on account of the tortures she suffered with her eyes, and a bee-hive shaped head-dress such as working women wear. On her work-table was a housewife, a rosary and a crucifix. Her face is common enough, with strong nose and chin, prominent cheek-bones, a large mouth, lips almost in a dead straight line. But her penetrating glance and her radiant smile forced the respect of the poor stray. Anna made him sit down, told him in a few phrases the deplorable story of his life, and turned his sophisms inside out. Conversation continued. He was abashed and silent while with her, but his pride gripped him anew as soon as he left. One day the Beata cut matters short: "My good Sir, you have no time to lose. The end of your days is fast drawing near." A few days later he fell gravely ill, and Annette sent him this message: "You will never get up again." The priest's resistance was broken: he abjured his errors, went to confession, and died in peace.

The Process tells numerous other stories, now concerning her miraculous powers, now concerning her faith. The story of conversion we are now to relate cost her twenty years of prayer. It was a question of a Job-like man who formerly believed, but was driven to rebellion by a series of misfortunes. Several times Anna came between him and suicide, and by a wondrous practice of vicarious suffering habitual to her, she took upon herself the hell wherein he struggled. He found his faith again, while she sank into indescribable darkness. He survived the Beata and bore witness to her. This strife for the salvation of shipwrecked souls is never paid for except by a thousand tribulations, but she accepted anathema for her brethren.

"The triumph of the Faith," says Cardinal Pedicini, "constituted her martyrdom, wrenching groans and cries from her when she used to come barefoot to St. Paul's-outside-the-Walls and there pray before the miraculous crucifix, or when she made the Way of the Cross at the Coliseum. It was there she became friends with the mother of Napoleon I and with the brother of Madame Mere, Cardinal Fesch."

She was peculiarly interested in the Jews, for she saw that their role in world-affairs was considerable for better or for worse. She foretold a great movement of conversions among them, and the important part they would take in the return of peoples to the Gospel. The conversion of Alphonse Ratisbonne at Saint Andrew delle Fratte happened four years after her death, but that of his brother Theodore preceded it by ten. She saw in her sun the foundations of the two brothers—the religious congregations of men and of women of Our Lady of Sion, the first congregations founded directly for the conversion of the Jews.

Sophie one day accompanied her mother to the church of the Holy Apostles where the baptism of a Jewess was to take place. The Queen of Etruria was the godmother. In order not to be seen by the Queen who would undoubtedly have come to embrace her "Sister Annette", the Beata hid herself in the recess of a chapel and fell into ecstasy at the sight of the harvest of which this conversion ushered in the firstfruits. On coming out she allowed her joy to burst out. "This convert is a great soul . . . She will go to heaven without passing through Purgatory."

V

TRIUMPHANT HOPE – POVERTY AND DETACHMENT

WHILE she scatters like seeds around her miracles of conversion, Anna goes deeper down into the depths of her nothingness. She is heard to sob out: "My God, have pity on me who am nought but sin."

She counts upon none but God. If she is lacking bread she tells Him of it, but refuses the presents of those who are under an obligation to her. She has, like St. Paul, a pride in retaining liberty of spirit. She has just cured a woman of patrician rank who wishes to reward her. "I do not serve God for interested motives," she says; "thank the Blessed Virgin, not me."

"At least accept this for your poor."

"You can yourself give them alms. Let us not mix up the works of God with money."

Even in 1815–1816, during the famine that followed the fall of Napoleon, when she was harassed by anxiety about daily bread, she asked for nothing, but worked twice as hard, prayed, said over and over again: "There is no one in whom to put confidence but God. Men are weather-cocks that turn with every wind. Only God is constant."

"But what about your numerous children? Are you going to let them suffer from hunger?" Thus spoke the wiseacres.

"*Please!* Do not insult God by suggesting that He can abandon us."

This imperturbable hope was rewarded by God. Let us glean among the hundred anecdotes given in the Process. She went to St. Paul's-outside-the-Walls to tell Our Saviour there was no more bread. He said, "Go back home. You will find some." She reached home and found a letter awaiting her from the Marquis Bandini containing a draft for a small amount of money.

Another day and there was again no bread. She went on her knees: "Lord, your unworthy servant expects her daily bread from Your hands." Someone knocked at the door. An unknown person handed in a letter sent from a very great distance. It contained an alms with this message: "I hear you are in need; allow me to come to your aid."

So she *does* accept alms after all? Yes, but only when they hold no threat either to her liberty of spirit or her poverty. From what was sent her she took what was necessary, but the rest went to the poor.

§

But what was stranger was that she gently imposed the same law upon those who worked with her, in particular upon Mgr. Natali, her secretary. Thrice the Emperor of Austria wrote to Rome to obtain a benefice for him, but Annette saw to it that the place in the Datoria was not accepted. Another time there was question of two benefices for him, but the Beata warned him that she was praying that the negotiations would fall through! "I had the happiness," said Mgr. Natali in his deposition, "to see the servant of God on intimate terms for a period of thirty years. So perfectly did she practice detachment from the good things of this world that she merited the highest praise for it." Did he always think on those lines? One may doubt it. And Domenico? "I used to say to her," he said, "why do you not think of speaking to such and such a one?"

"The Queen of Etruria," deposed Cardinal Pedicini, "because she wanted to have her counsellor ever at hand, suggested employing Domenico as butler in her palace at a high salary. The family would come with Domenico, and the future of all concerned would be secure. Anna refused for the following reasons: "We must not excite jealousy, nor raise the family above its own status, but we must live ever in liberty of spirit for the service of God. Engagements contracted with the great expose one to the temptation of betraying the truth in flattering them." Consequently she thus replied to the Queen: "I beg Your Majesty to leave us in our mediocre sphere. God wishes us to remain where we are. Nought that is necessary will ever be wanting to us."

Here is another picture. The Queen, distressed

because the poor woman never asked her for anything, one day opened a drawer full of gold before her eyes: "Take some, take some, 'Nanna Mia' (my Nanette); take all you want." Annette smiled, and, with that freedom of spirit which brought home to the great their true poverty, answered:

"You are very simple, my poor lady. I serve a Master who is richer than you. I trust in Him and He provides for my daily needs. Ask yourself whether I can leave Him in order to attach myself to such childish things." The Queen understood and, in the end Domenico understood. "It seemed to me," he said, "that she obtained one long miracle in providing for all the necessities of so large a family. What could I have done with my wages of six "ecus" per month? I let her go her own way, because I noticed that when she prayed or did some good work Providence came to our assistance."

People had to resort to tricks to make her accept an alms. A rich English Catholic whom she had helped wanted to guarantee her a life pension. She refused it. The good man had recourse to some anonymous people, so that when Anna lacked the very necessities of life they would be able to force, as it were, an alms upon her—necessities, for there was never any question of superfluities. Tortured with various complaints, she yet refused a worn covering that Mgr. Natali offered her. Oppressed by her asthma and unable to rest on her bed, she refused an armchair, and would use nothing but a straw chair without cushion or back. Cardinal Pedicini, seeing how uncomfortable her narrow quarters were, offered her a room in the vast palace of the Chancellery. She refused. Cardinal Fesch again and again made similar offers, only to meet with the same refusal, and yet, according to Sophie,

"Our mother had hours of unspeakable pain."

In spite of her grievously hard work her children had to be content with a piece of bread moistened in oil and vinegar for dinner. In 1799, while Pius VI was in exile, Prince Chigi no longer paid Domenico any salary. Over and above that, as we have seen, there was scarcity of food, and the need of queueing at the bakeries where there was free distribution to the indigent. One sympathises with the emotion of Domenico in his old age, as he recalls the painful memory: "Ah! my poor wife; her health was so frail, yet she had to wait the live-long day in cold, or wind, so as not to let her family suffer." "Although she was with child" (it is Mgr. Luquet that gives us the detail) "and overwhelmed with other causes of weariness, she did this throughout the time of acute misery." It was at this time that she was at pains to make sandals and shirts, bodices and dresses. Providence intervened. This work put her in touch with the nuns of Saint Dominic, and with their assistance and that of the Queen of Etruria, who obtained orders for her, it produced five crowns a month for the upkeep of the night watcher of the oratory. All other gifts were refused by the Beata.

She was criticised, but she was praised by the Lord, who in her case desired this contempt of earthly goods, and this confidence in Himself. When, without as much as a fraction of a farthing, she sometimes made a pilgrimage round the basilicas and contented herself with saying "Think about it," He thought! He does not love timid characters who hesitate for fear of risks. "When you see difficulties in things, know that therein lie trials that make you dear to My Heart, and that will have a happy issue, if you put yourself in My hands. Easy things at first sight seem good, but a hidden poison of self-love rots them . . . They begin well enough, but soon go from bad to worse."

"Mary, Mother of Holy Hope," she used often say, "pray for me." "Jesus, Father and Support of the Poor, have pity on me." And They heard her prayers.

Her ecstasies

VI

CHARITY – ECSTASIES – THE EUCHARIST UNVEILED – DEVOTIONS TO THE HOLY TRINITY – TO THE SACRED HEART – TO THE PASSION – TO OUR LADY OF SEVEN SORROWS – TO ST. JOSEPH AND THE HOLY ANGELS

"HER charity was a volcanic flame." Nature for her was a measureless poem. It was a great effort for her to withdraw herself for one instant from the thought of God. She would be cleaning saucepans, and suddenly Our Lord was there. She hastened to avert her gaze, and then, being overcome, remained in ecstasy, saucepan in hand. Sophie depicts her sweeping cobwebs and being suddenly levitated while the hairs of the broom turned on empty air. Sophie would cry, "Mamma, where are you going? Up there there is no dirt."

Another day it would be at the stove that God would transport her to the third heaven. As one stricken she would have to sit down, and Sophie would say, "Mamma, you are tired. I will do that for you." When Anna came to herself she would sigh: "My God!" and take up the plates and saucers again. Another time it is at table when, fork in hand, she stands still, her eyes on heaven. Domenico, who understood none of these "eccentricities", calls out, "Annette! Marianna!" No reply. He shakes her in his fear of a stroke of apoplexy and prepares a dose of lime for her. But in the end he got used to it and took it for convulsions or drowsiness. When Annette came back to her senses he grumbled at her saying: "How can you doze at table? You are stupefied with sleep. You must go to bed earlier." After the death of his wife he suspected the true nature of things: "I do really believe that my wife was favoured with heavenly gifts. As to ecstasies, I could never discern any. I remember, however, that at night-time, as we said the Rosary, there were times when she did not answer. At table, also, it often happened that she was absent-minded, sometimes with a fork in her hand, sometimes without movement. I spoke to her and she took up again what she had left off, giving me a smile."

At bottom, Domenico was a near relation of that good fellow Chrysale, and attached more importance to his saint's tasty soup than to her ecstasies. After all, the old man of ninety-two years was a little put out about all these marvels of which people spoke to him, but of which he had seen nought. In time he could no longer smoke a pipe on the Corso without someone laying siege to him. He either refused to answer or was content to say: "Oh, yes! she surely was a good woman," and then, shrugging his shoulders, "but she was always going to sleep."

But if you attacked her, *then* you "drew" the old porter. "So it seems she was lazy. . ." Swift as an arrow at the mark he proved that never since the beginning of the world was there seen so valiant a woman. Then people would succeed in getting some details out of him.

When she thus went to sleep with her eyes towards heaven, Mariuccia would say tearfully:

"Mamma is dead. Mamma is dead." "No! she is praying." Sophie would say by way of correction. "Be quiet, she's asleep," Domenico would growl. "Let her alone; she had no sleep last night."

At the saying of the Rosary, ecstasy was the rule, and at this Domenico was still more shocked. "It is shameful to go to sleep like that during prayers, when one has the whole night for sleeping" (The Process and Summary).

"When I used to go to see her in the morning," says Cardinal Pedicini, "I often found her in ecstasy, and was obliged to wait patiently till she came to herself. Ecstasy would again seize her in the middle of our conversation. I would wait again. Only obedience had power to call her to herself."

Her confessor says, "I was often the witness of her ecstasies when we used to visit the seven basilicas in company with Cardinal Pedicini. At that time she usually went to Communion in the chapel of the Holy Crucifix at St. Paul's. Immediately after Communion she entirely lost herself in transport, yet, as we had to continue the pilgrimage, I used to order her quickly in the name of obedience to recall her mind and follow us without delay. She obeyed."

The Beata, in the end, complained to our Lord.

"Leave me alone, Lord. Withdraw from me. I have my work to do. I am the mother of a family."

After Holy Communion, when she felt ecstasy overwhelming her, she cut matters short and hastened back to her kitchen, but the Spirit mastered her in the road, so much so that she had to have a companion. The sight of a cross, of a flower, or of a statue of Our Lady, would halt her, ravished in the middle of the Corso amidst the traffic, to the anger of the drivers. She used to take refuge in a neighbouring church. Naturally the gossips missed nothing.

Some admired, but most burst into peals of laughter.

Cardinal Pedicini confessed his inability to give any idea of the favours with which she was loaded at her daily Communion. With her head and shoulders in her white veil, and her hands joined, she wept with long-drawn sobs; her sighs made her bosom heave. A witness goes so far as to say that the flames and rumblings of Vesuvius alone could give an idea of such consuming charity.

§

She detected souls in a state of grace by the sweetness as of a personal fragrance; on entering a church she divined at which altar the Blessed Sacrament was reserved.

A secular priest (this we are told by Father Salvatori) saying Mass in St. Ignatius' Church, sure she was a hypocrite, had the odd idea of testing her by giving her an unconsecrated host. Anna detected the imposture, and Our Lord ordered her to inform her confessor. Father Salvatori severely reproached the priest, who confessed his fault. Another day, says Cardinal Pedicini, Annette was preparing for Holy Communion in the church of the Trinitarians. When the Irish Franciscan who was saying the Mass turned round to say the *Ecce Agnus Dei*, the Host he held in his hands left them, floated through the air, remained poised for a moment, and then came to rest on the lips of the Beata. The good Father took the matter very badly and returned to the sacristy crying out against such abuse of the Liturgy and against witchcraft. He made a note in his pocket-book of the name of the guilty party in order to denounce her to the Holy Office. Two Trinitarians who were present succeeded in pacifying him and making him see that God is Lord of the Liturgy.

Many a time at the moment of Communion she saw the Host come to life. Jesus was there, sometimes in the form of a child lying upon the petals of a white lily and saying to her: "I am the flower of the fields and the lily of the valley;" sometimes in the form of a King dressed in purple: "In this crowd of people that you see in the church," He said to her one day, "there are scarcely two souls truly sincere in their love. The others are equally ready to come to church or to go to the theatre."

For many of these facts Cardinal Pedicini is a never-failing witness. He remarked this incident at the moment of its happening. Anna was going to Communion in the chapel of the Pieta, in the Piazza Colanna. Receiving the Host, she fell down as though struck by lightning. All near were alarmed. When she came to herself she was confused and complained to Our Lord, as St. Teresa used to complain, and with the like lack of success.

He answered: "You must expect to suffer these pains on many other occasions." "Indeed," adds the Cardinal, "on receiving Our Lord she was ravished by ecstasy. Often after giving her Holy Communion, I had, in order to save her from attracting attention to herself, to order her in a silent gesture to leave the altar, and thus restrain the emotions of her heart, which broke forth in burning sighs. It cost her much to repress her fervour. I used to see her face bathed in sweat, even in winter-time. In unfrequented churches, like Saint-Paul's-outside-the-Walls, I did not interfere with her fervour. I have often seen her fall, after Holy Communion, as if she had been struck by lightning, and remain a long time in that condition."

One day Annette was kneeling in ecstasy after Communion in the church of the Pieta when an alarm sounded outside among the French soldiers. There was a tumult, the cracking of rifles, the rolling of drums. Everybody fled. The sacristan shook his keys and hammered on the doors: "Quickly! Get out quickly! There is bloodshed." Annette heard nothing, she remained in ecstasy while the sacristan ran to shelter in a wardrobe in the sacristy. . . . I have just visited that wardrobe; it is spacious and solid. When she came to herself Anna was greatly astonished to find herself locked in. She knocked at the sacristy. But the sacristan, in the depths of the wardrobe was more frightened than ever and did not stir. In the end he came and spoke through the keyhole: "Who is there?" Hearing a woman's voice, he summoned courage to open the door and crept stealthily to the entrance of the church. The tumult was over, but the soldiers were still standing to arms there in the Piazzo Colonna. Calmly Anna went through their ranks and returned home.

But matters did not always have such a happy ending. It was in vain that she made herself small and effaced herself during her thanksgiving by drawing her veil closely around her; there were pious women of the Pharisaic type, and with them some "scribes" mingled, who in time raised cries of "scandal" and "devil-possession". She bowed before the storm, changing her church each morning. But Our Lord intervened and told her to put a bold face on the matter and to scorn this mockery.

The battle began over again. Anna often went to receive at the chapel of the Pieta, which was near her home and was always open early in the morning. A distinguished parishioner had sworn to expel this hypocrite. As she approached the holy table he snatched away the Communion cloth. Annette said nothing, went back to her place, and waited for another Mass. The good man left her alone in the end. But it was the celebrant who took up the glove a second time, and on reaching the Beata passed her by without giving her Communion. If she came by herself he refused to open the tabernacle. Anna suffered the affront, but Mgr. Natali, on being informed by witnesses, came and reminded the priest of his duty, at the beginning of the Mass. The priest shrugged his shoulders and again passed over the Beata. Mgr. Natali indignantly went into the sacristy and threatened the priest with a formal denunciation. Surprised that a priest of such eminence should interest himself in a poor woman, the celebrant reflected, and in the end made excuses. But it was against Mgr. Natali that the Beata turned: "What have you done?" she said. Mgr. Natali replied wisely: "If you are pleased at being insulted, well and good; but as for me, when I see such things I cannot allow them to continue." The two different points of view are each right. It is sometimes praiseworthy to accept caddish behaviour directed against oneself; it is never so to approve of it when directed to others.

§

When Gregory XVI, on account of her continual ill-health, had granted her the privilege of a private oratory, Anna's little house became a cenacle, where, hidden from the eyes of men, she could surrender herself to the transports of her faith. Cardinal Pedicini thus describes the exterior manifestations that followed Anna's Communions at that time: her face was suffused as with fire, and a noise such as a flame makes was heard, and her bosom heaved as if it would burst.

There were similar manifestations when Anna

spoke of the Trinity, of the Sacred Heart, or of
Mary. She began her letters with this invocation:
"Praised be the Most Holy Trinity," an invocation
which she repeated at the beginning of every action.
All her Fridays were consecrated to the Sacred
Heart. But it was more in the mysteries of the life of
Jesus themselves than in treatises of devotion that
she studied the Sacred Heart. Bethlehem, Nazareth,
the Divine Infancy, Joseph's workshop, Calvary—
these were the objects of her contemplation. As long
as her health permitted, she went at intervals, for
forty successive days, barefooted, to venerate the
crucifix at the Mamertime prison. Like St. Catherine
of Siena, she heard the Crucified invite her, as we
have seen, to make her choice: "Which do you want,
to follow Jesus stripped of all things, or Jesus in
triumph?" "I embrace the cross of my Jesus," she
answered, and the whole of her life showed how
seriously she meant what she said.

The Virgin of Seven Sorrows: "My own dear
Mother," as she called her, was queen in her little
oratory. A votive-lamp was always burning before
her. Yet as the wealthy benefactors, cured by Anna
with the oil from this votive-lamp, soon grew tired
of paying the expenses of the poor little light, Anna
being wretchedly poor, allowed it to go out. For this
Our Saviour rebuked her, blaming her want of
confidence. The votive-lamp was re-lit, and hence-
forward the oil was punctually renewed in the silver
lamp provided by the Queen of Etruria.

As she was praying one day in the church of the
Ara Coeli, near the figure of the Blessed Virgin,
painted on a column, the picture came to life, as it
were, and Anna heard it say: "My daughter, tell
Father that I am without a light and that I wish to
be specially honoured here. If the Fathers will not

do what I ask I shall compel them to do it by working miracles." The Fathers turned a deaf ear, but miracles brought *ex-veto* offerings, and the *ex-veto* offerings effected the conversion of the priests.

Sophie gave witness to this effect: "Mamma used to say the Angelus on her knees; she kept the vigils of all the feasts of Mary by penitential practices. She had given her name in to the confraternity of the Holy Rosary and caused all our names to be inscribed therein also. She was also a member of the confraternity of Our Lady of Mount Carmel, and wore the scapular.

In the course of an ecstasy the Blessed Virgin Herself dictated to the Beata a prayer, which spread rapidly. It was printed under the names of certain pious ladies, for Anna wished to remain unknown, and was presented in 1809 by Cardinal Pedicini to Pius VII, who approved it and enriched it with indulgences. Here is an extract from it which recalls the grand style of St. Teresa:

"Prostrate at Thy feet, O Great Queen of Heaven, I venerate Thee with the deepest reverence, and I confess that Thou art the Daughter of the Father, the Mother of the Divine Word, the Spouse of the Holy Spirit. Thou art the store-keeper and the almoner of the Divine mercies. . . . For this reason we call Thee Mother of Divine Compassion. Behold me here in affliction and anguish. Deign to show me how truly Thou lovest me. . . . I beg Thee to ask the Holy Trinity most fervently to grant us the grace ever to conquer the devil, the world and our evil passions; the efficacious grace that sanctifies the just, converts sinners, destroys heresies, enlightens infidels and brings Jews to the true Faith. . . .

"Obtain for us this great gift, that all the world may form but one people only, and one Church. . . ."

This Church was the object of all her thoughts. She recommended it to the angel-defenders of the Faith and to her guardian angel, whose daily counsels enlightened her even in the management of her home, "in an extraordinary and sensible manner" (Process).

VII

THE HEART OF A SAINT – CHARITY TOWARDS THE SOULS IN PURGATORY   CHARITY TOWARDS THE SICK – CHARITY TOWARDS THE POOR. TENDERNESS TOWARDS ANIMALS

THE suffering souls never ceased to claim her prayers, but their deliverance cost her the pains of a continual purgatory. For souls she would drag herself to the cemetery. Her visits took place for forty consecutive days. She always made them, whatever the season, in spite of sun, rain, cold, mud; and recited over every grave three times "Eternal rest . . ." and a prayer. She prayed especially for the souls of priests.

One day, while she was assisting at Mass for the sake of some soul, she suffered untold anguish. Cardinal Pedicini said the second Mass and at the GLORIA the Beata saw the soul delivered and entering Heaven; she felt ready to die for joy at this ravishing sight. To souls delivered from Purgatory she recommended the interests of the Church and of the Pope, "the Christ on earth", as she called him, after Catherine of Siena.

Yet it is in the presence of the sick that this heart, infinite in its manifestations of tenderness, reveals itself to greatest advantage.

"When she was summoned by the sick," says Domenico in his disposition, "she went straight away, whatever time it was. I had given her the fullest permission."

Her motto was "Never refuse a poor person." During her absence her mother did send one away. On returning, Anna begged with tears, "In the name of Heaven, my good mother, never send any-one away without giving him an alms. If there is nothing else you will always find a loaf in the cupboard." During the famine it was an astonishing miracle to Domenico that that cupboard was never empty of bread. Legions of beggars called, and, as if they were not sufficiently numerous already, Anna went round the doss-houses, and even to the luxury hotels, where the Revolution had multiplied the poor who were ashamed to beg.

One day in winter, when she came out of the Pieta church with Mgr. Natali, she met in the street a young man who was almost naked; his eyes were haggard; he was crying with cold and hunger, a veritable spectre covered with filth, from whom the passers-by drew aside as from one smitten with the plague. Anna ran to him, took him by the hand, led him to her home, warmed him, washed him, dressed him, restored him, consoled him, gave him alms, and sent him away with a thousand expressions of regard, so that he wept and could find no word to answer.

Another day she had reached the church of Our Lady of Consolation when she came upon a poor woman stretched on the road, foaming at the mouth, in a fit of epilepsy. The passers-by shunned her with averted heads. Anna drew near, wiped away the slaver, lifted her up and went to a neighbouring shop to buy her a cordial. Charity is contagious. The crowd stopped, a voluntary collection was organised and given to the poor woman. Once she had restored her, Anna effaced herself and went to

the church. There an ecstasy awaited her. Like St.
Martin of old, who had just shared his cloak with a
poor man of Amiens, she heard Our Saviour say to
her: "Thank thee, my daughter, for the care thou
hast given to *Me*."

At the hospital of St. John, for Incurables, in the
St. James quarter, there were similar incidents.
Sophie, who accompanied her, saw her mother going
from bed to bed, distributing sweetmeats and helping the sick to bring up phlegm. The patient she
singled out was a woman whose face was eaten away
by a cancer. Her head had been covered by a veil.
The moment she heard Annette a murmur of joy
came from behind her mask. Anna went to her,
caressed her, washed her, and, while rocking her
like a baby, spoke to her of heaven.

"At this hospital of St. James" (it is still Sophie
referring to the same case) "there was a woman
called Santa whose husband had given her a contagious disease that ravaged her face. For that reason
her head was covered in a hood. I think, too, she
was no longer able to see. When she heard Mamma s
voice, she used to cry: 'Here is my angel'. My
mother would remain a long time with her. I would
press her to come away, for the stench was very bad.
But she would answer: 'But smell the fragrance of
her soul: she will go straight from bed to paradise.' "

Another day, when she heard that the daughter of
one of her bitterest persecutors was ill, she went to
pay her a visit, and to comfort her mother. At every
visit she took some sweetmeats. In the end she made
the sign of the Cross over her with her statue of
Our Lady, and the sick woman recovered.

Cardinal Pedicini says she had a special gift for
consoling the afflicted, but that she was not content
with a barren expression of sympathy, but rather

employed her "relations" in the aiding of others.

Her kindness extended to the very animals. "These poor animals," she used to say, "have their sole paradise in this world, so it is only just that we should try to sweeten their lives." When, because of illness, she went by carriage on the Pilgrimage of the Seven Churches, she would ask the coachman if the horses had enough to eat, and would buy some hay for their refreshment while she was in church. She caressed the wounds of these good creatures, as also the injured dogs and cats, and thus cured them.

The Society for the Protection of Animals could scarcely fail to take the Beata for patroness. I wonder if we must go back to her example to explain why the people of Rome are so kind to cats? Who has not seen round the Pantheon, about five minutes' walk away from Anna's home, that foregathering of sickly, scraggy and mangy cats lying down among the debris of the columns? They wait there for the daily dole that a few poor women never fail to bring them. The fact is (so I am told by a learned and most friendly professor of the Gregorian University to whom my book owes much), that in Anna's time the sickly cats had a splendid camp in the Forum of Trajan, but recent excavations have driven them to the Pantheon.

VIII

UNIVERSAL   CHARITY – POWER   OF   HEALING –
BODILY   INFIRMITIES – SPIRITUAL   INFIRMITIES –
CHARITY FOR ENEMIES

THE process treats at length of cures worked by the Beata. After repeating some of them, Cardinal Pedicini adds:

"I have left out several *hundreds* of which I took

a note on the spot, and *thousands* which were not written down at all." During her lifetime she was one of the greatest, if not the very greatest, of the wonder-workers of modern times.

This power of healing was bestowed upon this humble woman, as it was formerly upon the Apostles—in an *official* manner. Soon after her conversion, when she was gravely ill in the little street called Sdrucciolo, she was preparing herself for death when our Saviour appeared to her, dressed in a great blue cloak; He took her by the left* hand and told her He took her for His spouse and granted to that hand the gift of curing the sick. Then he said: "You may get up. You are cured." She cried out aloud and got up.

Sometimes Anna was content with touching a sick person with this sore hand which bore the invisible mark of her power. More often, so as to avoid admiration, she made use of a statue of Our Lady, or St. Philomena, of a relic, or of oil from the votive-lamp. Here are a few anecdotes: A lady of the princely house of the Albani was dying of cancer of the womb. She appealed to Anna's confessor, and he appealed to Anna. The Beata gave him a drop of oil from the votive-light, saying: "Let her put the oil on the affected part and invoke Our Lady." It was done. The following night the tumour broke painlessly and the invalid was cured. Overwhelming gratitude followed. The noble lady multiplied her offers of kindly offices and Anna ended by allowing her to undertake the upkeep of the votive-lamp, the oil of which had been the instrument of cure. The first bottle of oil was brought with demonstrations of eternal gratitude. Anna, though still a young woman, knew enough about the durability of gratitude

* Another statement says "the right hand."

among men and women. She smiled and said, "Quietly, daughter! You run too fast, and will grow cold. Remember, however, that you have made a promise, and, if you fail to keep it, misfortune will follow." Some months later the noble lady made an excuse for no longer sending the weekly bottle. She had to economise and was cutting out unnecessary expenses. She had scarcely sent the message when a series of disasters occurred among her extensive properties. A long illness completed her ruin. Anna pleaded for her, but Our Lord declared He had a peculiar horrror of ingratitude. All that she obtained was the conversion of the poor woman.

A Princess Doria, a religious of SS. Dominic and Sixtus, was similarly afflicted with cancer of the womb. She sent a secret message to Anna, saying: I do not wish to show my complaint to anybody, wherefore *it is your duty to cure me*."

"But what," Anna replied, "do you imagine I am? I am only a poor woman and a sinner at that."

"It is useless for you to make excuses. You are what you are, but I *will* you to obtain my cure. I have told you; it is for you to think about it. It is your business." So Anna therefore spoke to Our Lord, and the same evening she sent some cotton fabric soaked in oil. The following day the growth had disappeared.

The same thing happened to a religious oblate of the Child Jesus, only she had no confidence, and had a poor opinion of Anna. Anna was not even a religious, but a laywoman of no birth! Her confessor rebuked her. In the end, the day before the surgeon was to operate, the religious, in desperation, made her decision to use the cotton soaked in oil. The next day the surgeon found that he had only to put back his instruments; the evil had vanished. The doubting

Thomas was never finished praising the sanctity of that woman, even though she was married and the mother of a family.

And here are scenes that are the Gospel over again. Jesus had just cured the mother-in-law of St. Peter at Caparnaum. The sick heard of it, and flocked to Him by every road, and even by way of the roof. So also Anna, with Mgr. Natali, went to the house of a woman whose daughter was dying of the croup. The doctors had given her up, only the mother pleaded with Anna in the tones of the Chananite woman. Anna consoled her, saying: "It will be nothing." She made the sign of the Cross upon the swollen throat. The little girl was cured. The whole neighbourhood was stirred. Another mother, whose daughter was smitten with the same epidemic, asked for help. Anna cured this one also. There was a third neighbour. Her little boy was tormented with an abscess in the ear. With a caress of her right hand Anna cured the child. The mother had not finished thanking her when the second mother, whose little daughter had been cured ran up to her, bringing her little boy, smitten with diphtheria. The child was freed from the disease by a sign of the Cross. It is said that the series of cures continued, and I know well that smiles are likely to be raised by such tales, but I content myself by answering with Pascal's astonishment at his own folly: "What a fool I am! If Jesus Christ is God, what difficulty is there in it?"

§

A cure that made more noise, and one of which I have already said a word, was that of Marie-Louise de Bourbon, the dethroned Queen of Etruria. Expelled from her State, General Miollis had placed her under house-detention in the Convent of SS. Dominic and Sixtus, where she lived surrounded by a small court. But the sadness that gnawed at her developed into epilepsy. She had to be shut up in apartments covered with thick carpets, where she rolled about uttering frantic cries. After these attacks she lay motionless and as though dead. Remedies proved ineffective.

The Queen having heard of the cure of Princess Doria, summoned Anna, and begged her to plead with God for her. Anna told her to have confidence in the Blessed Virgin, and then, with her little statue of Our Lady, made the sign of the Cross. The attacks of epilepsy fled for ever, and the Queen was able to go out and about in Rome without hindrance. The medical world made a great to-do about the cure of a queen such as it had not made for two broom-wielders, and that is why Anna preferred to cure the broom-wielders. But the Queen showed a royal gratitude towards her benefactress, made her her adviser, her sister in God unto death, and faithfully kept alight the votive-lamp that had been so speedily deserted by the other noble lady.

This cure was the beginning of a new series. It was Anna's confessor who recommended a young man also smitten with epilepsy. She found the invalid in bed, broken by a crisis of the disease. His parents stood by in distress. Anna said, with the utmost cheerfulness: "Come on! Up you get! Quick! I can't abide seeing people in bed. You will not die of that, at least."

The sick man threw off the bedclothes and rose, cured. His stunned parents had not recovered from their amazement before Anna fled. The gratitude of the now miraculously cured man lasted a good month, during which he came often to assure Anna of his undying thanks and to offer her his services without wages. She smiled and said: "You will very soon forget."

He forgot so soon that he was not seen again. He was speedily punished, was smitten with a fresh complaint, did not dare to approach his benefactress, and ended sadly. But as in the case of the votive-lamp, God soon sent a faithful servant who asked no wages; it was Luigeto Antonini, who, in spite of banter and sarcasm, remained loyal to his bene-factress until death, and made a deposition at the Process.

We owe to the Princess of Palestrina the account of the cure of her brother-in-law, Cardinal Barberini. "I used to love to confer with Anna. When I could not see her I wrote to her. She prayed to God for me, and for all that concerned me, and the result was always as she foretold. She was frank and friendly. If my children were ill I turned to her. My brother-in-law, Mgr. Barberini, was stricken with a fatal disease a little before his promotion to the cardinal-ate, and I told the holy woman this. The terrible illness grew worse, and yet she bade me fear nothing and not to be troubled, but to have recourse to St. Philip Neri. She also sent a relic of the saint."

It was an un-hoped for cure, and actually from the moment the Beata began to pray Our Lord had said to her: "The prelate's death is decreed by the divine counsel." Yet Anna only insisted the more for this impossible cure, and obtained it. Our Lord told her no one would attribute it to her, and in fact it was credited to St. Philip Neri. That, however, was fresh reason for insistence. Anna never believed in patenting her good deeds.

The Luigeto Antonini, whom I have just named, the knight and servant of the Beata, and the agent of her miracles, deposed that he assisted at a great number of cures. "Oftentimes I accompanied her on such errands. When she could not go in person she sent me with a little cotton soaked in the oil of the lamp that burned before her statue of Our Lady." And the good young fellow was no more astonished at being the agent of cures than were the little Indians sent on similar errands to the sick by St. Francis Xavier. He himself, when attacked by sciatica, which tied him to his bed, or constrained him to walk with crutches, spoke to the Beata, who cured him with a sign of the Cross. From then onwards he could go limping but alert here and there through the town at all times. If he caught a cold or a catarrh in going the Beata's errands, it was enough for him to tell his "Mamma", and a sign of the Cross put all to rights.* Headaches or pains in the chest, swellings and other miseries which he contracted in the service of the saint fled at a sign of the Cross.

Here is a moving incident. In Anna's last illness the Abbé, worn out with going for the doctor, the priest, her friends, fell ill of congestion. The Beata beckoned him to come near, and tracing on his breast the sign of the Cross said: "Go to bed. Go to sleep for half an hour and all will be well. I have too much need of you at this moment to allow you to be ill." Half an hour later he was cured, but Anna was in her agony.

§

Sometimes in the endless recital of this golden legend the sameness of the facts is enlivened by a spark of comedy. It might be said that Providence, in this life of terrifying austerity, mingled with so much

---

* Mgr. Natali enjoyed the same insurance against sickness.

that was tragic, loved—as in the life of Francis of
Assisi or Joseph Cupertino—to get smiles beside
tears, glad flowers beside grave lessons. The one
helps the other, fixing it, like a parable, in the
memory. "These parables made one smile and
understand," said the tailor, Ferdinand Crozier, one
of the last surviving parishioners of the holy Curé
d'Ars to me in January 1915.

The era is a sad one. "A breath as from a grave-
yard moves over the earth." Is it not, then, an act
of charity to afford souls (especially when God
sends it through His saints) an opportunity for
laughter? Caught in a torrent of rain going to confession Anna asks at a house: "Could you lend me an
umbrella so that I can get to Our Lady of Victories?"
The good woman, who recognised her, promised the
umbrella, but added: "Do you know we have a dead
person here? She led her to a poor lodger. He was
not yet dead, but the death-rattle was in his throat.
The priest, having given the Last Sacraments, had
gone. The relatives, crouched round the bed, had
already spread the shroud over his feet. Anna laid
her hand on the ice-cold face, made a sign of the
Cross, and fled, forgetting the umbrella. The storm
had ceased, and the "dead" man was on his feet.

The gift of curing maladies of the body was only
an outward sign of a more precious gift, that of
curing spiritual infirmities. Anna's first anxiety, like
that of Teresa of Avila, was to heal those whom she
directed, of what she considered to be the worst
cancer of all, namely, sadness. There follows an
explanation of the "fioretti" granted so prodigally
in this life of expiation.

"If the evil spirit," said Our Lord to her one day,
"succeeds in plunging a heart into profound sadness,
be sure he already has it in his toils. Knowest thou

what my faithful servant Philip Neri did when a sad silent person of little sincerity came seeking him? He chased him away. He would not listen to him, for he recognised therein a proud and incorrigible soul. On the other hand, when there came a sinner with his heart on his lips, even if he were loaded with the heaviest crimes, he gathered him affectionately to his breast and did not leave him till he had put him once more on the right way." Similarly, Anna anticipated only evil of those pharisaic men and women with long faces who knew not how to smile. She began by deflating the wind-bags of their pretensions by a few pin pricks. If the patient bent his head, all was gained; if he shut himself up in wounded dignity, all was lost.

Cardinal Pedicini tells us that a number of priests were freed from the snares of the devil during the course of a simple conversation with her. How many men caught in the toils of vice or of false religions were converted by one glance, "and from ravening wolves changed into lambs". Speaking of those condemned to death, for whom Anna had a special schedule, Don Rafaële admits that he had at times to be called to order. He avoided "difficulties", and when he saw Anna involving herself with those condemned to death, he remonstrated with her. "My son," she said, "would you wish to be treated thus yourself? Go! Go! Be off! It will be to your own good." He went with bowed head, to find the ruffians, while she scourged herself. At other times the ruffians came to her, and Domenico assisted at terrible, almost surgical conferences.

"I can assure you," he deposes, "that among those who came for advice to my wife, were some who were thoroughly exasperated, furious, and fuming with passion. But after a talk with the servant of God I saw them go with their heads down, pierced with compunction and restored to God." Restored also to their families, for very often domestic dramas were played out in her poor little room.

"How do you expect to have peace in your families," she would say briskly, "if you have no peace with God?" She pleaded for this peace with the holy audacity of saints. As she implored Our Lord, she used a saintly hardihood reproaching her Divine Spouse, telling Him He no longer loved her, and if He did not grant her His grace, she would find herself forced to quarrel with Him." You could hear her repeating: "You no longer love me, then: I can see that for myself quite clearly. I *want*, yes, Lord, I want the conversion of these persons. They are Your sworn enemies, but that is because they do not know You. How much would it cost You to make Yourself known to them for a single moment? I shall have to break with You, then, since You no longer wish to listen to me." In such terms do the good Neapolitans threaten St. Januarius, if he is not quick in performing his obligatory miracle. Often, at the end of such supplications, Anna would hear the reply: "Be it done unto thee according as thou desirest."

§

During her last years, when she could no longer stir, just as she sent Antonini to cure the sick, so she sent Mgr. Natali to act in matters of conscience—reconciliations between husbands and wives; warnings to prepare for death; to have done with such and such an entanglement; no longer to cheat in business, no longer to exploit the poor; to show less attachment to power, or to prelacies. The poor Mgr. often trembled at the prospect. A young woman, Ursule Annibali, beaten by her husband, a cook, made a lunatic by jealousy, escaped and took refuge with Anna. She kept her with her for three days, gave her a talking to, prayed with her, and then said simply to Mgr. Natali: "Go and find this man. He will turn on you bellowing and with a great cutlass in his hand. Have no fear, but rebuke him severely. The cutlass will fall from his hands. He will cry like a child, will throw himself at your knees, and will become as mild as a lamb."

Mgr. Natali made another act of contrition and went off! The scenario was as prophesied. The bellowings of a wild beast, the brandishing of the cutlass, and in the end, tears of contrition. I think of the storms unleashed so often among my own dear Alps of Valais—lightnings, thunder, torrents of rain, and then the smile of the sun upon the blue gentians. Anna pushed her queer behaviour so far as to invite the wild beast to eat, together with his wife, in her house. After a further lecture she made them embrace. They went off, arm in arm, and we are assured that their lives knew no more storms.

Cardinal Salotti speaks of her social apostolate, and he is right. To reconcile families was her speciality. "Once," recalls Giovanna Cams, a servant of Anna's, "there were a husband and wife, very rich and very miserable. Here it was the wife who was jealous, not the man. She suspected him of undue attention to a chambermaid. There were hellish scenes. Each of them sought out Anna, demanding: "Give us back our peace." To the woman Anna preached calmness; to the man the dismissal of the maid. Both obeyed, both drove together in open carriage so that the town could witness their perfect harmony, to give thanks to their peacemaker.

The Curé of Ars about that time used to weep, saying: "It is in the confessional that I have learnt what evil is." Anna's little house reminds one of the confessional of Ars. The husband of Agnes Adrover, one of Anna's friends, openly betrayed her for a married woman, who was his ruin. On Anna's advice Agnes kept quiet and prayed. "All will end happily," she promised. Quite so, but how, Agnes wanted to know. It was an unexpected climax. One day Thomas, the unfaithful husband, on his way to his mistress, stopped, according to pious habit, at the church of St. Lawrence in Lucina to say a prayer to Our Lady of Good Counsel. What does he see? His accomplice, who with equal piety, was going to Communion. Logic is a rare thing even among men. Thomas, who never looked upon himself as a comedian, regarded his accomplice's behaviour as farcical. "If she has the hardihood to be faithless to God, how much more capable is she of being untrue to me." He drew back, and penitently regained his marital hearth. Anna's friend's peace had returned.

This "social apostolate" was exercised beyond the frontiers of Rome. Directly or indirectly multitudes drank of the same well—Ministers of State, princes of the Church, Popes, saints of reform. Anna told the bare truth to all; no varnish, no flattery. Cardinal Pedicini, himself one of the great of the earth, remarks: "From the great of the earth she exacted detachment from earthly goods and kindness to their servants." There was nothing impulsive about her advice. She heard the interested parties, prayed long, took counsel with her confessor, while suppressing names, and then decided, and the decision was often: "Forgive! Forget!" Here, too, she recommended nothing she herself had not heroically practised.

§

Bourdaloue tells us that the forgiveness of injuries is the most difficult task charity has to accomplish. Anna was very sensitive and so inclined towards resentments, but her patience was only the more heroic. Men, and above all women, gave her abundant occasions for it. "One day," Sophie tells us, "I was at my mistress's, where I was learning plain needlework, and a neighbour by the name of Francesca came in and said: "That sorceress has just passed." She was speaking of my mother. I went and found my father, to whom I told all. He was in the prince's kitchen. Boiling with rage, without so much as taking off his apron, he ran round to the woman's husband, and after making a violent complaint, told him that if he did not succeed in making his wife control her tongue he would cut it out! The scatter-tongue, on coming home, was so beaten by her husband that she had to stay in bed for several days.

When my mother heard what had happened and the report I had made, she rebuked me severely, and, to give me a lesson, she put the pincers in the fire, saying she was going to burn my tongue. I begged her to do nothing of the kind. She replied that she would forgive me this once, but would not forgive me if I did it again. She then made me go without breakfast and sent me to school with a piece of bread dipped in water. For several days she did not speak to me, which was an intolerable punishment. I would have much preferred her to hit me. She told my father he was wrong to make trouble over a word. Finally she paid a visit to the woman, bought her some delicacies, prayed for her cure and obtained it."

"There were evil tongues," Domenico insists, "that gave her no rest. I remember among others a wicked woman who had the hardihood to calumniate her honour. I had the wretch put in prison, but my wife was grieved about it and did all she could to obtain her release. The ill-disposed creature began again immediately. If I saw that anybody was annoying her, that person paid dearly for it, but I could not follow her everywhere. Moreover, I saw that the servant of God was very upset when I meddled in these matters, so I finished by saying: 'Do as you wish'; 'Let things take their course,' she would say; "words can neither wound nor kill."

That was not Domenico's opinion. As to Our Lord, He sometimes revenged, in crushing fashion, the honour of His servant. "Examples are numerous. Her spiritual sons knew it well, and could testify from experience that if they interpreted any action of this good mother in a sense that wronged her they paid dearly for it before the day was out." Sometimes Anna chided Our Lord on the subject, but gained little by so doing. He said: "You indeed ought to pray for them, but as for Me, I must remember My promise to you, to avenge your injuries, and you must be content with obtaining a punishment for them that is confined to this life."

Once, in the Pontificate of Leo XII, an important person came to Anna, asking to see her secretary, Mgr. Natali. "He has not come back," replied she, courteously. "I know that he has come back," said the visitor. "No, he is not here. By God's grace it is not my way to tell lies, and I do not know at what hour he will return." Beside himself with rage, he called her a sot, an idiot, a liar. Anna only prayed for him, but, three days later he was arrested, and imprisoned in the fortress of St. Angelo. When he came out he was ruined and half deranged. His death was a wretched one.

Another important person had wronged her. He was smitten with apoplexy. His wife came and asked Anna to obtain a moment of lucidity for him to set his affairs in order, and begged her even to send the little miraculous Madonna. Our Lord would not allow it. "He who treats thee with contempt in his lifetime cannot have thee at his death, and whosoever refuses the Sacraments when he had his health, deserves to be deprived of them at the moment of death." Sadly, Anna said it was useless to send the Madonna and that very night the sick man died.

Domenico relates that when they lived in the Corso they had an evil neighbour who kept Anna's patience on the stretch over a period of several years. "Her name was Constanza Branci. She was a seamstress. She was either deranged or possessed by the devil for she could not possibly have invented out of her own head the accusations she brought against my wife. Anna-Maria paid no attention to the calumnies and did not seem even to be conscious of them. When she met her in the street or on the staircase of the house she was the first to greet her. She made a point of speaking to her, lavishing courtesies upon her, and went at times to ingenious lengths to provide treats for her. But this viper, so far from being moved, only increased her hatred and effrontery. She continued to attack Anna and her daughters, to tarnish their honour and to bring them into disrepute, not only before the people of the house, but in the shops." Domenico breathed fire and anger, and Anna succeeded by nothing short of a miracle in restraining him; meanwhile she "prayed always, without fainting."

§

It was Our Saviour who grew "faint". "The moment will come," He said to Anna, "and it draws nigh when this proud woman shall be humbled. Thou shalt see her stricken on thine own doorstep, begging for alms." The Beata wanted to turn aside the thunderbolt, but Our Lord said: "Be content to know that if I thus punish her in this world it is that I may spare her in the next." This woman, proud as Lucifer, poisonous as a viper, was fairly well off, but came to utter ruin and was soon seen begging and knocking at Anna's door. Anna was not satisfied with helping her, but made use of her relations to help her out of her beggary.

The depositions of Cardinal Pedicini, Mgr. Natali, and Sophie, make one rub one's eyes. The Beata's honour is daily dragged in the mire by shrews who go to the length of accusing her of selling the virtue of her two daughters, Sophie and Mariuccia, of swearing that they have witnessed abominable scenes with their own eyes. . . . When her daughters go out, scandal-mongering women follow upon their heels, insulting them. When Anna lived in the Corso there was a veritable demon of a woman (the Constanza of whom Domenico talks), who lived on the same floor. This woman's door opened upon that of the Beata. From morning till night she kept her door open and lay in wait, spying as to who came in and who went out. She had the duty of letting the apartments, and when clients were lacking she called the Beata a witch: it was she who kept applicants at a distance. Anna's answer was in the form of gifts. She went so far as to offer her one day half a roasted chicken. The woman was as gluttonous as she was avaricious and, upon half-choking herself, she screamed and screamed again on the stairway that the witch had poisoned her. Anna suggested that perhaps she had eaten too eagerly, for the rest of the chicken had poisoned nobody. The suggestion was very badly received. Old Santa took the opportunity of saying: "I told you so! You should not give her anything." But Anna contented herself with a request that Domenico should not be told. The shrew, upon falling shortly afterwards upon very evil days, came and held out her hand to Anna, who, says Sophie, was not content with succouring her, but "before her own death begged us to continue this charity, and we did as we were asked."

PART III

THE BASTION OF THE CHURCH

I

THE BEATA'S MISSION – EXPIATRESS – DESOLATIONS – SICKNESS OBSESSIONS

"Without the shedding of blood, no remission."

Now, God chose this humble woman to obtain the world's remission. Never, since the Great Schism of the West had the Kingdom of Christ been in such a pitiable condition. God flouted, hunted from thousands of churches, the clergy cut in pieces, the Popes dragged from one prison to another, Christianity foundering in a sea of blood. Not a priest in the armies of the Revolution and the Empire to absolve the dying.

There was needed a victim of expiation, a redemptress. Anna was chosen. It was a substitution unintelligible to rationalism, which the fact of universal solidarity (upon which M. Leon Bourgeois has built his laic philosophy) might none the less have made intelligible to it.

Mgr. Pedicini, Mgr. Natali and Father Philip attest that the Beata was "the victim for the Church and for Rome." Our Lord promised her in return that Rome should not be handed over during her lifetime for any long period to the enemies of the Papacy. For that one would have to wait, as the sequel showed, until 1870–1871. He promised her that the cholera would not force the gates of Rome while she lived, and as a fact it awaited the very day of her death. But it was for all the sins of Christendom that Christ constituted her a victim.

He had given her an inexpressible horror of sin. If she heard a blasphemy in the street she wept and said over and over again, together with her children, "Blessed be God", and on coming home prostrated herself on the ground, and struck her head upon the floor till it was stained with blood. Yet what is the sin of a carman the worse for drink compared with the infamous legal enactments thought out in those laboratories whither God directed her gaze, or with those millions of children taught to blaspheme God by the victorious Revolution?

The Soviets were not yet upon the scene, nor their little godless militants, but she foresaw them and saw already founded in Rome itself groups of young free-thinkers who swore hostility to the priesthood in life and in death.

§

From the beginning of her conversion Anna asked for expiatory suffering, and it was granted with a prodigal hand. But the waters of ecstasy rose like a flood, and she begged their withdrawal, and her wishes were granted to the full. Christ approved of her heroic sacrifice. "There are few, very few, My daughter, even among the servants of God, who renounce spiritual delights in order to embrace suffering by love. Oh! yes, very few renounce them." "I have chosen you, even you, for a place in the ranks of the martyrs. . . . Your life shall be a martyrdom longer and more meritorious than a martyrdom of blood, and it will be for the support of the Faith." And He added, using as He sometimes did, the language of poetry:

> *"Thy tortures other none shall know*
> *'Tis I, the Craftsman, I who know*
> *That formed thee: other none shall know."*

God gave a yet more precise outline of her vocation. "I destine you to convert sinful souls; to console priests, prelates, and even My Vicar. You will have to fight against a crowd of creatures subject to a thousand passions. You will meet many treacherous souls. You will be made a laughing-stock. You will endure it for love of Me. Your persecutors will be brought to book. I will punish them in this world and the next. But I will console those who treat you kindly even if they are great sinners. . . . I shall myself guide you by the hand to the altar of sacrifice."

At every step higher along the way of sorrow she was urged on yet further by a new hunger; hunger not for suffering for her own sake, but for redemptive suffering.

When the soul is ready for supreme sacrifices the knife falls. "Then," says Cardinal Pedicini, "consolations disappeared like lightning, leaving in their place dryness, pain, and labour. To tears of compunction there succeeded the most disconsolate aridity; to the joys of heaven, torture; to gaiety, sadness; to tender devotion, the most crippling weariness. Her soul passed swiftly from the splendours of the day to the darkness of blackest night. The heavens were like bronze. Tears would have been able to soften her dolorous exile, but even that satisfaction was denied her. She had to submit herself to the divine will in drinking in small draughts the chalice of cruellest torment without mitigation or relief. It was an abrupt passage from the extreme of riches to absolute penury. Her ecstasies did not cease, but in them she saw naught but the infinite distress of the world. "It was," continues the Cardinal, "a purgatory of twenty years. She saw God everywhere, but was unable to reach Him. She used to tell me at that time that she saw herself relegated to a corner of hell."

The "dark night" for twenty years! After Holy Communion she sometimes experienced a ray of light, but the darkness that supervened seemed all the deeper. The Master spoke, but only to invite her to climb the hill of Calvary. The crown of thorns with sharpened points that surrounded the mysterious sun took on its full meaning during those frightful nights when, tortured by illness and by devils, her soul seemed to her to be an arid desert. But never did she plead for the end of her martyrdom. On the contrary, she added new austerities and savoured it by praying the longer. Thus did she, as she put it herself, "row against the stream". In those days, when men were fighting on a thousand battlefields for paper crowns, and when heroism was talked of as never before, Anna spoke not that word; she only lived it!

Now, it was precisely when heaven was thus closed against her that earth became intolerable to her. Contradictions and calumnies and diseases showered down upon her like hailstones. Each of her senses was placed in the crucible of pain, as the evidence abundantly testified. She had continual headaches, which grew more violent on Fridays, and she suffered so much in this way that she was unable to stand upright, but to had lie down on the bed. If she had to get up to go about her household tasks the pain became so intense that, though she strove heroically to hide her distress, she shed hot tears and whispered: "What frightful pain. I can stand no more!" The sharp points that stabbed her head pierced also her eyes. Unable though she was to bear the light of day, she had to work at sewing and to stand in front of the cooking-range, which was torture to her. As her eyes usually showed no sign of disease and as she made no complaint, no one would have known of this torment if it had not been her duty to let her confidential priest know about it. In her last years she lost one eye completely and was all but blind.

The pains she suffered in her ears were so distressing that she had to wrap a band tightly round her head, and this stifled her when the weather was hot.

Her mouth was tormented almost continually with a taste as of vinegar, and to this she spontaneously added the penitential discipline of thirst. Distillation of poppies was suggested as a relief, but this gave her palpitations.

Her sense of smell was infected by the atrocious stench of the sins of the world, an affliction which increased when sinners came near her. Neither the smell of flowers nor burning aromatic herbs could lessen this stench, as of rotting corpses, that choked her.

Our list is not finished. Racked by pains in her bowels and in her joints, by chronic rheumatic troubles, by asthmatic shortness of breath, by a hernia that impeded all her movements, by the miraculous hand which was torn by invisible stigmata, everything about her was dislocated, so to speak, including the soles of her feet and the joints of her bones.

Yet scarcely anything of all this could be noticed, for she went on working, smiling, consoling others, disguising the waters of tribulation which overwhelmed her.

But for Giovanna, her maid, we should know nothing of that extra malady left with her from the birth of her last child—a large suppurating wound which learned surgeons thought to alleviate by stopping it with a thick wad of lead! "No man is a hero to his valet," yet Giovanna never ceases praising Anna's patience. ·Anna besought her to say nothing of these "trifles", lest it should cause anxiety to those around her. Giovanna, seeing her bending over the stove and gasping for breath, suggested her leaving it alone, but she gave a bantering reply: "Oh! the fires of Purgatory are more searching than that." The Mgr. Natali would question her about how she felt. "I am suffering unto death," she would whisper. "Thy will be done," he would suggest. "On earth as it is in heaven," she would answer with a smile.

It was in the midst of such distress that the "Grappin",* as the Curé of Ars called the Devil, played his part, but his assaults had just as little success as desolation in turning Anna away from her prayers.

Of old when the consolations of Holy Communion inundated her she used to fly from them; now, in the hour of dryness, she made longer thanksgivings. Bathed in cold sweat, harassed by temptations, fear, boredom, disgust, fifteen minutes prayer crushed her more than hours of labour. Thus, in summer she stayed for a long time motionless, in spite of stinging insects; in winter, in spite of chilblains, asthma, rheumatic pains, which seemed to await the time of prayer to revive; in spite, too, of the attacks of the evil spirits.

§

The intervention of evil spirits in the lives of the saints, the Curé of Ars, for instance, is too well

* The word means a "grapnel", but to convey the meaning we should have to translate by something like "the Clutching Hand" or "the Old Grabber" (Translator's note).

known for us to waste time discussing it with unbelievers. The whole question turns on admitting or denying the spiritual world altogether. If the soul, if God, exists, what difficulty is there in admitting that the devil exists? Jesus encountered him in His day; the saints have encountered him, and if we ignore him, while rubbing shoulders with him every day, that is perhaps because we are all too easy a prey for him.

Ernest Hello has some splendid reflections on this subject, which he develops as follows: "People influenced by the Devil deny his existence, for he only reveals himself to those who withstand him. . . . The Church provides us with several weapons against him, and Holy Water first of all. But the astonishing thing is that man, who has need of everything; man, the universal beggar, yet finds it possible to despise Holy Water. . . . Man who never dreamt of scorning the natural use of water unblessed, conceitedly scorns that water when it is raised to a new dignity. . . . The folly of man . . . belongs to the mystery of the Abyss. . . . The conceit of despising water would seem incredible to one who does not know mankind. It is true that he does not despise it till it is blessed, . . . that, in his eyes, constitutes the attenuating circumstances of the contempt. After despising it, he who a moment afterwards will be thirsty, is proud of his contempt, instead of ashamed of it, so proud that he wants his friends to know about it. . . . If the veil were lifted from his eyes, man would pay homage to that Spirit of justice whereby the Church puts matter in opposition to Lucifer, that reprobate who scorned matter on the ground that he was an angel . . . matter, which God did not despise, on which God cast a profound glance, over which God leaned as

He conceived the idea of taking a woman one day for his Mother. . . . Water is austere, deep, boundless, magnificent, above all a necessity. Its mission is to purify and to preserve, to put Satan to flight by providing little children with weapons against him: weapons of an extreme simplicity against him who so loathes simplicity and so loves a false glitter and has such theatrical tastes; against him for whom "despair" is synonymous with "never", for its continuity suffers nothing from interruptions of time: it has a robe with a train, the robe of eternity.

The Devil, then, did his utmost (so the Process tells us) to harass the prayer of the Beata, by obsession and by unclean imaginings; later he resorted to open onslaught, appearing sometimes in a loathsome form, sometimes in a seductive one. To this poor woman who knew indeed how to read, but not how to write, he propounded riddles, proving to her that she was an idiot. With never-ending arguments he demonstrated the absurdity of the doctrines of the Incarnation, the Holy Eucharist, the Resurrection, the Judgment, Hell: one syllogism followed hard on the heels of another.

"Who has proved to you that there is an eternity? When the body ends, everything ends. Have you considered what intellectual men think on these things? Look at the priests who retail these tall stories; see how they live! If they believed them they would not be such lunatics as to live so."* Annette contended at first by weeping and repeating her *Credo*; then with the Sign of the Cross, when the grimacing tempter fled like a whirlwind.

On other days tactics are changed. There is a gentle knock on the door. A bishop† in purple

* Quotation from the Process of the Beautification.
† i.e. The devil in the guise of a bishop.

appears, or a Cardinal in scarlet, perhaps a venerable religious, hands in his sleeves; in fact, the superior-general of a well-known order. Annette rises, embarrassed at being so honoured, kisses the hand of the distinguished visitor, asks his blessing, begs him to be seated. But little by little a vague disquietude disturbs her. The holy men surely give her the oddest advice: "This way of life, my daughter, befits neither your age nor your state of life. Take the word of those who have the grace of vocation. It is a very grave fault to shorten one's life by such austerities. You should think rather of getting food for your children and of educating them, instead of making yourself ill. Even a Carmelite, whose vocation it is to mortify herself, could not endure your régime. . . ." But always the serpent would show itself. "Why not have a good time like everybody else? You had more sense when you were eighteen, with your pretty red mantilla. Do you think God is so cruel as to take pleasure in suffering?"

At that the Beata took holy water, blessed herself, and sprinkled these high personages, who suddenly forgot their dignity and fled as fast as their legs would carry them. Yet they succeeded in disturbing her, and she remained for hours in tears, asking herself if all these suggestions, and others like them, had not received her secret consent. She multiplied her penances, yet found no peace except on the word of her confessor; yet a mere word from him was enough.

As mild methods did not succeed, the devils took to brutal ones. The howling of wild beasts, thunderous knocks on windows and doors, furniture overturned, invasions by animals out of the Apocalypse, punches, kicks, blows from sticks over the head and shoulders—all these in turn were adopted. Cardinal Pedicini says: "They took her by the neck, rolled her underfoot, subjected her to frightful torments, and tried to breakdown her purity by sensual apparitions." This witches' sabbath occurred at night, while the children were in their first sleep and before Domenico's return home.

Often demons would strive to drive her to her death; always at the last gasp a superior force would tame them. Anna was present at their meetings and heard them declare she was their cruellest enemy, that they had to protect themselves against her and have done with her. One night while saying her prayers, a whole pack of devils enveloped in a luminous mist, gathered about her. It was like a carnival of the diabolic where a panther rubbed shoulders with a yelling drunkard. As they did in the courtyard of the Curé of Ars they held council deciding "This is the moment to attack." Some caught her by the throat, some struck her with the fist, others gnawed her hands, yet others tore out her hair. "Fantasies of the Imagination," someone says. But wait! Mgr. Natali, who lodged in the room above, awakened by the pandemonium hastily threw his stole over his cassock, snatched up a flask of holy-water, and trembling, went downstairs. Annette was lying on the ground, covered with blood, from the murderous treatment. He sprinkled holy water about the room and Anna got up and took to her prayers anew. The priest went up to his room until the next alarm.

The next day the visitors again changed their tactics. They offered the Beata the delights of a Sybarite garden. She spat in their faces recommending herself to Our Lady, to St. Michael, and to her guardian angel, and the apparition vanished.

Then followed a whole cycle of obsessions—of blasphemy, of despair, of hate. She won through, but such struggles shattered her body and aggravated her infirmities.

§

According to the Process, these attacks were delivered with renewed violence at the period when Rome and Papacy were threatened by Napoleon and by the menaces which it was the Beata's mission to turn aside. Catherine of Siena, in moments of similar crises, underwent similar torments. She heard the devils cry out: "Curse you! You want to wreck our plans and hunt us from Rome. But we will kill you." And her body bore visible marks of their savagery.

Cardinal Pedicini testifies to having seen Anna many a time crying like a child as a result of the violent treatment she received.

Mgr. Natali says in his deposition: "She was beset by such onslaughts during the course of the night that without the special succour of Our Lord the strongest of spirits would have collapsed. During the first five years that I lived in the house, terrorising noises, uproars and monstrous apparitions of malignant spirits were so frequent, and so disturbing to the whole house, that I was forced to sleep lying on a sofa with my clothes on, to be able to run to her assistance at a moment's notice with holy water.

"I confess I was cowardly; if Our Lord had not given me special courage I should often have been tempted to quit the house, although I remembered that my bishop (the Blessed Mgr. Strambi) had commanded me never to leave it. But when evening came and I thought of the night ahead it seemed to me that there came down upon my shoulders an insupportable burden."

For those who are able to assess facts and the workings of the human mind at their value it is extremely difficult to interpret such plain and simple statements as auto-suggestion. This naïvete and "simplicity of the dove" delights me as it reappears on every page of the *Memoirs of Mgr. Natali*, but it was very often denounced by the promoter of the faith (the "devil's advocate") as contrary to the "prudence of the serpent" demanded by the office of the prelate. In it lay the danger of credulity, of blind admiration and of exaggeration. Granted! But one may ask whether too much shrewdness would not have tainted the testimony even worse. Moreover, Mgr. Natali was only one of thirty eye-witnesses, among whom were three cardinals, three bishops, three marquises, an English lord, three religious, two duchesses or princesses, without mentioning Anna's family, the servants, and the neighbours, both men and women—and of these some shared the characteristics of the serpent rather than the dove.

As with the Curé of Ars the diabolic onslaughts were the prelude or the aftermath of great conversions.

The lamentations of Christ which the Beata transcribed were mostly concerned with the laxity of priests, religious, and church dignitaries. It is for them above all that she suffered and multiplied her voluntary penances. One day Sophie discovered her mother's discipline in the drawer of the prie-dieu. "She scolded me for touching it without permission, and told me that she had made it to whip me when I was naughty, so as not to hurt her own hands."

II

CRUCIFIED FOR THE SALVATION OF SOULS AND
THE TRIUMPH OF THE CHURCH – THE BEATA AND
THE POPES – REPUTATION FOR HOLINESS AND
HUMILITY – THE "SMALL" VIRTUES: PRUDENCE,
JUSTICE, THRIFT AND GENEROSITY

ANNA's martyrdom lasted for forty-eight years,
and it is easy to grasp the words of Our Lord:
"Thy sufferings are beyond words, My daughter.
I wish them to be written down; yet in spite of all
people may read about them, no one will ever realise
the torments of thy soul. As for Me, I inscribe them
all in letters of gold, and in heaven alone shall the
grandeur of thy suffering love be known. There, too,
it shall be rewarded. Moreover, as I have already
told thee, I have chosen thee to be among the number of the martyrs, for thy life must be nought but a
long and harsh martyrdom." However, she knew
that the hour of suffering is the hour of redemption.
One could hear her cry: "Ah! let us thank God and
His Most Holy Mother! At this moment such and
such a sick person is making his confession. Another
soul is won for God."

"I remember," says Domenico in his deposition,
"that whenever there was an execution in Rome and
the condemned criminal would not repent, she was
very upset, and I noticed that in such circumstance
she was more unwell than usual."

Mgr. Natali tells us that one day she was going
to Communion at the Pieta church, though suffering
greatly, when he recommended to her prayers three
people condemned to death, one woman and two
men, who were to be executed at nine o'clock in
the morning. As hour succeeded hour an interior

voice kept Anna informed—the woman's sentence was commuted, but the two men who were to die remained impenitent. "So be it!" said the voice, "Let them die, and yet, less for the crime for which they are condemned than for their much greater crimes against their parents." Anna offered to suffer all things for their salvation, and the pains in her head became so acute that she had to lie down. She was heard to murmur: "Lord, what, I beseech Thee, can I do for these unfortunates?" Two heads fell. . . . But about six o'clock in the evening, in the midst of her agonising pain, she heard Our Lord say to her: "Thou hast given Me thy will, so that I am its sovereign ruler. On My part, I have, for love of thee, converted those souls. They are saved, but uniquely for the love I bear thee. Nevertheless, My justice can but expend its force upon thee."

The redemption of the guilty by the innocent! What a scandal to undiscerning minds! Yet therein lies the whole mystery of the redemption. Many are content to pass on hereditary evils to innocents born of a vitiated race, but in the Divine plan it is just the reverse for the innocent purify at their own cost the tainted spring.

§

The mysterious sun constantly presented a frightful picture to Anna's eyes—nothing less than a world empire of evil. Masonic conventions; the shambles of Europe, where thousands of soldiers were dying without priests: Austerlitz, Jena, Magdebourg, Eylau, Friedland, Wagram; Spain on fire; popes in prison; false councils held in Paris; the way made plain for schism; bishops and cardinals who showed resistance made captive; the Emperor administrating the Church as if it were an army, and giving it the shock-treatment one gives to a raw recruit. And always the voice repeating to Anna-Maria: "Thou shalt fulfil in thy flesh, what is wanting to My passion on behalf of My Church and My vicar."

In this rôle, played by Anna in regard to the popes, many parallels may be established between her and that other Sienese, Catherine.

Both the one and the other were sent to succour the Papacy in distress. Catherine saluted the pope as "the gracious Christ on earth". It was a salutation dictated by faith, for the Papacy of those days was undoubtedly far removed from the graciousness of Christ. Anna's also was the view inspired by faith, for she compares the pope to the eucharistic appearances under which Christ's presence is hidden. She realised that these appearances may be imperfect, or even sullied, as they were in a pope like Alexander VI, yet the reality abides. She saw such and such a pope undergoing a long expiation for his faults in purgatory, yet her esteem for the Papacy did not grow less. The poor, who came in crowds to her lodging, bewailed the bad temporal administration of the popes, but she bade them be silent, saying that the pope had so many things to think about he could not keep watch over all details.

This rôle of defending the Papacy was, however, only accidental. Her essential task was to support it by her prayers. It was a less brilliant rôle than that of Catherine, whose mission was to "restore the pope to Italy and Italy to the pope"; who went from the pope at Avignon to the Italian princes with her urgent and peremptory: "It is my will." "It is my will." Anna stayed in Rome and hid herself in a tiny street. The princes of the Church came there at times to ask her advice, but the weapons she most favoured were those of silence and self-immolation.

§

In 1798, thanks to Napoleon, and his brother Joseph, at work in Rome, the Roman republic was proclaimed. Massena carried off Pius VI, taking him to Siena and then to Valentia—it was there the pope died a year afterwards, as an old man of eighty-two years.

In Rome Anna witnessed and described the pope's death-agony, and announced the coup d'état of eighteenth Brumaire, following upon which Napoleon reopened France to the clergy. The widowed Church would have another pope on 14th March 1800. Pius VII made his entry into his capital, and Anna knew the trials that awaited him and what their sequel would be. The Pope, on his side, did not disguise his veneration for the humble labouring woman. He approved the lovely prayer composed by her, from which we have previously quoted. Cardinal Pedicini, knowing the calumnies that were being bandied about concerning her, had it in mind to give up visiting her, and consulted the Pope. He enjoined a continuance of the visits: "You realise," he said, "that I should have summoned her to me, if I did not fear to increase the gossip." Subsequently he expressed a wish that she should write to him; she did so, but with great confusion. He did not stop there, but "communicated with her several times" (so writes the Cardinal) "and he always asked news of her whenever I had audience; asked her prayers and charged me to take her his blessing."

On 2nd February 1808 the troops of Napoleon entered Rome and trained their artillery upon the Quirinal, where Pius VII was living. When all the Pontifical States had been attached to the Empire, a sentence of excommunication was inflicted on the

invaders, but the Pope's subjects were instructed
to abstain from all violence. Napoleon, who was then
on the Danube, sent two letters to Murat, the King
of Naples, couched in these brutal terms: "I hear
that the Pope has excommunicated us all . . . the
Pope is a raving lunatic who must be locked up."
On 6th July, Radet, at the head of some soldiers and
a gang of bandits, scaled the Pontifical Palace at
night and with strokes of the hatchet broke open
the doors behind which the venerable old man stood
upright, awaiting them. While Napoleon was winning the battle of Wagram, Pius VII was thrown into
a carriage. Locked in it, he was dragged from
Florence to Turin, from Turin into France, and
from there to Savona. Communication with the
Pope was forbidden, and an ecclesiastical commission
declared the excommunication of 10th June to be
without justification. Napoleon continued to make
appointments to bishoprics and suppressed the
Monastic Orders in Italy. Finally, just as he was
beginning that duel with half Europe in which he
was to be beaten, he had Pius VII transferred from
Savona to Fontainebleu. On the heights of Mt.
Cenis the aged Pope's agony overtook him and he
received viaticum and extreme unction.

President Segiuer declared that "Napoleon was
outside human history and beyond admiration".
Blinded by flattery of that sort the master acted as
one inspired. Count Ségur attributes these words to
him: "I find myself urged on to a goal I know not,
and when I have reached it and I am of no more use,
then a mere atom will be enough to level me with the
earth."

At this period Anna-Maria heard our Saviour say
to her: "Why have I raised up Napoleon? To make
him the tool of My anger wherewith to chastise the

iniquity of the wicked and to humiliate the proud. One wrongdoer destroys other wrongdoers." Napoleon unconsciously served the Papacy. The Concordat of 1801 gave peace to the Church in France, was the death-blow of Gallicanism, and acknowledged the universal jurisdiction of the Papacy. When his work was done, Providence swept away Napoleon. In defeat it was at the palace of Fontainebleu where he had imprisoned the Pope that he signed his Act of Abdication: "The Emperor Napoleon declares that he renounces, for himself and his heirs, the thrones of France and Italy." Pius VII, a free man, progressed through that same France and that same Italy, under triumphal arches, while the Emperor made his journey to the island of Elba and eventually the island of St. Helena.

Anna-Maria followed the tribulations of Pius VII hour by hour without intermission in her mysterious sun. By her means the cardinals, the prelates in residence in Rome, the faithful generally, learnt of the sufferings of the prisoner. She foretold the end of his trials, described the triumphal return. The Marquis Bandini, among other witnesses, testifies that about a year before the return of Pius VII, she told him the Pope would come back to his See with glory: "She told me the exact date, saying that he would pontificate in St. Peter's on Whit-Sunday. All fell out precisely as she had said. Thus on 24th May 1814 Anna assisted at the entry of the Holy Father into Rome.

However, the Papacy comes through one storm only to enter another.*

When the Empire went down in ruins, the secret societies began their campaigns of riots and plots,

---

* Cf. Fernand Hayward *Le Dernier Siecle de la Rome Pontificale*, 2 vols., Paris, Payot, 1928.

which were to trouble the Church from then till
the taking of Rome on 20th September 1870. The
people of Rome were in a ferment, political assasina-
tions multiplied, Carbonarism penetrated the Roman
courts of law, education, administration, the army,
the nobility, the very clergy. Cardinal Severoli's
own nephew (and he was the leader of the anti-
liberal party) swore by dagger and poison to destroy
throne and altar. Anna knew of this underground
work through her sun, and also paid for its frustra-
tion through her sufferings. She warned the Pope
or the cardinals not to take such and such a walk,
not to pay such a visit, for ambushes had been laid
for them. She was by the will of heaven a sort of
Minister of the Interior without portfolio.

On 6th July 1823 the aged Pius VII had a fall
which broke his thigh, and though he seemed to be
recovering, Anna warned Cardinal Pedicini that
there was no cure: it was necessary to give him the
last sacraments without delay. Her advice was taken,
and the Holy Father died in the morning of 20th
August at the age of eighty-one. At the same time
the 1,400-year-old Basilica of St. Paul's-outside-
the-Walls, where Pius had been rector, went up in
flames as Anna had prophesied.

§

There followed a disturbed Conclave, where the
"moderates", partisans of the reforms, confronted
the "zealots". The latter were led by Cardinal
Severoli and Cardinal Della Genga who was to be
elected. The "moderates" gathered round the
former ambassador of Napoleon, Cardinal Fesch,
and his two former adversaries, Cardinal Consalvi
and Chateaubriand, minister of Louis XVIII. As
always lampoons and satires, often violent and

sometimes coarse, filled the streets of Rome; among them this singular Litany was chanted:

"From Consalvi, the despot, deliver us, O Lord!
From the licentiousness of Alban, deliver us, O Lord.
That Thou would'st deign to make neither of them pope,
We beseech Thee hear us."

A masquerade inspired by the Masonic Lodges paraded the cardinals in the costumes of Harlequin and Pantaloon. Handbills stated that the offices of street sweeper and wigmaker were to be filled by Cardinal Fesch, and all the princes, dukes, marquises and other enslaved Romans, who had long been accustomed to such employment.

Hawkers sang couplets caricaturing the future Pope, Cardinal Count Della Genga. A popular lampoon at the expense of "Don Juan the unfortunate great hunter", declared:

"When the Pope is a hunter,
His States are the forests,
His ministers the gun-dogs,
And his subjects the game. . . ."

And ended with these blasphemous lines:

"Give us a pope, O Holy Spirit,
Who fears Thee, loves us,
And lives but a short time."

This digression is necessary if the reader is to understand the background in which the expiatress was involved.

§

On 28th September 1823 Della Genga succeeded Pius VII as Leo XII. Thanks to the Blessed Strambi, whom the new Pope made his counsellor, the relationship between Anna and the Vatican was drawn closer still. Mgr. Strambi consulted her in

the interests of the Church, in the name of the Pope
day by day, and conveyed her answers to him. It is
Mgr. Natali that gives us the information: "Every
evening," he says, "Mgr. Strambi told me under
strict secrecy about important affairs of the Church,
such as questions of reform, in order that I might
question the servant of God. He implicitly accepted
her counsels passing them on to the Holy Father.
One day, when one of her legs was causing her
trouble, I saw the Pope's surgeon at her house; he
had been sent by the Holy Father to get news of
Anna's malady and to ask if she had need of his
attentions."

Leo XII had reigned only a few weeks when a
serious illness threatened his life. Mgr. Strambi
offered his own life in exchange for that of the dying
Pope, and asked Anna through her confessor for
prayers for him. Anna, in the midst of her cooking,
consulted her sun and saw that the heroic prayer
had been heard. "No," she said, "the Pope will not
die. For yet a while longer, he will bear the burden
of the Church. Mgr. Strambi, however, must
prepare to die in the Holy Father's place." A few
days afterwards the holy prelate died.*

Anna lived on to be, more than ever, the angel
guardian of Leo XII, who was not to die for another
six years. By the designs of Providence Mgr. Natali
was made secretary to the Master of the Chamber.
Now the lodges had decided to "liquidate" Leo XII.
Leo's measures against drunkenness, and the bandits
who terrorised the Roman campagna; the execution
of two young nobles of the Carbonari for attempted
murder—anything and everything was made a pre-
text for stirring up discontent. These Carbonari died

* Mgr. Strambi was canonised in 1950. He has outstripped his spiritual
mother (*Translator's note*).

defying God and the Pope, were hailed as martyrs, and oaths were taken to avenge them. It was no sine-cure having to sift the visitors demanding an audience. Mgr. Natali was constantly asking Anna's advice; she would answer: "Send this visitor about his business; keep an eye on that one." Her instructions were so miraculously to the point that Leo XII, in the absence of his Master of the Chamber, set etiquette aside and ordered the secretary to remain.

During the last illness of the Pope, the Beata was warned of its fatal issue: "Arise and pray for My Vicar," said Our Lord to her; "he is about to render an account of his stewardship at My tribunal." On the following day Leo XII died; it was the year 1829.

Pius VIII succeeded him, to reign only twenty months. While the conclave was in session and no one could foresee how long the election would take, Anna declared it would be finished in eight days, but that the new pontificate would be a very short one.

Then Pius VIII's death. Cardinal Pedicini gives the details: "Pius VIII fell ill, though it was not thought to be serious. He was, in fact, on the point of resuming his audiences, when Mgr. Natali came to tell me that the servant of God had seen in her sun the catafalque crowned with the Tiara set up in St. Peter's. I warned the cardinal's secretary, who was thunderstruck, but he had no doubts upon the matter, and three days later the Pope died.

After a painful and long conclave of three months, wherein the intrigues of various States, especially of Austria, had free play, Cardinal Cappellari was elected as Gregory XVI. This was in 1831. Anna died in his pontificate. The sects made yet another resolution to finish with the Papacy and used the

long interregnum to prepare for it. Plots were of
daily occurrence, and the Carbonari in the end
declared that if the Papacy could be destroyed in no
other way, then Rome would have to be blown up.
Bomb-making was at full pressure. Anna-Maria
watched, warned, suffered. As the tempest, of which
God revealed to her the details, swelled in violence,
so her sufferings became more intolerable. Become
the scapegoat for sinners, she could be heard saying:
"I have sinned, O Lord; be merciful to me."

Mgr. Natali tells this charming story regarding
the election of Gregory XVI: "I was with the
servant of God at St. Paul's-outside-the-Walls, when
Cardinal Cappellari entered. Anna, in ecstasy,
occupied the only prie-dieu. I shook her so that she
should give place to the cardinal, but he signed to me
to leave her alone. Coming out of her ecstasy, Anna
fixed her gaze upon him, and as we returned to Rome
she said to me: "That was the future Pope." In her
sun she had seen a dove settling upon him; it was
bathed in golden light, but surrounded by gloomy
clouds, foreshadowing the coming revolution.

§

An amusing incident is told of the conclave. During
its progress Anna saw in her sun that Cardinal
Cappellari would be elected within seventeen days.
Now the saintly Camaldolese used a capacious snuff-
box, from which he often invited Mgr. Natali and
Cardinal Barberini to take a pinch. This was now to
end, so Mgr. Natali thought, for etiquette does not
allow one to dip into the snuff-box of a Pope. Something of a schoolboy, the Monsignor was probably
eager to let out the secret, and so, meeting Cardinal
Cappellari, he took a large pinch out of the future
papal snuff-box, sighing: "If only this were not the

last time!" "What's that?" asked the cardinal, but Mgr. Natali had not the courage to let out more. Soon he was no longer bound by the secret, and seventeen days before the election he found a means of calling Cardinal Barberini to the guarded lobby, which is the only link between the outer world and the conclave. "Take," said he, "seventeen pinches from our friend's snuff-box, for in seventeen days you will have no further opportunity."

The cardinal, who was one of Anna's miraculous cures, understood. He joined Cardinal Cappellari, asked for a pinch of snuff, and in leisurely fashion took the full seventeen, but, as will be readily understood, could not use all of them and scattered most on the carpet. Upon this, his friend got vexed. "What are you up to," he said, "wasting my snuff?" "You will understand—in seventeen days," came the answer. The cardinal understood, and later Mgr. Natali told him how, since the visit to St. Paul's-outside-the-Walls, Anna had foretold not only his pontificate, but the joys and trials that awaited him. The result was that Gregory XVI, ignoring etiquette, continued to offer the Monsignor first rate snuff from his snuff-box whenever he received him in audience.

What is more, he was a good pope, though by no means perfect, and Blessed Anna-Maria knew it, for holiness made her indulgent but not blind. The Romans, those wilful railers, multiplied libels against the former Camaldolese. But Ernesto Masi, who had no love for him, nevertheless wrote: "He was not the man that libel and satire made him out to be." He emulated Fesch as a great collector of pictures and works of art, and died in 1846, nine years after the Beata.

She also foretold the election of Pius IX and his

tribulations. One day, as she offered her tears and sufferings for the Church, Our Lord showed her "the horrifying sins of people of all kinds", which would bring down the lightning of His wrath. "How," she asked, "will so great a disaster be remedied?" "My Father and I will set all to rights, and after the chastisement those who survive must behave in the way I shall explain to you."

§

Here we touch upon mysteries. . . .

"Five years before the death of Pius VII," the narration of Mgr. Natali tells us, "she described to me the great ordeal ahead. Rome would be battered by revolutions; tribulations would be lessened by the supplications of the saints. The tares would be rooted out and the hand of God would reduce all to order where human efforts were unavailing. The scourges on earth would be lessened, but those of heaven would be universal and terrifying. Millions of men would die by the sword in war and civil strife, other millions would perish in unforeseen death. Then entire nations would return to the unity of the Church, and many Turks, Pagans and Jews would be converted and their fervour cover with confusion the original Christians. In one word she told me that Our Lord was intending to cleanse the world and His Church for which He was preparing a miraculous rebirth that would be a Triumph of His Mercy."

The same vision was presented to the eyes of the Beata on many occasions. She saw the earth enveloped in flame; darkness covering it; immense edifices flung down; the earth and the heavens as it were in agony; the ordeal followed by a universal renewal. And all that would come to pass when the

Church seemed to have lost all human means of withstanding persecution. The ordeal would make manifest "the secret thoughts of the hearts". "Those," said Our Lord, "to whom I shall grant the spirit of humility, those will be the victors."

People have tried to see in the Church's tribulations under Pius IX the great apostasy for which the wars of 1870 and 1914 were the punishment, and have supposed that we are drawing near to the great renewal.

Cardinal Salotti compares the revelations of Blessed Anna with those of the Venerable Elizabeth Canori-Mora. "The time of purification," Our Lord is supposed to have said to her, "will not be as long as you think. Time is in My hands. I can cut it as short as I wish. All that is necessary is that the five trees of heresy that infest the forest should be torn out by the roots." Cardinal Salotti calls these five trees nationalism, liberalism, freemasonry, modernism, socialism, and he sees them on the decline and concludes that the great renewal is at hand. Let us hope so!

At any rate, the Beata had clearly foretold that Father Mastai, then attached to the Chilean nunciature, would become Pope with the title of Pius IX and, in the midst of the trials without number which would reduce him to beggary, would govern the Church long and with holiness.

The elegant Count Mastai was formerly a willing and frequent visitor at the picturesque Armellino hostelry, so dear to Stendhal. He had become a priest at the age of twenty-seven years, afterwards Canon of Santa-Maria-in-Via-Lata (the Church of the Blessed Anna) and Bishop of Imola. At Imola, Count Pasolini instructed him in the theories of Balbo concerning a greater Italy and its reformation.

He became Pope, as the Beata had foretold, in 1846, after a conclave of forty-eight hours.

His reforms, the amnesty for political convicts and the granting of a liberal constitution produced indescribable enthusiasm, but the politicians made this very liberalism serve their own turn. The Prince of Camino (son of Lucian Bonaparte, the protégé of Pius VII) provoked a rising. In November 1848 the Minister Rossi was assassinated and Pius IX had to flee to Gaeta in the middle of the night. Mazzini and Garibaldi proclaimed the Roman Republic, but were themselves overthrown. Priests were hunted in the streets of Rome; there were sacrileges and masquerades. Eventually the French troops under Oudinot arrived and restored the keys of Rome to Pius in 1850. A precarious peace. There was the defeat of Castelfidardo, victory of Mentana, and the final collapse. On 20th September 1870 General Cadorna at the head of the Piedmontese troops of Victor Emmanuel, occupied Rome. By 40,785 votes against 46, the plebiscite of 2nd October declared the temporal power of the popes at an end.

If Anna-Maria had accurately foretold all these tribulations, she was equally exact in saying that Pius IX would be a holy Pope and would do great things during his long reign. It is somewhat distressing to find at the side of the last pope-king a man who was in too many ways the imitator of Mazarin, namely, Antonelli, the Cardinal Secretary of State; but this shadow on the picture cannot make one forget either the sanctity of the Holy Father or the fact that he defined the dogmas of the Immaculate Conception and the Infallibility of the Pope, or that he convened the Vatican Council—the most important event of modern times since the Council of Trent.

Pius IX recognised himself in the description of him given by the Beata, and on two separate occasions urged the promoter of the Faith to hasten the Process. Giving an audience in 1871 to the Confraternity of St. Peter, to which was committed the work of St. Peter's Pence, he said, "Mgr. Rafaële Natali, the zealous promoter of the cause of the venerable Anna-Maria has told us wonderful things about her, and of her prophecies concerning the times in which we live. He has told us often, as having heard it from her, that a moment would come when the Holy See would be reduced to living on alms subscribed throughout the world, and yet that money would never be lacking. Truly it is easy to recognise the truth of these prophecies."

Anna welcomed all.

Anna's humble house was known and visited, not only by messengers of the popes, but by all the saints of those troubled days—the Blessed Mgr. Strambi, the Venerable Mgr. Menocchio, sacristan to Pius VII, and the Venerable Brother Felix of Montefiascone, the Capuchin.

She welcomed a cabman, or a minister with equal charity. "A fly was as much to her as a camel, a flea as much as an elephant," says one witness. She did not refuse to give advice to statesmen, but she gave it with greater joy to that poor woman, for instance, who complained to her one day that her affairs had come to a crisis: "It's come at last! The keeping of hens is my livelihood," she said, "and it does not pay. It is a case of perversity in the fowls themselves, for they do not lay." The Beata instructed her in the best way of looking after hens, telling her it was the only thing to make them lay. With people of this sort her hunger for self-effacement was less in jeopardy than in contact with the great. Noble visitors abounded, Sophie tells us, but she herself never spoke of them, and if anybody else made allusion to them, she was confused.

The Duchess of Saxe, of the Bourbon family, Princess Giustiniani, and Lord Clifford, gave her their respectful friendship, but she never spoke of them. The Queen of Etruria wished to visit her, but she opposed it, and would not go to the palace unless expressly bidden. "Whenever my mother," says Sophie again, "caught sight of the Queen in the distance she would turn back to avoid being greeted, and because of her bad sight she bade me warn her of such encounters.

One day the Queen received Pius VII in her house and seized the opportunity to present her friend Anna to him. Anna at first felt a great joy at the thought of speaking to the Vicar of Christ, but the desire for self-effacement immediately rose uppermost. The interview would be witnessed; she contented herself, therefore, with prostrating herself at the feet of his Holiness without whispering a word; then feeling the approach of an ecstasy, she arose immediately and went away.

This reserve of hers was the reason why many who were beholden to her did not know the name of her who had cured or advised them till after her death. We give here the testimony of the Ven. Don Vincent Pallotti, the gifted precursor of Catholic social action.[*]

* The 4th April 1935 was the centenary of the foundation by Don Vincenzo Pallotti of "The Society of the Catholic Apostolate". It was later named "The Pious Society of Missions", or "The Society of Pallottine Fathers". Vincenzo Pallotti, born 1795, died in 1850, at the age of fifty-five years. He was one of the most illustrious Roman priests of the nineteenth century. The process of Beatification was introduced soon after his death. . . . On the occasion when the Decree upon the heroism of his virtues was promulgated, Pius XI said: "Pallotti forestalled both the name and the purpose of Catholic action when he founded

He spoke to the Marquis de Gregorio of a saintly woman who wished to remain unknown, but whose counsels would be salutary for him. The Marquis saw her several times, and in the belief that she was the intermediary of the saint, begged for advice and for graces. It was only after her death that he learnt the truth. She had even hidden her identity for a while from the Ven. Pallotti himself, in spite of the continual appeal he made to her prayers and counsels.

However, Anna could not entirely avoid tributes of admiration. She bemoaned the fact to God. Her confessor says: "Withdrawn into her own little room, she wept to see herself honoured; she complained, telling Our Saviour that He was unkind, that if He loved her, He would let her walk in the ways to which she belonged. Seeing that He led her by others so different she feared it might be a trick of the devil's. Therefore, in so far as she was allowed, she hid herself from the eyes of all," even from her own folk, even from the good Domenico.

"She always said to us" (Dominico's testimony), "but above all, when a neighbour had been guilty of a shortcoming, 'If the Good God did not take us by the hand, we are capable of worse behaviour'. She

the Society of the Catholic Apostolate for this in its essence is the same as Catholic action."

It was 4th April 1835 (two years before the death of Anna-Maria) that Pallotti, aged forty years, with the help of priests and laymen, created the Society of the Apostolate, a society with a very modern trend about it, for a large share in social and charitable action is given to the laity. Like all pioneers, Don Pallotti encountered ceaseless opposition, and dying prematurely, may well have asked himself whether anything of his achievement would remain. The layman's hour had not come; susceptibilities of every sort fettered that liberating movement which could have saved so much from ruin. The "Circle of Lay Conquest" rapidly declined, but the Community of Priests and Brothers survived, and turned its attention to less insecure ground—missions to the infidels, to emigrants and colonists. To-day the society numbers 115 houses in Europe, America and Africa. It is worthy of notice that Pius XI takes up anew the master-thought of the "gifted pioneer, protector and model" of Catholic Action, whose holy audacity Blessed Anna-Maria encouraged.

quoted the words of Saint Philip Neri: 'Lord, hold
me tightly, for if You do not, I am capable this very
day of becoming a Jew. . . .' She never said 'I have
done this or that', but always sought to put herself in
the lowest place, and to put it in a few words, she
would have obeyed the cat. She avoided praise, and
never argued. To tell the truth, I must confess that
a fault of mine when maintaining an opinion, was to
say: 'Be quiet; you know nothing.' Upon this she
smiled and answered: 'That is true, I am a fool; I
do not know how to do any good.' "

Sophie bears witness:

"When anybody asked my mother to recommend
some intention to God, she answered: 'Yes, let us
pray for one another.' People said to me 'You are
happy to have so holy a mother'. If I artlessly
reported this to her, she answered: 'My daughter,
you speak wrongly, for saints do not belong to this
world, but let us pray God that we may all die saints.'
At other times, when people said 'Pray for me, for
you are a saint', she was troubled and answered:
'What are you saying? I do not know how Our
Lord tolerates me on the earth. Don't talk such
heresy. God alone is just and holy. I am only a poor
specimen of a woman'."*

Sophie, with nice discernment, further emphasises
the fact that there was no pose in her mother's
lowliness only an extreme simplicity, a simplicity
that drew little children to her as it drew them to
Jesus. *Mas love for children*

§

The desire to avoid fuss made her, as I have said,
set aside as a temptation, the role of foundress or

* The French word "femelette" conveys, for a woman, what we convey for a
man when we speak of a "mannikin", or colloquially "whippersnapper" (*Translator's note*).

superioress. In the Process we read "With the light she possessed and the relationships she enjoyed she could have made herself famous by founding some pious work. Such ideas were entirely foreign to her, for she did not like novelties, was extremely afraid of self-love. She frequently recommended those who consulted her to re-establish or put new life into old works, rather than create new ones. "By so doing," she said, "you do good and mock the devil, for he has no way of slipping himself in by self-love and ambition."

Although she was daily carried away by ecstasy, Anna, as a matter of fact, had a strong leaning to the small virtues, and most of all to the virtues called "natural"—"Those humble plants," as St. Francis de Sales puts it, "that grow in the shade." Domenico, answering the close examination wherein the virtues of his wife were passed through a sieve, said with great appositeness: "Passing on to the virtue of prudence, I declare that the servant of God chastised her children with such moderation that they are all safe and sound to this day, thanks be to God. She noticed with sorrow that some parents are so carried away as to beat their children about the head, and she tried to stop them." He failed to say that he was in great need of that piece of advice himself.

Cardinal Pedicini adds: "Anna-Maria was always prudent in her penances. She performed bodily mortifications without ruining health. At the bidding of her confessor she relinquished the extremes she practised in the first fervour of her conversion. She advised her spiritual sons to submit entirely in such matters to the counsels of their director, for it often happens that the devil urges extravagant austerities, so that souls may be wearied and rendered impotent in the service of God.

She loved her spiritual sons to make holy resolutions, but not to bind themselves too readily to such vows. She followed a rule in pious exercises, but had the wisdom to disregard it when charity or family peace demanded it, nor did she hesitate to stay away from Mass and Holy Communion when her husband or children needed her care. She loved seclusion, but came out of it immediately if charity demanded. She loved praying in solitude, but she also knew the power of public prayer, and did not fail to attend the stations of the Cross on Fridays at the Coliseum."

"Of a mild, gay, and patient temperament," writes Mgr. Natali, "she none the less knew how to reprove her spiritual sons with great energy, and to speak frankly to great personages like the Duchess de Lucques, who followed her directions blindly, even in the governing of her estates."

She did not think that perfection dispensed with honesty. "Not only," says Domenico, "did she pay what she owed, but I remember her noticing a mistake amounting to no more than a sou in her daily expense accounts with Luigi Antonini, and returning it even before dinner. When she did needlework for the religious of St. Domenic, she returned everything left over down to the last bit of thread; she never got into debt, for one of her sayings was that 'the length of the stride must be measured by the length of the limb'. But she was equally conscientious in guaranteeing bread to her family in spite of profiteers. If she were forced to contract a small debt, she first of all warned the tradesman, and then made haste to pay without waiting for him to send in his claim." Happy creditors!

Happy also were her maids; for this labouring woman, the wife of a servant, had servants herself from time to time. Domenico says: "She could have been waited upon, because I almost always provided her with a servant, but she put her hand to everything in order to serve others. Anna paid these servants every month the agreed wages, but added gratuities if she had asked them to perform any unusual task." "I might add," he grumbled, "that these maids showed very little gratitude."

But surely he exaggerates, for he was himself no easy master to serve? In any case, we owe to the depositions of these women piquant details about the Beata, her thrift and generosity. They fill in the gaps in the following brusque and ungracious testimony of Domenico: "My wife never allowed her family to go without anything. On the other hand, she did not go in for junketing, as they do in Rome, but not as we do in the Valteline. Here people eat one day enough to burst their bellies, while the next day they have not a bite to put in their mouths. That is what happens above all, at carnival time and in October. But in our little cottage, under my wife's direction, everything was orderly and went like clock-work in the peace of heaven." When he had spoken like that, no doubt the old man aired a grievance. Cardinal Pedicini had put the matter more graciously: "Far from imitating the Romans, who, as the saying goes, spend twenty sous when they have only ten, Anna practised a very careful thrift, combined with the very greatest charity."

Her maids are as eloquent and practical. Listen to Annunziata: "In the Taigi household we were numerous. There was a dozen of us, including Mariuccia, Sophie, Sophie's children and Don Rafaële. Dinner usually consisted of soup, a dish of boiled or roast meat, with vegetables, such as potatoes. We bought two or three pounds of beef or veal, some-

times more. The Venerable Anna-Maria's husband
ate as much as three. For breakfast there was café-au-
lait for all, except on days when milk was forbidden.
For supper what was left over from dinner was served
again, or there was cheese, to which salad was always
added. At the midday as well as the evening meal
wine was measured out—a bottle of wine watered
to make it go a long way, and one of pure wine, of
which one bumper was served at the end to each
person (except the Beata, who said wine did not
agree with her). In a word," adds Giovanna, "there
was always plenty of food; the Beata did not suffer
anyone to go hungry."

She was austere to none but herself; she made the
servants sit down and stood herself to serve them
first and herself afterwards. All of the maids emphasise her careful thrift; even when sick and in bed, she
asked for the accounts, and commented if something
had been bought at too dear a price or of bad quality.
When her income was improved in some unexpected
way, she did not spend more lavishly, but economised
and multiplied her almsgiving. In one word she
treated her domestics like sisters. "One day,"
continues Giovanna, "I was carrying a large bottle
of about twelve paoli in value, for it was encased in
wicker-work and glazed. It broke in my hands. I was
very upset, but the Venerable Anna-Maria consoled
me by saying: 'It is nothing. We had a dozen
bottles of that sort and they are all broken, and that
one would necessarily have gone the same way as the
others.' To comfort me she poured out a little wine.
There were other occasions on which I broke plates
and saucers. She consoled me with the words: "It
is nothing. We must, after all, feed the crockery-
makers'."

The witty Sienese shows herself here. She shows

the distinction between a sad saint and a saddening saint. Anna wanted those around her to be gay. She knew that one ounce of good will and cordiality towards inferiors is well worth ten ounces of crockery. Giovanna also shows how servants miss nothing. The Venerable Bernard Clausi, of the Order of Minims of St. Francis de Paul, came to dinner two or three times. He only ate macaroni, but Giovanna had prepared macaroni with meat in it, and the Minims may only eat it without meat. "But," she says, "Pére Bernard must have had permission to eat 'fat' macaroni, for neither the Venerable Anna nor Don Rafaël would have put a forbidden dish before him."

III

THE MYSTERIOUS SUN – BLESSED ANNA BRINGS ALL THINGS TO LIGHT – THE LOT OF THE DEPARTED – THE SUPERNATURAL ORDER AND THE MORAL ORDER – THE SECRETS OF NATURE – SICK- NESS – THOUGHTS – THE FUTURE

ANNA spoke the popular language of Rome in her revelations, and Our Lord used the same language. So also the Blessed Virgin spoke the local dialect of Lourdes to Bernadette. But sometimes Our Lord spoke to Anna in poetical vein, but the poetry was none the less of the popular kind. On 31st August 1816, in the church of St. Charles at the Four Fountains, she was ravished in ecstasy after communion and heard and recounted this bridal song: "My Well-Beloved, thou dost repine, and yet thou art at rest in the arms of thy Well- Beloved. I am in thee and thou art unconscious of My presence. Yes, each day thou dost repine. Be at rest and fear nothing, my Well-Beloved in My loving arms. Thou shalt be well paid for thy sufferings. For I shall give thee every succour. I want to make of thee a valiant woman. Take thy buckler in hand and fear nothing. Reflect, My daughter, that thou must be My spouse, that thou must live close to Me. Whither I carry thee, thou shalt be happy and one day thou shalt die in My arms. Happy are they, My daughter, who live with thee. They may be called blessedly happy. What would it avail them to possess silver or gold, if when their lives ended, they should be damned? No, I have told thee before, and believe Me, my well-beloved, they who are at thy side are happy in their sufferings, for they shall share thy joy."

There follows the Master's lament over the new Jerusalem: "Oh, Rome! Rome! criminals, children! You ignore the good I have done you. I have taken note of your response to it. But when once the order is given by My heavenly Father. . . . My well-beloved, then thou shalt thyself see what will be the ending of Rome!

"Know that at this moment souls are falling into hell like flakes of snow. Let them weep and sob in their bitterness of soul. Rome can no longer be called holy Rome. Thou thyself dost see it, see it clearly with thine own eyes, how they live like beasts.

"Men seek nothing here below but luxury, pleasures, and the satisfaction of all their blameworthy lusts. And many of them complain to me that they can no longer support the weight of their miseries. But if only I could tell thee! . . . I would like to open My heart to thee. I shall revenge myself on them. It will be necessary for me to overwhelm them on account of their sins."

§

"To overwhelm them." Twice already the waves had carried off St. Peter's barque; Pius VI and Pius VII exiled, the cardinals dispersed, the Roman people trampled by the imperial armies . . .; the waves continued to swell under Pius IX; the Pope in flight to Gaeta and returning to Rome for the agony of Gethsemani; the populace yelling under the windows of the Vatican: "Death to Pius IX"; the priests attacked, the churches pillaged, infamous masquerades along the Corso, parodying the Feast of Corpus Christi, mocking the crucifix. A frenzied crowd dancing the Carmagnole and crying: "Long live petrol! It was petrol that burnt Paris; petrol shall burn Rome!" Statues of the Blessed Virgin Herself defiled and the grave of Pius IX dishonoured. . . .

One must keep such things in mind if one is to understand the terrifying visions in the mysterious sun, for it was there Anna saw the miseries it was her vocation to expiate or to obviate.

The gift of the sun was so singular that we must refer to it at this point once more, quoting the Acts of the Process and the Decree of Beatification. "I have done for thee," said Our Saviour to her, "what I have hitherto done for none of My servants; I have granted thee a gift that none of them ever had."

It is possible, as I have said, to discover similar gifts. Saint Columbanus, for instance, once saw in a flash, and as it were in a ray of the sun, the entire universe. Saint Frances of Rome enjoyed for twenty-seven years the permanent vision of an angel who played a rôle comparable to that played by the sun of Anna-Maria Taigi. He discovered to Frances the slightest faults, and enlightened her on the state of men's consciences. Anna read in her sun the most secret thoughts of men, and her own imperfections showed therein after the manner of a shadow. "And she possessed this gift in a continuous manner," affirms Cardinal Pedicini, that illustrious witness, who insists more than anybody else upon this matter. This was a difficulty for the "Devil's Advocate". His attacks took the line of insisting that such singular endowments could not be admitted in a creature not yet enjoying the beatific vision, and that therefore they should be attributed to self-suggestion or diabolic interference or suchlike.

Indeed, Anna herself had known fear, at first, thinking herself the victim of an illusion, from which she strove to free herself. Consequently any talk of auto-suggestion is to make light of facts, and to ignore Anna's character. Moreover, when her confessor required her to give an explanation, Our Lord answered: "It is a mirror that I show thee, in order that thou mayest know good and evil." Not satisfied the priest ordered her to insist that the gift should be withdrawn. To this Our Lord answered: "God is free. No one may have the effrontery to penetrate His designs. Let the confessor confine himself to his duty and not step beyond it." Our Lord, without, of course, denying the possibility of diabolic interference, gave her this criterion: "When it is the evil spirit, thou wilt experience great anxiety; when it is Myself, thy heart will feel a great sweetness."

The sun grew in splendour as she progressed from conversion to greater and greater purification. In the end its splendour was brighter than several suns, and yet Anna could look into it without wincing, although she was nearly blind. She saw tableaux of the present life and of the future, one after the other, sometimes by representations of reality, sometimes by symbols.

Sometimes Our Lord explained the symbols, sometimes He did not; yet He wished her to memorise them even unexplained. This, be it noted once more, disposes of any supposition of trickery or illusion, but what disposes of it most of all is the fact that numbers of her prophecies were manifestly proved true. Further, she did not look into the sun except when she felt herself invited thereto, and sometimes her glance was accompanied with a fear bordering on terror.

"As," says Mgr. Natali, "she saw therein her slightest faults; for instance, her too great attachment to her disciples, it left her no alternative but to walk always in the presence of God, to have a constantly clear recognition of her lowliness and nothingness, and to become more and more prudent in her actions, more and more ardent in her charity."

The disc of the sun was surrounded by a crown of thorns. The tableaux were never seen in the centre of the disc, but only in the surrounding rays. Yet one day she saw the sun opening, and from it issued torrents of blood, while the Blessed Virgin interceded to mitigate the scourges God had prepared. This was a symbol of the great and critical tribulations through which God was going to purify the Church. A terrifying cyclone seemed to be loosed: the heavens took fire, there were earthquakes, plagues, revolutions, riots, massacres, battles, black airships traversing the skies and covering the earth with fire and darkness. When she looked at the sun to discern any particular object, all the rest vanished.

She saw the peoples of most distant lands in detail as clear "as the façade of a neighbouring house"; she saw the scourges threatening each nation, the causes of them, their remedies; the disorders of each class of society whether clerical, aristocratic, or lowly.

"I do not claim," said her confessor, "that she is able to grasp the inner meaning of the mysteries of our holy religion, for that belongs exclusively to the blessed who see the face of God; but, though she was unlearned, she spoke of those mysteries as profound theologians would have spoken of them. As for other questions accessible to human intelligence, questions moral, scientific and so forth, she gave exact answers, no matter what the subject, so long as obedience or charity called upon her to do so."

§

The Beata saw in her sun the fate of the departed, the duration and the cause of their expiation. She never gave the name of any soul who was damned. When Mgr. Natali remarked to her that the damned have no right to charity, she answered: "Their relatives and friends who are still on earth have a right to it none the less."

Here are some instances of her knowledge. She saw a priest whom she knew, saved for doing violence to himself in favour of an importunate beggar. It was an act of virtue which brought in its train other graces and meritorious works.

She saw an ecclesiatic held in high esteem for his activities, his preaching and his zeal, cruelly tormented in purgatory, because, instead of seeking the glory of God, he sought the reputation of a great preacher.

She saw one of her friends who had had supernatural light suffering in purgatory because she had not kept silence about those favours.

Again, two religious friends of hers were in purgatory, the first having died in the odour of sanctity, the second with a great reputation as a director. The first had shown too great attachment to his own judgment; the second had given too little attention to the exercise of his ministry.

Count X . . . had died two days previously, he was saved though he had led a very dissipated life, for having pardoned an enemy. He had, however, to spend as many years in purgatory as he had passed in frivolity. A lay disciple of Anna's who had a great reputation for virtue was condemned to grievous punishment for having flattered people in authority.

She saw the catafalque prepared for Leo XII, and some years after his death she saw his soul like a ruby not yet purified by the flames.

At the funeral service of the wealthy Cardinal Doria she saw that his soul would get no assuagement from the hundreds of Masses which he had taken care to secure for himself. These Masses would serve the turn of the poor, and his turn for succour would not come till later.

The Beata flattered the great as little as Catherine of Siena or the art-craftsmen of the Middle Ages flattered them. . . . Quite the reverse. She saw the soul of a Capuchin lay-brother, Felix de Montefiascone, going straight to heaven; the same thing happened to another lay-brother of the Friars Minor, to Valory, a young Jesuit novice, and to two priests of the mission.

While confessing to Father Ferdinand, the Trinitarian, she said: "The General of the Trinitarians, who is in Spain, has been murdered, together with his companion, by French soldiers." She described the ill-treatment they received, and how their martyred souls had sped to heaven. A month later letters from Spain announced the death of the two Trinitarians in the circumstances described.

Even if we do not blindly accept all the assertions of Mgr. Natali and of Father Callistus of Providence,* we yet find that many of her visions were less consoling than these, and then Anna's face

---

* Father Callistus (*Vie de la V. Anna Taigi*, 5th edition, p. 371) writes: "The priest who was her confidant one day had a discussion with another person on the small number of the elect. He contended that the greater number of Christians of to-day were damned, and his opponent defended the opposite opinion. The holy woman hearing of this discussion, looked into her sun and saw the destiny of those who had died during that day. Very few, not as many as ten, went straight to heaven; many remained in purgatory, and those cast into hell were as numerous as flakes of snow in mid-winter." This quotation is taken from the deposition of Anna's confessor.

It would appear that this is a question concerning Rome at a particular period. Other points: on page 405 Father Callistus, referring to a phrase in the depositions that "during many successive days she saw impenetrable black darkness cover the earth", says in a long note: "There would seem to be question here of physical darkness." Mgr. Natali, on being asked about this point by a great number of people, was quite definite in telling them all that the darkness would last three days, and during that time only blessed candles would give any light," etc. Upon this Father Callistus writes: "The author of another life of Anna-Maria seems to be astonished that we spoke to our readers of darkness and other extraordinary events which Anna was said to have foretold." To this criticism he replies by referring to the approbation given to his book, and to the good it did to "soft and sensual souls, who pulled themselves together in order to consider their evil ways: for it was absolutely necessary to reach such a state if the arm of God, ready as it was to smite us all, was to be arrested."

On page 407 Father Callistus, following Mgr. Barbier de Montault, cites in a note other words of Mgr. Natali uttered in 1869 (thirty-two years after Anna's death, on the very eve of the confiscation of the Papal States): "Italy will return to the Pope what she has stolen from him and will be subject to him. Pius IX will see the triumph of the Church. The Pope is of one mind with Anna-Maria, who watches over him. Pius IX will be a saint. Her prophecies extend even up to Anti-Christ, whose days are drawing near. There is still a great number of popes to come, but their reigns will be short."

"Short! What about Pius IX, Leo XIII, Pius X, Pius XI? I know well that the prophecies attributed to St. Vincent Ferrer about the imminence of the coming of Anti-Christ militate against neither his sancity nor his miracles, but the memory of Anna-Maria would have lost nothing, I think, if her historians and confidants had shown a little more discretion."

The Beata is rich enough for us to be content with the riches that belong to her without question. From 1869 onwards Father Callistus thought himself justified in deducing this conclusion from Anna's words: "The hour of the complete deliverance and triumph of the Papacy cannot be long in sounding." Sixty-seven years have passed. Do not let us put weapons unasked into the hands of the "soft and sensual souls" we set ourselves to convert. Let us also reflect that the Church does not take count of all prophecies and visions of saints, even if they are supposed to be authentic.

became clouded with an expression of infinite sadness.

She saw lightning, and in the midst of the lightning laymen falling into the abyss; ecclesiastical dignitaries, and also priests and men and women of religious orders. The promoter of the faith thought this disrespectful and lacking in charity on her part. She gave no name, but when she heard that anybody, especially an ecclesiastic, had died leaving much money, she shook her head and said: "There are so many poor people to succour. Salvation is very difficult to speculators, to those who cause famine among the people." These truths, true under the Empire, are truths still.

"If she was questioned on a point of doctrine, for example, on how predestination could be reconciled with the goodness of God, she had only to look into her sun in order to give answers of astonishing exactitude." The scenes of the life of Christ appeared to her in detail: the house at Nazareth with its poor sticks of furniture, the place where Mary slept, and meditated, "for the very short time she gave to sleep was all the same a meditation."

Let us remark in passing that, if we are to understand "the interior life of Mary", we shall never have a better model than this labouring woman, this spouse, this mother whom we call Anna Taigi.

§

She was very devoted to St. Joseph, and saw him, not as a certain type of hagiographers represent him, a hoary old man, but as a strong, handsome young man, just a little older than Mary. She did not, however, speak of these things except with her confessor and those whom she guided. To the latter she recommended above all strength of purpose. As to her own relationship with them, Jesus required of her utter detachment. "One cannot," He said more than once, by way of preparing her for ingratitude, "One cannot count for long upon the good will of creatures. Man is like a weather-vane, God alone is changeless."

Cardinal Pedicini summarises this subject in a few words: "How often have I sought her advice on divers matters connected with the offices I have held! Her knowledge of things as profound as it was universal came indubitably from the wisdom of God. She related to each comer the different circumstances of his life, revealed to him his most secret thoughts, and she did all this quite artlessly in the form of a friendly conversation. It was easier for her to know the state of a soul, or the progress of an affair, than it is for us to read a book: she had only to throw a glance at her sun."

One is reminded of the good Rénan demanding that the Lord should come and work His miracles in the presence of five united academies, if He wanted them to be taken seriously. Rénan was fifteen when Anna died and thirty when Domenico made his deposition at the canonical Process. What would he have said if he had been told as follows: There was recently a good woman in Rome. She had no education, yet she knew the secrets of nature and even certain details of ancient history better than M. Rénan. Her glance travelled over the immensity of the skies, the abysses of the earth, but without regard to self-interest, and opposed to self-advertisement, she made no use of her knowledge except when charity demanded it. She knew diseases and their remedies and even the reasons for which they were sent, but, for using such knowledge, asked not even her daily bread.

§

Let us gather a few more gleanings. The only son of a great Roman family was dying. Anna was consulted, and looking into her sun recommended a very simple remedy, but added that the doctors would have nothing to do with it, would be mistaken about the nature of the complaint, and the child would die. This is exactly what happened. Historians who want the details, which would be out of place here, have only to refer to the folios of the Acts of the Process.

When she was consulted she mostly began by referring the petitioner to the doctor, but if she saw the doctor was mistaken, she said, "My son, try such a remedy, for your trouble comes from such a cause." The son of a trader was dangerously ill and his aunt recommended him to Anna. She answered: "He will be cured on this occasion, but in five years time will have a fall from a horse, will be carried away half dead and bereft of speech. Invoke the name of Jesus, and he will return to consciousness. Make him go to confession forthwith and receive the sacraments. He will die shortly afterwards, not from the fall, but from an incurable ailment of the bowels from which he is suffering." Five years afterwards events turned out as had been foretold, the autopsy showed that the disease indicated by the Beata and not the fall from horseback had caused the death—a thing which thoroughly bewildered the doctors.

Reaching St. Peter's one day with Mgr. Natali she encounters the magnificent train of Cardinal Marazzani, who had just been promoted. She looked into her sun and murmured: "To-day great pomp; in a month, the tomb." The cardinal was carried to the grave a month later.

The Queen of Étruria was gravely ill. Blessed Mgr. Strambi organised a solemn triduum of prayers to obtain her cure through the intercession of the Ven. Paul of the Cross, the founder of his congregation. He begged Anna's prayers, but she replied: "Do not go on with this affair, for you and your founder will cut a sorry figure." The sick woman at first made a noticeable improvement, but soon grew worse, and nobody dared tell her of the turn things had taken. Messengers came to Anna for help and she charitably warned her friend of her approaching death, and urged her to put her affairs in order. The shock was painful, but in the end the queen made her sacrifice and died a few days afterwards.

Anna frequented the church of Saint Andrew in the Quirinal, where the novitiate of the Jesuits is. Father Rossini begged Anna to pray for Brother Marcelli, who was ill with the stone. "No," said Anna, "it is not the illness that brings the brother so low; it is a great interior suffering." The brother, on being questioned, admitted the truth and got better. On this occasion Father Rossini recommended the Company of Jesus to the Beata and she looked at her sun and saw and foretold the trials that awaited the renascent society in the near future.

Among her disciples were some who were tempted to abuse the gift of their mother. One of them actually asked her to tell him the lottery number that would win the big prize! The Beata said it was not her business to be a prophet of good luck.

Others lost their keys or tobacco pouches and wanted her to fill the rôle of St. Anthony of Padua. Anna would smile and say, "Look for it! Must God look after stupid people?" If they search in vain, sometimes she who cured even sick animals would take pity on them and say: "Look in such a place: that is where you have left your key," or, "Such a person has found it; make him return it, but be more careful another time."

The good Luigetto, her man-of-all-work and disciple, used to talk to her like a child: "Mamma, have I made a good confession?" Anna looked into her sun: "When you accused yourself of such a fault you left out such a circumstance." "Oh, yes! That's true," cried the good cripple. Mgr. Natali and Mgr. Guerrieri testified that they sometimes experienced qualms of conscience during Mass, and that the Beata, when Mass was over, would show she knew of these trials of soul and would give them excellent advice.

If a carbonaro or a freemason came to her (and it was often the case) the sun was covered with darkness, but, on the other hand, it became brighter when a holy soul like Don Pallotti, for instance, was there.

She smiled when Cardinal Franzoni was told by a visionary that he would be Pope, and sent a message asking her if he could count on it. "No," she answered, "he need have no fear, or is it consolation he needs!" As the tares grow side by side with the good grain, so would-be rivals of the Beata multiplied.

A good religious who was conducting a difficult project thought he saw two angels appearing to him in the night, assuring him that his enterprise was admirable and would succeed. However, he questioned the Beata, who smiled and said it would fail lamentably—which it did.

A religious of the Poor Clares, Mary Agnes Firrau, was gifted with a genius for intrigue and set the whole town buzzing with stories of her visions and mystic graces. She had already initiated a reform in the Franciscan third order. One of her sisters, either from fear or from ambition, helped to lead priests, prelates and directors astray by attributing to her the genius and sanctity of St. Teresa. The cabal grew. Indeed, the poor woman spoke and wrote almost as well as Teresa—at any rate that was the opinion of doctors, who had their suspicions of the humble Anna.

Anna saw the sad truth—pride, self-interest. She went to see the wretched women twice, and though unable to speak to them openly, yet made them see by the glances she gave them that she understood their tricks. They opposed a brazen front to her, but justice was at hand to undertake their humiliation. "Another time," says Mgr. Natali, "the Most Reverend Father Capistran, general of the Friars Minor of the Observance, told me he had in his care a holy religious from Monte Castillo, whose virtues and gifts he highly praised. He none the less asked me to consult Anna as to what she thought of this sister. She did not answer, as she was of a very delicate conscience where charity was concerned, but as I insisted, she said: "It is useless for you to ask my opinion. Do not waste your time with all these visitings." I understood. A little while afterwards the Most Reverend Father and his nun were summoned to the holy office, and were punished.

Under Leo XII the future Cardinal Cristaldi met Mgr. Natali in the Pope's ante-room and said: "I am going to Naples in great sadness, for a religious has told me that I shall die there, and although I make little account of prophecies, I am sad. Do you know anybody who has supernatural gifts?" Mgr.

Natali asked Anna, who questioned her sun: "Let him make himself easy. He will have an excellent journey and a happy return. At Naples let him go to such a convent. He will find there two nuns, one of them in great repute for sanctity, but let him avoid her, for she is deluded. The other is reputed a fool and he will not be allowed to see her, except with difficulty. She is the wise one and will give him useful advice."

So it came to pass.

The cardinal, returning to Rome, wanted to show his gratitude. Anna would accept nothing, though she recommended a family which her own poverty did not allow her to assist. The cardinal guaranteed a monthly allowance. Shortly afterwards he took to his bed and the doctors said his sickness was not serious, but Anna saw his death in her sun and sent a message of warning to him. The cardinal made an act of resignation, settled his affairs and died a few days later.

Another time she sent Mgr. Natali in great haste to one of their friends. The friend was ruined and, afflicted with neurasthenia, was on the point of suicide. The priest went quickly, and finding the unfortunate with a gun in his hand, consoled and saved him. Someone will say this is a trivial story, but the salvation of a soul is theme for a great story. However, here are some more striking experiences. Cardinal Pedicini relates that before going to his diocese of Palestrina, he always went for advice to the Beata and did not lift a finger without it. She saw in her sun and told him all the disorders that existed among the people and the clergy, what reforms were necessary and what difficulties would attend them.

§

In 1815, when Blessed Mgr. Strambi begged Pius
VII to relieve him of the burden of the episcopacy,
so that he might return to his life as a Passionist,
Anna told him that, in spite of the assurances of
Cardinal Pacca, Pius VII would give him a bad
reception. "This time," said Mgr. Strambi to Mgr.
Natali, "the holy chirper has chirped wrongly. I am
going for the precise purpose of thanking His
Holiness, who has already agreed to my resignation."
But Pius VII received him with a severe expression
on his face: "We know why you have come," he
said, "but whom are we going to send in your place?
The night-sweepers? Go away and go at once!"
The "holy chirper" had seen the truth. She consoled
the Beatus by telling him that he would return to
Rome, but only to "leave his bones there".

Leo XII did in fact make Mgr. Strambi his
counsellor, and, says Mgr. Natali, "he begged me
to see him each evening. He let me into the secrets
of the conversations he had during the day with the
Holy Father, so that I could get Anna-Maria's
comments upon them." When he had secretly
offered his life for Leo XII, while the latter lay
dying, he asked her prayers for the Pope, and she
answered: "The Pope will not die; it is Mgr.
Strambi that will die; let him prepare himself for
death." To objections that Monsignor was in good
health, she only replied: "I tell you that within a
few days his remains will be exposed in the church."

No one believed her, but the Beatus was suddenly
stricken down with a loss of his faculties.

The Passionists were very distressed that he had
not been able to receive the viaticum, and besought
Anna through Mgr. Natali to intercede for him.

Mgr. Natali says: "I found her knitting with a table in front of her. She gave up her work, put her head between her hands, prayed for a while, then lifted her eyes towards heaven. "Warn those in attendance upon him to begin Mass at dawn in order to give him Communion. His mind will be clear and active and he will be able to receive. He will even have time to make his thanksgiving. Then he will fall back into a coma and from thence will pass to eternal rest." All fell out as she predicted. The depositions, given in detail and taken under oath, are in the Process.

Incidentally, one may say in passing that the miracles of which there is so abundant a harvest in the life of this saint, miracles contemporary with the First Empire and the Restoration, may well cause the incredulous who are of good will to ask themselves this question: "If even one of these miracles is historically proven [and they are very difficult to deny], is not the whole supernatural order also involved? For there is question of a co-related whole. The believer, faced with these facts, is completely free, for he has no need of the miraculous, and nothing, apart from loyalty, compels him to accept it. But are not the incredulous bound by a similar, nay, by a greater loyalty—the loyalty of impartial examination of evidence, when faced by a disconcerting document? To refuse to accept facts, or to turn the blind eye to them in order to keep a prejudice intact is to make history the most arbitrary of all sciences.

In 1805 Anna announced the Spanish Revolution, the abdication of Charles IV (which was to take place three years later) and his exile in Rome.

In 1836 she predicted that the cholera would break out in Rome on the morrow of her death, but she told Giovanna and Sophie that the scourge would spare them and theirs. It came to pass.

And here is a story that relieves the strain of these high matters. In 1816 she quietly informed Mgr. Natali, that some sectaries would poison him, but he would recover. Now, on the afternoon of the Feast of the Holy Innocents, about four o'clock, four ruffians pressed him to take a glass of punch with them at the Monte Citorio café. Somewhat indiscreetly the priest accepted the invitation, entered the café, noticed that he was surrounded by ne'er-do-wells who watched him closely, but he drank his punch. At five o'clock, as if it were in a melodrama, the adventurers cried out "The deed is done! It is five o'clock!" The priest ran away and began to suffer pains like death which lasted the whole night, but when the hour of Mass came, the pains ceased abruptly. He arrived at the Church of the Pietà where Anna was waiting for him with a smile on her face. As he was thoroughly spent she took him to that same café (which was about fifty paces from the Church) to revive him. You see she was by no means averse to a joke. The owner of the café, more dead than alive, thought he was seeing ghosts, but served the snack that was ordered. Anna smiling all the while urged her secretary to make a good meal, and then, telling him what had happened, read him a little lesson in prudence.

A Bavarian minister came asking advice. She began by telling him his life-story and his faults then she turned to politics, surveying the European situation in a way which amazed him. She dealt clearly with the affairs of various courts the plots hatched by men and foiled by Providence the secret intrigues, and the results so different from those aimed at. An hour's conversation convinced the ambassador that she had the entire world under her eyes as he had his snuff-box in his hand; that she knew all while he and his fellows, old in diplomacy, did not even know what was contemplated in the courts to which they were accredited."

§

According to the testimony of Mgr. Contratto, Bishop of Aqui, General Michaud, aide-de-camp and friend of Alexander I, Emperor of Russia, while staying in Rome in 1825, heard a vague rumour that the Czar was dead. Hastening to the Russian Embassy, he was told that the rumour was without foundation, having been started by the liberals. Dissatisfied he went to see Anna, who told him that the Czar was indeed dead, and that news would reach the Embassy the following day. Then she consoled him by saying: "The Emperor died a Catholic, and is in purgatory. He is saved for his charity to his neighbour, and for protecting the Pope and the Church." If one may believe an article in the *Civilta* of 4th November 1876, General Michaud was sent to Rome for the special purpose of discussing with Leo XII the conversion of Alexander I and the return of Russia to Catholicism. The general assisted in St. Petersburg at his friend's funeral, and, it is said, learned that the Emperor had secretly abjured his schism shortly before his death. He told the Emperor Nicholas this, hoping to induce him to follow that example. Father Pierling, S.J., in a letter to the *Monde*, confirms the general's statements. In any case we may observe that without any doubt the Beata would have had reason for what she said even if the Emperor had died a Catholic only at heart.

Before returning to Russia, Michaud, touched

by Anna's poverty, wanted to help her. She refused everything. There are some, even men of good will, who would try to belittle such prophecy by saying that Vespasian, Cagliostro and Mme de Thèbes also seem to have made them, and that if ninety-nine out of one hundred mediums are cheats, there also remains one per cent that makes his profits justly and whose visions are authentic.

But Anna's refusal of all assistance should make them think twice about such reasoning. We may also insist that there must be some method of discerning the counterfeit from genuine coin—people like Teresa of Avila and Joan of Arc, who are genuine, and not imposters. History and psychology, no less than theology, supply us with such a method. They take into consideration the quality of the facts and the purpose they serve, no less than the quality of the witnesses from a moral and human standpoint. The credulous disciples of Charcot have not grasped this point, but Henri Bergson and Dr. Carrel have had the conscientiousness and the intelligence to recognise it.

Anna's royal singleness of purpose makes us understand with what freedom of spirit she spoke to the great. An eminent personage in Rome, high in the employment of the Apostolic Chamber, as rich as he was pretentious, consulted her because, as he said, many saintly souls had told him that together with the Pope, he would do great things for the Church. He asked her to cure his wife who was ill. Anna kept silent looking into her sun; only on being pressed did she say eventually: "God intends to punish certain families for failing to fulfil their obligations."

The man bowed his head admitting his guilt. A few days later she sent him this stern warning: "Le you and your wife prepare for death. Your family will be destroyed before the close of the French occupation." A few days after his wife died, and the whole family found itself ruined by the misconduct of the children. The patrician had the courage to return and ask for the full truth. Anna delivered it: "You will be declared bankrupt and will die soon after."

Again all happened as she had said.

About the same time a young woman of the aristocracy and her husband who had a Prelate of indifferent life living with them got to know her. The young lady was converted by her and brought her to see the Prelate, counting upon a similar conversion. He was very high with this insignificant bit of womanhood who did not hesitate to make known to him the deplorable state of his conscience, and sneered at her. The Beata withdrew not to return, but sent word by the lady to the dignitary that though Pius VII would return from exile at such and such a time, he would not see the Pope.

Her confessor asked Anna's prayers for an illustrious family of Pistoia. "My daughter," answered Our Lord, "this family must suffer. It will be reduced, and its head will die a terrible death." Much disturbed by this answer, her confessor begged for a revision of the sentence, but Our Lord's answer was unrelenting: "It is useless to plead. They must be uprooted because of their sins, and you will see the death of the head of the family as has been said." Some time afterwards this nobleman was condemned to be shot and was taken to the place of execution, but eventually the sentence was commuted to imprisonment for life.

One day Anna was praying in front of the Crucifix of St. Paul's-outside-the-Walls when Our Lord told her that because of the sins committed in it he intended to make of the Basilica a heap of ruins. A little while afterwards the Basilica went up in flames.

The future Cardinal Lambruschini going to Paris in 1827 as Nuncio, feared a bad journey and asked Anna to pray for him. She saw in her sun that the journey would be prosperous, but that the Nuncio must prepare to undergo at Paris a veritable martyrdom of soul. The Nuncio had many opportunities to reflect upon these words, which were only too true, before the idiotic and irreligious Revolution of July 1830 forced him to leave Paris. In her sun she followed the revolutionary movements of Europe, and the rise of Socialism, and described them to those who were in her confidence. These visions were to render her burden as expiatress more and more crushing.

IV

SHE WHO "VANQUISHED NAPOLEON I" AND CON-SOLED THE MOTHER OF KINGS – ANNA-MARIA AND THE "NAPOLEONIDES" – ANNA-MARIA AND NAPO-LEON – ANNA-MARIA AND CARDINAL FESCH – ANNA-MARIA AND LETITIA

I HAVE reserved for this chapter events to which other writers have made little allusion. The silence is explained by the reticence of the documents, and also by the fact that they touched too closely people then living. To-day the facts belong to history, and it would be childish to ignore them. Moreover, they make the Blessed Anna-Maria a figure in the great epochs of history, and give to her life a universal interest.

What was the nature of her contact with Napoleon

I and the "Napoleonides", above all with Letitia, Mother of Napoleon, and with Cardinal Fesch, uncle of the Emperor—Letitia and Fesch who have rightly been called "the conscience of Bonaparte's family?"

Until now we have known Napoleon and his creatures from the memoirs of contemporaries and the publications of F. Masson; Cardinal Fesch, through his Vicar-General and apologist Lyonnet; Mme Mére through her fervent admirer Barron Larrey. More recent works such as *The Letters of Letitia Bonaparte* published by Marquis P. Misciatelli in Milan 1936, Lancelotti's book *I Napoleonidi* published in Rome 1936, and above all the learned and critical work of Latreille *Cardinal Fesch as Ambassador* published at Alcan 1934, allow us to make a more objective study of events. Certain unpublished documents drawn from the Vatican Archives clarify those events still further. Napoleon, Fesch, Letitia on one side; the Blessed Anna-Maria Taigi on the other.

It seems that Providence was at pains to set these two types of humanity, as if on a co-related diptych, in contrast to one another; to give a modern application of the Ignation meditation on the *Two Standards*. On one side there is the contempt of the world, its glories and its rewards, united to an indomitable pride in the service of the true and the good: the nothingness of human efforts ending in the exaltation of Divine Omnipotence. On the other the devouring yet insatiate hunger for crowns and benefices; the choice (which became unconscious but was justified in Napoleon's eyes by family interest) of mediocre talent in his lieutenants; and finally that formidable engine of destruction, which, after crushing the world and piling ruin upon ruin, itself disintegrated.

§

Napoleon and Anna-Maria

Letitia's correspondence opens with a lecture by the poor mamma (upon whom, though she is not yet a widow, rests the education of five sons and three daughters) addressed from Ajaccio to the young Napoleon, a scholar at Brienne (2 June 1784). He is not yet fifteen years of age, but demands money from his father in peremptory tones:

> "Sir,
> I am tired of advertising my poverty. What! Is your son to be continually the laughing stock of a few noble clowns? No, Father, no! If fortune is absolutely set against the improvement of my lot, then take me away from Brienne, if necessary make me a mechanic."

One wonders if it would not have been better for Napoleon, for Letitia, for the whole Napoleonic clan, for the world itself, if the future conqueror had become a carpenter. I know well that some would consider this a monstrous suggestion. Letitia went on mortgaging her property down to the last patch of land in order that Napoleon might not be degraded to the rank of a mechanic; yet she answered sharply: "If I ever receive a letter like that again, I shall wash my hands of Napoleon. Where, young man, did you learn that a child could talk to its father as you have done? As to the deprivations you suffer, you ought to know that it is nothing short of the impossibility of helping you that is the reason of our silence."

Neither she nor her brother Fesch ever thought of coming to Anna-Maria's conclusion—"As we are poor, let us stay in our simple state." Already Letitia was dreaming great dreams: Napoleon was dreaming greater ones. After swinging now to the right and now to the left, behold him at the age of sixteen a lieutenant of artillery; at twenty-four a general; at twenty-six a Commander-in-Chief of the Army of Italy; at thirty, First Consul; at thirty-five Emperor—distributing crowns and principalities to five Napoleonides. Would that make him great?—or them?

Stendhal wrote: "Napoleon would have been much better off without a family." Napoleon exiled at St. Helena admitted: "My relatives did me much more harm than I did them good." He forgot to add that his own example must be made in great part responsible for the follies they committed in conducting themselves like demi-gods—scandals, cupidity, fatuous pretensions and treacheries. But, though bitterly chagrined by them, he took care, to keep up the imperial tone towards them, for the edification of the rest of the universe.

Emperor of the West, heir of Charlemagne ("I am Charlemagne," he wrote to Pius VII), it was not enough for him to have France and Europe at his feet; popes must also be at his service. Pius VII must submit not only to crowning him Emperor, and to yielding the Papal States, but also to giving or ratifying the divorces necessary for imperial politics —his own, Jerome's and Lucien's; and even again to abandoning to him the nomination of bishops and recognising him as "bishop" for the exterior. "I had my Councils," he dictated to Las Cases. "What is there unseemly," said he to M. Emery in 1810, "in the Pope being subject to me now that Europe acknowledges no master but me alone?"

§

In Rome, the Blessed Anna-Maria followed in her sun the career, thoughts and actions of the conqueror from the year 1791, when he was only a petty lieutenant. She was present, so to speak, during the conflict of seventeen years that bathed Europe in blood and glutted the Napoleonides' craving for domination. Not one of the acts of violence committed against Pius VI and Pius VII, not one distress of mind they themselves suffered escaped her. As the threats of schism, during and after the Two National Councils of Paris, became more evident, so did she pray and offer herself in expiation, "that the arms of the wicked might be broken, and their power dispersed". Her prayers were heard, as she foretold and described, more than a year ahead (so says the consensus of evidence from Marquis Bandini, Mgr. Natali, Father Philip and Cardinal Pedicini), the disastrous return from Moscow, the liberation of Pius VII, his triumphal progress across France and Italy, and his first Pontifical Mass that was to be celebrated in St. Peter's on Whit-Sunday 1814. The witnesses took note of those unusual affirmations at the time, for humanly they were absurd.

Her vision followed Napoleon the Fallen to the Isle of Elba, to St. Helena where he died 5 May 1821. The Emperor's mother and his uncle, Cardinal Fesch, did not learn the news of his death till 22 July two and a half months later, but on the day itself their neighbour Anna, gazing into the sun, described to Mgr. Natali the death of the exile: "She saw his bed, the dispositions of his soul, his grave, the ceremonies at the funeral, his destiny in time and in eternity." What destiny? The documents are silent on the point. But the Beata who always kept a warm corner in her prayers for his enemies could not abandon this enemy.

Cardinal Fesch, by then a disciple of the humble woman surely echoed the substance of their conversations when he said: "God did not break him; God humbled him and in humiliation lies salvation." For in truth no humiliation was spared him on that farm at Longwood where the roof let water, where rats and lice and bugs were a pest, where the pitiless Hudson Lowe parcelled out bread and wine to him with sordid meanness, and above all doled out measures of freedom, curtailing it little by little so that in time he could not stir from the house, then from his room, and eventually could not show his face at the window, under pain of being insulted.

Lowe controlled and spied upon his words and letters, so that correspondence became impossible between him and his mother, or his son, the King of Rome, or his wife, Marie-Louise. It is true that as regards Marie-Louise he knew enough of what was only too certain that she was shamelessly faithless to him. In very truth to this erstwhile master of the world, heaven alone remained. Did his faith, lulled to sleep by success and the world's worship, wake again? The answer remains uncertain* even after one has gone through those twenty or so volumes in which Montholon, Las Cases, O'Meara, Gourgaud and the rest reported the conversations of the Outlaw in the course of his six years agony. There were materialistic aphorisms worthy of M. Hormais: "My dear Gourgaud, when we are dead,

* There would appear no uncertainty about the only way men can judge, namely the external fact that Napoleon in his last hours ordered Exposition of the Blessed Sacrament and received all the Last Sacraments, save the Viaticum which his sickness forbade; he could see the Tabernacle from his death-bed. See the moving account in Belloc's "Napoleon" (*Translator's note*).

dead we are."—"If I had to have a religion, I would adore the Sun."—"Providence? Why, honest men are always unfortunate, and scamps fortunate. You will see: a man like Talleyrand will die in his bed." To-day he apes the Mussulman, to-morrow the Protestant. According to him, Francis I should have supported the Reformation—"The Head of the State ought to be the Head of Religion." There was no remorse for his iconoclastic violence: "I am not a man like other men."

Stendhal suggests that the chief cause of this giant's fall was, "his love for mediocre talent." He wanted about him tools, not ministers. He could not tolerate near his person any acknowledged merit; he kept his marshals at a distance and was parsimonious in the praise he gave them. It was this state of mind that suggested those unpleasant phrases about Christ—"that poor Jewish fanatic of an idealist". Then he would turn back on himself, and in the grip of that uneasiness about religion which never forsook him, he would study the Bible and theology, assist at Mass with devotion, snub Dr. Antomarshi's materialism,* confess his faith in God, and in Christ whom he called "the only One eternally loved", go to confession to the young Abbé Vignali, and ask for the Viaticum and Extreme Unction. He bade Vignali expose the Blessed Sacrament in the next room and therein celebrate the Forty Hours. In a word, the soul was more important than words and actions to this victim of a too perilous destiny. "Let us not leave the class we were born in, but abide in our lowliness," said Blessed Anna-Maria Taigi.

At the hour of his passing, at the setting of the sun, a storm uprooted the last tree of Longwood. That

---

* See Belloc's "Napoleon" (*Translator's note*).

same day at Rome, according to the account of Baron Larrey* (who follows Mme de Sartrouville, Letitia's reader, and her chamberlain, the chevalier Côlonna) a stranger whose voice, manner, figure and bearing were those of the Emperor, demanded a private interview with Mme Mère, forced the sentries, and said in the voice of a seer, as he presented a Crucifix to Her Highness: "At the moment—at which I speak to you, Napoleon is set free from pain and is blessed. Kiss the Saviour of your well-beloved son." Is this a legend? Is it reality? True or false in the two and a half months that preceded the cables which brought the fatal news, Letitia still maintains her desperate efforts for liberating the captive. The Beata, with whom she was in touch, had evidently not informed her. In any case would she have been believed? Had she not something better to do as expiatress? To succour by her prayers him who had made his "Ego" the centre of the world, and had pressed the sufferings of others into his service that the universe might be his slave state. Had she not to succour him by her own sufferings, her own expiations according to her own scale of values?

That method of hers had crushed the giant. We have just used a phrase which will be belittled by those whom Péguy calls the perverse, namely the doctors of bibliography. "Where are your documents and your references?" they cry. I could answer with the sally of G. Duhamel which lately called forth the applause of the French Academy: "M. Lenotre says what is true. Alas! he says what is better than Truth: he says what smacks of the Truth."

* Cardinal Lepicier makes a study of this extraordinary experience in his book *Le Monde Invisible*, pp. 473-476.

§

Should we be much better off if we had found in some
unpublished papers of Napoleon's the words: "I
have been beaten by the prayers, the expiations and
the prophetic wisdom of a poor woman in Rome?"
To that also the critics would cry: "Where are your
documents?" if indeed they did not prefer to stifle the
whole debate with Rénan's: "There is no supernatural." It is the eternal conflict described by Paschal,
between the spirit of the man with the foot-rule and the
man of discernment. "What makes geometricians
somewhat blunt of perception is that they do not see
what is in front of them, and that being used to the
clearly defined yet common place principles of geometry, they are at a loss when it comes to matters of
delicacy which are not patient of such handling. Refined things are perceived with difficulty, or rather
sensed more than seen. Such things must be instantly
grasped in one glance. And thus it is rare for
geometricians to be men of acute perception,
because they try to apply geometry to subtle matters
and become ridiculous in the attempt."

With a glance let us scan the Acts of Process.
Many a time Jesus said to the Beata: "Your sufferings are essential for some purposes which you
recognise, and for others you must be content not
to recognise. Your life will be a long martyrdom in
support of the Faith and the Church." Pius IX, in
the Decree of Introduction of the Cause, assures us
that her vocation was "to humble in the dust the
pomp of the world, and to outwit the schemes of the
wicked, to which God opposed, as it were, a rampart
in the form of a lowly woman". Among these
schemes none was more constantly before the mind
of the Beata than Imperial politics. Daily she saw

its activities, aims, outrages; its partial successes, its final overthrow. She described to Cardinal Pedicini, to Mgr. Natali and to her confessor (see the Process folios 342, 1318 and throughout) the events that were to cast a shadow of gloom over the pontificate of Pius VII. She foretold, giving even minute details, his five years captivity, the Moscow Campaign, which was the dawn of the Emperor's chastisement, Napoleon's abdication, and the Pope's return; she thereby encouraged and guided Churchmen; disarmed God and broke the force of His scourging. "God expressly promised her (her confidants attested) that the plans of the wicked would be brought to nothing, that if He allowed them a free field of action, He would halt them when their prosperity seemed on the point of triumph; but, as for her, she must dispose herself to satisfy His Justice. Once she began to see in the mysterious sun those plans going by default, she reminded Our Lord of His promise at the risk of subsequently paying the price in the graces she won by fresh sufferings. This astonishing contract lasted all through her life."

Her confidants are inexhaustible on the subject. Not only did she see in her sun the sufferings she would have to pay for her "Austerlitz" victories of the invisible world, but her physical heart was like a thermometer wherein she felt the flood of expiation rising as the power of her great adversary dwindled. So that she could prepare for them these sufferings were heralded by double knocks which she felt distinctly in her heart. They were stronger or weaker according to the intensity of the pain to follow." Never were they louder than in the fifteen years during which she measured her strength against her great adversary Napoleon, those fifteen years when

three million Frenchmen perished for the sake of
one man afflicted with war-mania* and Caesarism.
During those fifteen years she was not content with
the dreadful trials showered on her by both God and
man, but she multiplied her prayers, penances and
pilgrimages. These last she made in bare and blood-
stained feet, to the Basilicas of St. Peter and St.
Paul: and all this was to obtain "victory for the
Church, its purification, peace and liberty, and ruin
to the persecutors". And God, after each battle
where none but herself was the victim, said to her
"It shall be done according to thy will." Cardinal
Salotti may well have said: "The prayer of Anna-
Maria before God triumphed over the power of the
Imperial armies." Louis Veuillot expresses the truth
in other words when he says: "She was God's
answer to the victors of every kind; on the battle-
field, in politics and in the acadamies."

§

And indeed who will deny that there contributed to
the fall of the giant all things—the intrigues and
betrayals of a man like Fouché, the scandals and
voracity of the Napoleonides, France bled white,
the revolt of the nations, the burning of Moscow,
the pride of an upstart dictator who allowed no
human being whatever, not even his mother, to
speak to him familiarly, or call him other than
"Sire"? The Beata would deny it less than anybody.
She knew that God makes use of secondary causes
to achieve His purposes—the pebble cast by the
sling of David to flatten Goliath to the earth, the
follies of Roboam, son of Solomon, to ruin the House
of David. It is written that Roboam spoke arrogantly
to the people "for Jehovah guided all things towards

* The French word "guerromanie" was coined by Stendhal.

the accomplishment of the word He had spoken by the Prophet Elias of Silo to Jeroboam: 'behold, I am about to snatch the Kingdom from the hand of Solomon, because they go prostrate before Astarte, the goddess of the Sidonians'." Bossuet is not at issue with the laws of the School of Charters,* but supplements and goes beyond them when, in his *Discourse on Universal History* he shows, intermingled with the operations of men, the operations of Him who reigns in the heavens and upon whom all Empires depend. The plan of Divine history does not wipe out the plan of human history, but is superimposed upon it. This is a commonplace reflection (at least for the believer) upon which it is salutary and consoling to muse in days when might in its arrogance declares itself universally to be right.

§

Anna-Maria and Cardinal Fesch

It remained for the Beata to give consolation and enlightenment to those whose hopes were shattered by the Emperor's death—Letitia and Fesch.

Fesch! Like his nephew, Napoleon, he knew the "bewitching of vanity", the "luxury of domination" as St. Augustine called it. What of his career? Child of the same mother as Letitia, bursar at the Aix seminary, he succeeded his uncle as archdeacon of Ajaccio within sixteen months of his ordination (clan-solidarity already!) Head of the family group he urged it towards the Revolution, which he saw as a coming thing. A "juring"† priest, he became Vicar-General to the intruded Bishop, and took

---

* A college founded in Paris 1821 for Librarians and Paleographic Archivists.
† i.e. a priest who had sworn (jurer) allegiance to the National Convention and thus thrown in his lot with the Revolution against the Church (*Translator's note*).

possession of the goods of his own Chapter. He and all his clan were eventually banished by the Paolists* in 1793. Unfrocked, reduced to living on his wits, his fortune began with the Italian Campaign wherein he was (together with the gloomy Collot and his future friend Torlonia from the Auvergne, officer of the commissariate,) and thus had opportunities of easy loot in the matter of works of art and banking accounts.† Returning to Paris and installing himself in a pretentious hotel, he indulged in the theatre, fashionable restaurants and the gaming table. Despite irreproachable morals he seems to have forgotten his vocation for eighteen years. But Napoleon having signed the Concordat needed a Churchman devoted to his service. Here was a fresh application of the "family system" that was to inspire him to a thousand follies. Napoleon's uncle was asked to don the soutane again, so as to become Archbishop of Lyons and Cardinal, an affair regularised within three months.

In June 1802 the First Consul nominated Fesch as Archbishop of Lyons. M. Emery absolved him of his irregularities behind closed doors, and gave him a retreat. Fifteen days later the Archbishop was consecrated at Notre-Dame by Cardinal Caprara; within thirty days he was a Cardinal at the age of thirty-nine. There followed honours more and more fantastic—minister of religion "in partibus",‡ Ambassador to the Holy See (without restoring what he had previously acquired), Primate of Gaul; Grand Almoner of the Empire (an office which allowed him to regularise on the eve of the Coronation, the marriage of Napoleon and Josephine, and, later, to

---

* A party of Corsican Nationalists resisting France (*Translator's note*).

† The Napoleonic marshals looted art treasures, as well as other things.

‡ "in partibus infidelium", i.e. "for infidel areas".

declare this marriage null and void and to bless the union of the Emperor and Marie-Louise); Chevalier of the Golden Fleece, Primate of Germany, with the rank of King. . . . The 600,000 francs or more these various functions brought him were not sufficient for his extravagance. His letters to the Emperor are full of recriminations on his poverty. He borrowed money from Torlonia the erstwhile commissariate officer, who had become the Roman banker and marquis, Giovanni Torlonia.

The Beata saw the soul of Duke Torlonia saved because of his acts of charity, but Cardinal Consalvi, Secretary of State to Pius VII, could not bear this " 'Mr.' Torlonia on account of his monstrous thefts". This caused trouble between Consalvi and Fesch, trouble which grew worse when the Pontifical Court gave the Embassy's secretary Chateaubriand, author of *The Genius of Christianity*, a reception at which the puerile vanity of the Ambassador took offence. "He has genius," someone had the courage to say. "Yes," said Fesch, drily, "sufficient for the signing of passports." The over-brilliant secretary was sent about his business.

However, opportunities were not lacking to the susceptible Ambassador to emphasise his own importance. There was the preparation for the Coronation of the Emperor; ranging the Pope in the right camp for the war against England; manipulating the three divorces demanded by Imperial Politics. He succeeded in the matter of the divorces* of Napoleon and Jerome, but failed with Lucien who snapped back at him with the words: "At any

* It should be noted that the word "divorce" is sometimes loosely used to cover the word "nullity". The "divorces" of Napoleon and Jerome do not involve the integrity of the Pope, even if certain local ecclesiastics come under suspicion. See for instance pp. 357, 358 in "The Question Box" by Bertrand Conway, Paulist Press, 1924 (*Translator's note*).

rate conceal your base sentiments in the folds of your purple, and go your way in silence on the broad road of ambition." The Imperial nephew expected yet further ignoble services from the Cardinal—to obtain recognition of his coronation as King of Italy, which put the Holy See in vassalage to him; to declare legitimate the kidnapping of Pius VII. The Cardinal dared to demur at that and the nephew wrote "Take a cold bath." For the rest he had so little doubt of his uncle that he added to the titles of Primate of Gaul and Primate of Germany, that of Archbishop of Paris. This last put Fesch in a position to have the first marriage of Napoleon annulled, to bless the second, and to organise the National Council. And yet the nephew was not satisfied! Fesch dared to write a letter of filial devotion to Pius VII during his imprisonment. From the depths of Russia Napoleon, who had the letter intercepted, threatened to send him to join Pacca at Fenestrelle, hit him where it hurt most by withdrawing 300,000 francs of his pension, and exiled him to Lyons. There Fesch showed himself a zealous and exemplary Prelate. These signs of the Emperor's displeasure made him lose nothing of his enthusiastic and blind devotion to the demi-god who was the architect of his fortune.

The documents published by André Latreille justify that author's conclusion: "Of all the Napoleonides he was the most conscientious in the service of Napoleon and of the Family, for he never separated the two. We would say that Fesch's Gallicanism was fashioned out of this fidelity."

After the Russian débâcle he hurried to Paris to draw up the pseudo-concordat wrested from Pius VII which granted Napoleon the right to nominate the bishoprics of France and Italy without allowing the Pope power to eliminate the unworthy. France was already invaded, and Pius still a prisoner while Fesch was writing edict after edict celebrating in flamboyant language the new Cyrus, the elect that Heaven was opposing to the barbarians—"Foregather, ye peoples . . . you shall be conquered because the Lord is with us."

Then came the abdication of Fontainebleau, Fesch put his collection in a safe place, and gained the Italian frontier together with his sister, Letitia. At Cesena their path crossed Pius VII's who opened the gates of Rome to them. There followed the Hundred Days, that last ray of glory. While Pius VII was in flight from Rome, Fesch was once more named Ambassador and then Viceroy of France. Back in Rome Anna saw the disaster of Waterloo on its way and the exile of St. Helena.

While Napoleon was bound for that island hell Fesch, without batting an eyelid, claimed from Louis XVIII the arrears of his salary. The answer he got was exile. He left for Siena (homeland of the Beata) with Letitia. The Grand Duke Ferdinand VIII refused to allow him to stay. Once more Pius VII opened Rome to the exiles, but asked Fesch to renounce the Archbishopric of Lyons. The request was met with a firm refusal, maintained under three pontificates right down to his death.

Metternich calls Fesch a singular mixture of avarice and bigotry. Should we not say that he also was a victim? He had the makings of a perfect notary, even of an excellent parish priest, but an unfortunate destiny coupled with ambition made of him, unto his own undoing, a "vice-god". His last historian remarks that, by a twist not uncommon to upstarts and the creatures of courts, he came to identify might with right, and "to argue from the

uselessness of resistance to its lawlessness". To his
confidential friend the Abbé Isoard he wrote with
the typical Napoleonic violence of expression: "The
prosperity of the Catholic Church rests, after God,
with the Emperor. If one must give in on points
that do not involve an article of faith, is it not
obvious that the feeble should yield to the strong?"
... "Tell it bluntly to the Romans that it is their
lack of confidence that ruined them, and their pride
finished them off. If they had only listened to me, the
Pope would not have come to his present pass."
What was it then that he so widely advised? For
one thing the identification of ecclesiatic and
imperial law in the matter of marriage and divorce;
to hold as null and void unions declared such by the
State. Henry VIII asked for nothing more!

§

Happily in him, as in Napoleon and Letitia, heart
prevailed over head. Condemned to inaction, the
Cardinal divided his time over a period of twenty-
five years between his oratory, his library, his eternal
art-gallery, his cardinalitial functions and his daily
visits to "Madame Mère". From a distance he
prepared the Emperor for death by sending him
two chaplains, also Letitia, to whom each evening he
gave a devout instruction. He had recourse on
Letitia's behalf and on his own to the prayers and
counsels of the Beata Taigi.

He had a genuine piety, and he formed the habit
of joining every Friday evening at the Coliseum in
the Way of the Cross enacted on ground sanctified
by the blood of the martyrs. Anna-Maria was an
habitual member of the small group of faithful
souls that gathered round him. It became a Confraternity, the presidency of which was conferred

on the Cardinal by the Pope. The women's section to which the Beata belonged, was directed by Princess Gabrielli, Fesch's niece. This enabled Letitia, a stickler in etiquette, to take part in the gatherings. In any case her brother set her an example of humility. With a penitential garb over his purple, and bare-foot, he carried the Cross at the head of the procession, intoning the chants, and reciting the prayers. It was there, among the ruins of the Coliseum, not far from the expiatress who hid herself in the background, that the Cardinal revealed what was best in him.

Anna's fame and the material distresses with which "she who vanquished the Emperor" had to cope, made her speedily known to him. He generously offered her lodging in the Falconieri palace where he was already sheltering Napoleon's mother, but she, as usual, rejected the offer. Fesch did not let the matter rest there (as Father Philip, confessor of the Beata, Mgr. Natali and Cardinal Pedicini notice); "Desirous of seeing her, and of introducing his sister to her, he asked her to pray for them and to tell him what light she might receive in their regard." Anna's replies we know only from herself. She wrote to Fesch that in response to his request, he was to tell his sister "to meditate upon three points—what she had been, what she was, and what she would soon be: and to prepare herself for death". It was advice from which the Cardinal could himself draw great profit. Did His Eminence do so?

His apologist, Canon Lyonnet, after quickly skimming over the embarrassing episodes (the schemings of the Napoleonides against the Pope), shows us the Cardinal at the age of seventy-six, confined to solitude (Letitia and then Anna had died), tortured by a tumour in the stomach, saying over and over again: "I do not fear death. I trust in God who knows I have wished to serve Him." He died 13 May 1839, fortified by the Sacraments of the Church and the Papal blessing. The only thing Canon Lyonnet regrets is that the ingratitude of the people of Lyons deprived their city of the royal munificence with which His Eminence dowered his Corsican homeland in his will—his library, his priceless collection of pictures, academy of sculpture and painting, that glory of Ajaccio, the immense palace that would have looked so splendidly among the façades of Bellecour.

His fortune, like Letitia's, exceeded 4,000,000 or, as it would be to-day, twenty or thirty millions of francs. By contrast the former little storekeeper of the Army had not long before witnessed the death of a poor woman who spent as much energy in remaining in her state of laborious poverty as the Bonaparte clan had in emerging from it, and who left to her numerous family a legacy of four crowns. And Fesch must have heard her grieve over those, and "particularly those churchmen, who left immense fortunes behind them".

§

The Beata and Letitia

The opposing sides of the diptych are more clearly contrasted when we consider the two women, Anna and Letitia.

Such a study could not have a better guide than *The Letters of Letitia Bonaparte*, recently published by Pierre Misciatelli.

It must, however, be borne in mind, that these letters habitually written or dictated in popular Italian (the Italian more or less that Anna used) had to be translated into French by Letitia's secretaries.

The volume opens with the forceful letter to the young Napoleon already quoted. Wife of a wayward husband (the kin, so far as that goes of the Giannetti) who gave her thirteen children and left her a widow with eight, together with the responsibility of the poor family and its connections. The weight was shared by old uncle Lucien, the Archdeacon (and he was a model of far-seeing thrift), and by the Abbé Fesch who succeeded him and kept to his methods. In the following letter "the widow of Bonaparte" "lays at the foot of the Throne and presents to the generous and sympathetic heart" of Monseigneur, the Minister of War, this petition: "Burdened with the education of eight children, widow of a man who had always served the King, and bereft of all resource" she begs for her son Louis a burse in the Military School, even though he has failed his examination: "eight wards, Monseigneur, shall be the mouthpiece of the prayers she pours out to heaven for your good estate."

On the page after this "the citizeness Letitia Bonaparte", now gone over with her brother Fesch to the Revolution, expresses her republican loyalty towards Citizen Chiappe, Representative of the People at Nice, in order to obtain an advancement for her son Lucien. Next a refugee at Marseilles, as badly housed as the Blessed Anna-Maria, she trades the paltry pittance of her family with the women of the market place, and waits her turn, like the Beata, to receive the bread ration doled out to the patriotic refugees. But this miserable state lasted only some weeks. Napoleon, nominated Captain-Commander, finds a place in the administration for Lucien and Joseph.

Suddenly a great piece of news: "the little

whipster", at the age of twenty-six becomes, thanks
to Barras, Generalissimo of the Army of Italy. The
Napoleonic fairy story which was to last for eighteen
years has begun, but already it showed at what cost.
Without a word to his mother or brothers, the young
demi-god married civilly Josephine de Beauharnais
"the perverse and brainless friend" of Barras.*

§

Letitia was chagrined. This scandalous misalliance
would furnish an excuse for the escapades of her
other sons, would emphasise the odious harshness
of the Emperor towards Lucien, Jerome, Elisa, and
Pauline, would instal in the very heart of the clan a
permanent element of discord and hate. Yet wounded
though she was, the mother bowed her head to that
will which suffered none to dispute it, and offered
her motherly congratulations to "Citizeness La
Pagerie Bonaparte" of whose infamous conduct she
was well aware. In that letter dictated by Napoleon,
Letitia still used the word "citizeness". This plebeian
language was soon to vanish; the film was unwound
with dizzy speed. Crowns and demi-crowns poured
like rain upon the seven sons. She betrayed no
astonishment, and from the tenth page onwards
takes up her rôle with the greatest solemnity. "Sire,
Your Majesty (thus she addresses her son, Napoleon!)
has given me a lovely palace, but the allowance of
480,000 francs is not enough: one or two million
registered for greater security in the account of the
public debt would be essential. Your Majesty's
Mother must be honoured by the peoples as much
as you honour her." She must also have an official
title. She suggests to him the titles "Majesté Mère"
or "Impératrice Mère". He chose "Her Imperial

* cf. *Letitia Bonaparte*, by L. Peretti. Plon. 1932.

Highness, the Mother of the Emperor". If the Napoleonides were going to exasperate Napoleon for a period of ten years with their pretentions, they surely learnt in a good school! Lucien (the most sympathetic of the Bonapartes) to whom the Emperor owed the success of 18 Brumaire and after that his crown, was the only one to show a disinterested singleness of purpose. Rather than repudiate his second wife, Alexandrine Jouberthon, he braved the Master's anger and contented himself with a principality instead of a crown. It was a species of folly that left Letitia at a loss. Her letters are full of remonstrances. As late as the year 1810 she was writing "your obstinate behaviour will shorten my life". She encouraged him by the example of Napoleon divorced and re-married, of Jerome divorced and re-married, of Louis separated from his wife. Lucien replied: "I love my wife and I love the children she has given me. Moreover, I am a Catholic." As if that mattered! What mattered was to be a king like the others! So Letitia went so far as to write to her daughter-in-law: "The Emperor wills your divorce. Do not hesitate. Your children will be recognised by the Emperor and may succeed to crowns." The unanswerable argument! Poor Anna-Maria! She was at that very time opposed to everything that could lift her or her children out of their obscurity, or that could revive anything of the glory of her ancestors.

But Letitia was a Catholic; she gave alms, had a devotion to the Madonna,* attended Mass and sometimes Vespers and lived an irreproachable life so far as was consistent with pride of race. This pride went to childish lengths. She deliberately served Cardinal Fesch with meat on Fridays, and when he

* To whom she consecrated Napoleon.

expressed surprise, she retorted sharply back: "Do you not realise that the Court of France has always been dispensed of this abstinence?"

In her palace in the Rue Saint-Dominique the flower-garden of her royal children was in full bloom: Napoleon, Emperor of the West; Joseph, King of Spain; Louis, King of Holland; Jerome, King of Westphalia; Lucien, Prince of Canino; Caroline, Queen of Naples; Elisa, Grand-Duchess of Tuscany; Pauline, Princess Borghesi.

Was she at any rate happy? Far from it. At the height of her triumph she wrote to Elisa: "I think I was born for nothing but suffering." The scandals, rivalries over matters of precedence, and treacheries of the Napoleonides never ceased to torture her. "All declare that I am the happiest mother on earth" (she admitted to her confidante, Rosa Mellini), "but my life is one long succession of the sufferings of the martyrs." The phrase is the same as that used by the Beata, but the cause is different, and while the poor woman never lost peace, the Queen never possessed it. People poked fun at her avarice, and asked her if she had not the fortune of five kings under her fingers. "Will it last," she answered: "who knows but one day I may have to supply food for all those kings?" "Whenever the postman knocks I fear he is bringing me news of the death of the Emperor fallen on the battle-field." The end was much worse than that; it was disastrous: he fell, but only to die by inches in that atrocious gaol on St. Helena.

§

A refugee at Rome with her brother Fesch, she lived over a period of twenty-one years in the vicinity of the Beata. Those two lives already so intimately interwined in the invisible world were from then till death interwined in the visible world. It was a diptych wherein two mutually exclusive concepts of life were etched in striking contrast. And yet everything seemed to predestine the two women to follow the same path. Both were of Italian blood, both of almost the same social class, both dowered with beauty and courage, both fashioned in the hard school of poverty, both glorified by the crown of many children, both crucified in youth and in grey hairs by the same material cares and by a series of physical and moral trials which etched on their faces lines of sorrow, giving them a striking resemblance the one to the other.

Do not think of the splendid marble of Canova which depicts the Mother of Napoleon as another Agrippina (Letitia said artlessly that it was a "perfect likeness"), but the plain water-colour of Charlotte— the aged Queen in her decline seated at her table with hands joined, her eyes unseeing, her face wrinkled, her lineaments furrowed, her mouth large and sad, her nose straight and strong, her head-dress oval and made of grey material. Put that living "Pieta" side by side with the model in wax that encloses and outlines the face of the Beata under the altar of San Chrysogonus. Except for the impression of serenity which irradiates the latter, the resemblances are astonishing.

In 1818 Letitia bought the Rinuccini Palace at the corner of the Corso and of the Piazza Venezia, facing the Capitol and the Palazzo Venezia where the late Mussolini* had his quarters. Massive iron railings, lofty brick-coloured façades; on the ground floor a marble plaque representing the death of

---

* The book of which this is a translation was published in 1936 (*Translator's note*).

Letitia; a grand staircase, in the middle of which looms large the gigantic Napoleon of Canova in the rôle of Caesar (it is a nude that holds the terrestrial globe like an apple in its hand); corridors of enormous rooms garnished with the imperial arms; in the last room is a loggia that opens upon the Piazza Venezia.

There the exiled Queen* passed her days, received the uprooted Napoleonides, Louis, Lucien and the rest, and wrote or dictated the letters which the present master of the Bonaparte Palace, Marquis Misciatelli, has just published.

Up to 1821 one thought dominated her mind, the prisoner of St. Helena. She wanted to join him there. As she was refused permission, she laboured together with Fesch to send him provisions of one sort or another (which never reached him), furniture, books, a cook, a surgeon and two chaplains. She urged the Napoleonides to club together to help him. Unfortunately they claimed succour rather for themselves, for they had not given up the idea of playing at kings. It did not enter their heads that men of their race should forego idleness and petty intrigues of love or politics for work. It was said that "they were incapable of anything but ruling". Letitia, with some hesitation, bade them govern their own selves. "Retrench the expenses of your household," was the advice she gave to Jerome erstwhile King of Westphalia, who asked her to buy him a splendid castle: and she asked him to think of the Exile of St. Helena.

With a thoroughly Roman dignity she addressed herself to England, to Metternich the pitiless, to the Kings of the Holy Alliance, asking them to

* I am well aware that the sole official title was "Madame Mère" (*Author's note*).

soften the prisoner's lot and to see to it that her letters were delivered to him, instead of going to London, there to enrich the collections of auto-graph hunters: "In the Name of Him who is Goodness Itself, have some concern for my son, and put a term to his torments." Only one Sovereign, the former Exile of Fontainebleau, Pius VII, listened to her appeals. Meeting Madame Mère on the Palatine, or the Appian Way, the aged Pope would descend from his carriage, and walk up and down with her asking: "How is the good Emperor?" Nor was it a matter of polite formula with him. Through Consalvi, Pius VII intervened in 1817 with the Regent of England, asking him to soften the lot of him "who had re-established religion in the great realm of France". Letitia excused herself later on for grave infringements of courtesy towards the Pontifical Government, arguing that she was confined in Rome as a State Prisoner, but two eloquent letters addressed to Consalvi in 1818 gave her the lie direct in advance: "I am the mother of all sorrows, and the only consolation vouchsafed to me is to know that the Holy Father forgets the past, and remembers only the affection he shows to all that belong to me. We found support and asylum with none but the Pontifical Government. I speak in the name of all my family of outlaws, and above all in the name of him who is dying by inches on a desert rock. His Holiness and Your Eminence are the only ones in Europe who strive to soften the evils he suffers and to put a term to them."

The Emperor's death became known to Letitia only eight weeks after her neighbour the Beata had seen it and described its stages. When she was informed of it by Fesch, she did not weep, but with a silent gesture bade him begone and remained alone with the stupefied bitterness of her grief. The following phrase gives the substance of all the very brief letters in which she notified the Napoleonides of the death: "There remains to me nothing of such a son but a lifeless corpse. Leave me solitary to live out my days in affliction of spirit," she wrote to Caroline.

§

There remained also a soul . . . and she was too much of a believer to forget it; and yet not one appeal for prayer in all these letters. She had now but one thought—to have the remains of her son brought to Rome. She claimed his body from England:

"The Mother of the Emperor Napoleon comes to claim from his enemies the ashes of her son. In the Name of God, in the name of all mothers . . . let me not be refused the ashes of my son."

Her letter was left unanswered, a thing which increased the bitterness of her soul without breaking its ambitions. She who had not wept when they told her of Napoleon's death, wept with joy when Jerome told her that the Chamber of 1830 had voted the replacement of the Emperor's statue on the Vendôme column. The son counted less than the hero, for she refused to give any details of the hero's childhood to Louis Napoleon. What had to go down to history was "his exploits. It must be the figure of the Emperor that stands out in his colossal proportions". We here touch upon the saddest element of mystery in this life which was yet so noble in so many ways. The head of the family had disappeared, Letitia (blind as ever to the miseries, scandals and sufferings of every kind that had attended the rise of her sons), shifted her indomitable will for a "restoration" to "l'Aiglon" and Louis Napoleon, the elder son of Louis, King of Holland, and Hortense, the future Napoleon III.

In 1831 Gregory XVI was scarcely crowned when a revolution fostered by the Carbonari and their allies, Pépoli, son-in-law of Murat, the two sons of Hortense, Prince Gabrielli, and the Marquis Potenziani, the treasurer of Letitia, and the rebels broke out in the environs of Rome and then in Rome itself. The aim was to overwhelm the Pontifical Government, to imprison the Cardinals, to crown l'Aiglon as King of Rome in the Capitol, and to confer the regency on Louis Napoleon. In the Apollo Theatre, built by Prince Torlonia, the banker of the Bonapartes, this refrain was heard:

> *The wicked sectaries (i.e. the priests) must fall*
> *Fall they must beneath the axe of vengeance.*

The Beata followed in her sun the riotous gatherings in the Café della Barcaccia, and the Café Nuovo where Carbonari and Bonapartes, priests and seminarists shouted: "Long live Napoleon and Liberty! Liberty or death!"

Thanks to the support of Austria the plot failed; Louis Napoleon fled; his eldest brother Charles died on the journey. Now Letitia (so the police records assure us) was privy to the plot. She had promised a million francs for the treasury of the future king, had made overtures to the rioters. Yet at that time the Papal Government was giving asylum to her, to Fesch and the Bonapartes. Her letters to Hortense do not betray the slightest remorse, only a fear that the fugitives might be arrested and that l'Aiglon, Duke of Reichstadt, might be reft from her hopes. But no, she asserted to Prokesch, 21 July 1832, "he will ascend the throne of his fathers".

The very next day l'Aiglon died prematurely, worn out by the bitterness of his exile, the gilded boredom of Schonbrun, and the harshness of Metternich; his soul corroded by the desertion of his mother, Marie-Louise, who, in her Duchy of Parma, lounged among her lovers and hen-parrots; his own health ruined by his dissolute excesses.

He died at twenty-one filled with bitterness, saying over and over again: "To end so young a life so pointlessly. My birth, my death, that is my whole history." He also was a victim, the most tragic and the most blameless, of that megalomania which made all his breed a rootless race.

Marie-Louise, with her son at his death, broke the silence with which she had hitherto received Letitia's letters: "God has so disposed things. We have nought to do but to submit ourselves to His Supreme Will." Letitia replied by the pen of Fesch: "To my infirmities God has willed this blow, but therein lies a new pledge of His mercies, the firm hope that He will have amply made up by the glory of Heaven for what was lacking in the glory of the world." O. Aubry goes on to say that "while the mother was quickly consoled, the grandmother consoled herself never. The Mother of Kings had nothing left but death. She had hoped for her family's revenge in the King of Rome. She had served but one obsession, Napoleon, with the disappearance of the visible heir she wrapped herself in the shroud of night. She did not hope for revenge through Louis' son, the future Napoleon III. The letters published by P. Misciatelli, suggest on the contrary that she carried her unconquerable hopes of revenge into the night of her blindness and half-sleep that preceded her death.

§

Of Louis, "my own Napoleon", it was only from eternity that she was to see his short-lived triumph and the disasters that broke him. Who would show to that old Corsican woman the vanity of "the glory of this world"? A hundred paces from her palace, facing the little church of Santa Maria in Via Lata, a poor woman, Blessed Anna-Maria Taigi, who read as in an open book the soul of the Queen and paid by deadly pains for the overthrow of the final plot, never ceased praying for her unconscious enemy. She had promised to pray for her. What then was necessary in order to detach the octogenarian Queen from this world and its vanities? God continued to beat upon her heart as upon an anvil. Her griefs multiplied; three of her children (not counting five who had died young) and five of her grand-children were gone. "They all die," she wailed, "and I live on alone to weep over them. I am like a tree that loses its leaves. I have no longer any tears left to lament them. God's will be done!" In 1830 a fall broke her thigh and left her practically powerless; then, as happened to the Beata, the light of day little by little went out, ending in complete blindness. She no longer saw before her loggia the Tower of the Capitol, that symbol of so much vanished glory. If only a little peace would come to her from her surviving children, but their quarrels and importunities saddened her. "I have nothing left," she replied to them. As a matter of fact she scarcely left four million francs—a mere drop of water for six princely heirs of the direct line. Of course the Beata left only four crowns to a greater number of inheritors!

We have already noted the message sent her by the

Beata through Fesch: "Yes, I will pray for your
sister, and will let her know what light I receive
concerning her. Meanwhile let her meditate upon
what she has been, what she is, and what she is soon
to become, and let her make ready for death which
will not be long in coming." Were there any direct
conversations between Letitia and Anna? It is
probable even though we have no documentary
evidence. But the facts guarantee at least this conclusion—Providence drew these two lives together
as they drew to their close and they were fused like
two metals in the one crucible.

During a period of nineteen years the Queen
frequently encountered the Beata for they dwelt
in the same street; she saw her at the Coliseum and
in the churches of the Corso. But during the last
two years the contact became closer. Anna lived
within a hundred paces of the Bonaparte Palace.
The two women belonged to the same parish, that
of Santa Maria in Via Lata. A tradition has it that
the crypt of this church, in front of which was
Anna's dwelling, was the first prison of St. Paul. It
was also the church of the Bonapartes. In the chapel
to the left lie the ashes of Joseph Bonaparte and
Zénaïde. Lucien, who had his quarters almost in
front of it, came there also, to pray or to dream, by
the side of Letitia.

The narrow nave with columns of red marble
must often have seen the old Queen arriving,
clothed in a black dress, blind, her steps faltering,
leaning on two attendants. Quite near to her, who
but yesterday was saying proudly, "I am more than
an Empress; I am the Mother of Napoleon, the
Mother of Kings," but had now become "A
shadow longing for death"—quite near to her (for
the space is confined) another old woman, not less

infirm, and also nearly blind, is at her prayers. Her head covered with her veil to hide her tears and ecstasies, she saw again a picture that was familiar to her—the glory and servitude, the rise and fall of this family against which she had had to fight a war lasting forty-five years. If she better than anybody knew their faults and mistakes, she also knew how they had suffered and served, for she was well aware that Napoleon also served. Did the nearness of the saint, her prayers and her tactful advice eventually console the inconsolable and restore serenity to Letitia's soul? The Countess of Blessington one day meeting her as she wandered among the groves of laurels and myrtles on the Palatine, spoke to her of Napoleon: "I shall rejoin him soon," she replied, "in a better world, where weeping is no more. I thought I had lived out my time, but God sees what is best for us." In her letters which were still steeped in worldly interests, the calmer tone of Christian confidence appears: "We cannot alter any of the decrees of Providence. God alone is good." When she could no longer go out she attended Mass daily in her little private chapel.

On 1st February 1836 the Mother of Kings felt herself failing and asked for the Last Sacraments. They were administered (as they were soon to be administered to the Beata) by the parish clergy of Santa Maria in Via Lata, at dusk. Cardinal Fesch, who was present at the Extreme Unction and brought his sister the Papal Blessing withdrew, not thinking there was any immediate danger. She who had for a long time lived surrounded by an eager Court in the midst of the nursery of Kings, was to die alone as was Anna-Maria. Rosa Mellini, the Queen's reader, had retired into a corner when at eight o'clock in the evening the Queen breathed her last. Rome, amidst the noisy gambols of the Carnival scarcely heard the two modest bells of Santa Maria in Via Lata, and of the Ara Coeli, as they tolled for her passing, but, a few steps away a poor woman heard, prayed and wept.

The second will of Letitia was made after the death of l'Aiglon, for the first made him her sole heir. It begins, in Italian, with these humble words: "I declare that I wish to die in the Catholic religion. I am humbly sorry for my sins and I beg the assistance of my Guardian Angel, of my holy patrons and advocates, of my dear Mother and of my Creator. Let one thousand Masses be said for the repose of my soul."

Cardinal Fesch, ex-King Jerome, Prince Lucien and his wife (she whose repudiation Letitia had desired), attended the remains which were dominated by the portraits of eight princes or kings, the gigantic bust of Napoleon and the bust of l'Aiglon. The silver vigil-lamp, which burnt near the body of Napoleon, burnt near his mother.

"If," says Larrey, "she had died in Rome thirty years earlier, the vaults of St. Peter's would have reverberated to the sound of the bells announcing 'Urbi et Orbi', the death of the Great Man's mother."

Rome was not to see that triumph till sixteen years later when Napoleon III had the remains of Fesch and Letitia exhumed in order to have them taken from the chapel at Corneto to Ajaccio. There, in the Imperial Chapel, a block of black marble enclosed the tomb with the inscription: "*Mater Regum*," "The Mother of Kings."

§

Many whimsical accounts have been given concerning the death and obsequies of Letitia. The death register at Santa Maria in Via Lata, which I was able to consult in the Vatican Archives, allows us to reconstruct the facts, hour by hour. Under the noble official formularies of graceful Latin which give to the extract the charm of a page from Titus Livius the truth appears in its stark reality.

Only five years had passed since the troubles created by the Napoleonides, and demonstrations were feared. The *Journal de Rome* gave her eight obscure lines in which the name of Napoleon was not even mentioned, but correcting history by giving the date as 1 February, not the 2nd. The Government hesitated for a long time to authorise the taking of the body to Corneto. The coffin arrived at the little church late at night, its few followers being some nuns and princes without princedoms. Its solitude was broken by Letitia's faithful friend, Anna-Maria, who, six steps away on the opposite side of the road, could see the light of the candles, and watched in prayer. The next day she was there to hear the early morning Mass according to custom, and received Holy Communion quite close to the coffin. The nave was small. In order to avoid crowds it was forbidden to display the Imperial Arms at the door or on the catafalque. Fesch however succeeded in putting them upon the pall and the coffin: on the coffin, beneath the Imperial Eagle and the "N" the words *"Mater Napoleonis"*.

During the morning the chapter celebrated the Queen's solemn obsequies, then the coffin disappeared into the crypt to await the second nightfall. Towards two o'clock in the morning, the hour at which Anna usually took her rest, the Beata could see the doors of the church opening in the silence of the night. The coffin was brought out silently to a carriage: it left on its way to the Civita-Vecchia road and the Chapel of the Daughters of the Cross at Corneto, escorted by the little group of Napoleonides.

A year later between those same columns of red marble, on that same white flagstone edged with white, in that same church of Santa Maria in Via Lata, another coffin rested: it was that of the Blessed Anna-Maria Taigi. The entry is found five pages from the other in the same register.* Anna's entry is very short, and the registrar, bemused by the plague rife in Rome, immediately after the death of its Protectress, the secretary of the Chapter, was the victim of distractions. But even there the dryness of official formularies is eloquent. In spite of the terrors of the plague the humble woman was taken the day

* Here is the translation of the two entries:

No. 421. *Bonaparte Ramolino Letitia*

On 2 Feb. 1836 at eight o'clock on the preceding night (sic) Her Royal Highness Madame Letitia, née Ramolino, widow of Charles Bonaparte of Ajaccio, in the Island of Corsica, mother of Napoleon Bonaparte, former Emperor of the French, slept in the Lord, at the age of about eighty years, spiritually strengthened in her infirmities with all the Sacraments of the Church, recommended to God by the Prayers for the Dying, fortified by the Apostolic Blessing of the Holy Father *"in articulo mortis"*.

Her remains were taken on the fourth day after her death to the parish church during the night, in a carriage, after the style of the nobility. The following day she received the solemn obsequies with the assistance of the Chapter of Canons and of the College of Beneficiaries.

After the solemn obsequies the wooden coffin, enclosed in a leaden case and sealed, was placed, at the request of Notary Apollon, in the vault of the canon-curé, lately deceased.

Then at two o'clock in the morning, at the notary's request, the coffin was handed over by the Rev. Christopher Brenda (deputed by the canon-curé) and placed upon a carriage, and taken outside the city to the venerable convent of the Sisters of the Most Holy Cross and Passion of Our Lord Jesus Christ, at Corneto; that is to say, it was transported thither, there to receive ecclesiastical burial.

In witness to which . . . 6th February 1836 Tomas Landuzzi can.cred.

No. 463. *Gianetti (by birth) Taigi (by marriage), Anna-Maria (died in wedlock)*

On 9th June 1837 Anna-Maria Gianetti, born at Siena, daughter of Louis and wife of Peter (sic) Taigi, aged sixty-four years (sic), died piously, fortified by all the sacraments of the Church, assisted by the curate of this church.

The following day she was brought from her home, which is in this parish and where she ended her days, into this basilica.

On 11th June, exposed in the middle of the church, she received the solemn obsequies, and on the same day after sundown was carried to the public cemetery.

In witness to which . . . in the absence of the canon-curé, Pierre Minetti, can.adm.

after her death, on the 10 June, into the church. Already canonised by the crowd, her body remained *exposed in the middle of the church* from the 10th to the 11th. In spite of her poverty she received the solemn obsequies, then, after sundown she was taken to the Campo Verano where the cortège of pilgrims, swelling as it went, bore witness to her imperishable glory.

V

FINAL PURIFICATIONS – LAST ILLNESS – DEATH – GLORY

THE smart young woman of Rome from the Dei Monti quarter had become an old woman of sixty-eight prematurely worn out. For nearly half a century she had unceasingly walked the same road—poverty, suffering, love of her neighbour, passionate love of God, in the midst of a spiritual darkness bereft of consolation. Not entirely bereft, but the consolations she received from Our Lord were austere: "I am thine as I am of all who take up their cross bravely. The children of the cross are my well-beloved."

She advanced with great strides upon the royal road. The "tongues of vipers" were never silent, yet the veneration of better-disposed people accompanied her when she dragged herself along the streets of Rome. She hastily disengaged herself from these praises in order to get back to her poor lodging, there to feel once more her home-sickness for heaven. Three months after Letitia's death on reaching St. Paul's-outside-the-Walls in the company of Mgr. Natali, she said to him: "It is the last time." In front of the holy crucifix after Holy Communion she felt suffused by a deep peace. "Live in peace, My daughter," said Our Lord to her, "and do not trouble yourself over what people about you say. You have not spoken rashly. Adieu, My daughter. You will soon see Me again in heaven. Yes, My daughter, Adieu. Soon you will be with Me in My kingdom. Make haste to go where you will, for afterwards it is the end." There remained to her naught but to assuage her hunger for suffering over a period of seven months' agony.

On 26th October 1836 she took to her bed, never to leave it. Her body broken with pain, from the sole of her foot to the crown of her head, her heart pierced to see her numerous family in a state bordering on destitution, she yet preserved that miraculous peace that never left her. Therein lies a fact more eloquent than the innumerable prodigies of such a life. The documents are full of testimonies to this peace: "The peace of her soul," says Cardinal Pedicini, in his deposition, "resisted all onslaughts." And referring especially to the end of her life, when the flood of her tribulations reached high tide, her confessor declares: "At the end of her life, she achieved such a tranquillity of soul, such a peaceful union with God that it is impossible to describe it." Indeed, our poor little minds cannot explain this prodigy—peace in the midst of universal crucifixion.

She spoke of her death as of one of those journeys to the Pincian, where they ate chestnuts and took a little white wine. Her poor afflicted fingers continued to ply the needle, and up to the last three days she directed the house as the servant of all.

The moment came when, racked with pain, she could no longer move, while her interior desolation only became greater.

§

In her sun, that tragic mirror, the world was still reflected. It revealed the development of the secret societies. Their activities unchained a terrible persecution against Swiss Catholics. At Geneva, London, and Turin, Mazzini prepared the way for world revolution, but first of all for that revolution whence Italian unity was to arise. His programme included the total destruction of Catholicism. "The Italian people," he kept repeating, "is called to destroy Catholicism, therefore in the name of the revolution, continue. Humanity is the only Messiah!" There were persecutions in Germany, where the official watchword was already: "One German religion, one German philosophy in one German fatherland." In France the spirit of Voltaire and of a mystic form of socialism was triumphant; Lammenais had revolted against the Church; Cousin and Quinet were canonising German rationalism. In China and Indo-China, again, bloody persecutions. All these visions passed before the eyes of the agonised expiatress.

Yet to see her so amiable and encouraging, "one would have thought her to be lying on a bed of roses".

Domenico tells us that for many years she had eaten what would satisfy a grasshopper. "She had received an order from heaven to abstain from fresh meat, and therefore took only a little fish and a tiny piece of bread, with sometimes a little stewed fruit." But even this slender nourishment became intolerable to her. Her distress grew until she was dying on a veritable Job's dunghill. "I myself gave her," says her confessor, "out of a motive of charity, the covers of the bed on which she died. I collected alms, but they were not enough to support the poor family, and Don Rafaële was obliged day by day to go in quest of provisions. This was an unutterable torture for the poor woman, and God sent only what was strictly necessary. Yet, in the midst of this cruel distress she received a thoroughly unjust demand to pay a debt of her daughter's." The Beata withstood one last temptation of prosperity. The wife of the governor general of Savoy had known her at Rome and had obtained many graces through her. When she returned to Turin, she made known her intention of procuring Anna plentiful alms by making her needs known to the court. "The servant of God," says Mgr. Natali, "entrusted me with a reply to the effect that she was grateful, but begged not to be spoken of, because she wished to remain unknown." The attractive publicity was refused. "She said to me," continues the prelate, "that one should be content to live by asking alms for the love of God for a poor family, and not quit the path of humiliations." She received with gratitude certain delicacies—some chickens, some fine fruit, some old wine, but they became treasure for incurables.

Mgr. Natali bowed to her. He had understood rightly, and his devotion to her did not play her false. He said Mass every day in Anna's oratory and gave her Holy Communion. Towards the end Cardinal Pedicini obtained permission for her to receive Communion after taking the draughts of a poppy beverage that were given her to drink.

§

On Sunday 2nd June 1837 the sick woman was attacked by fever. After Communion on Monday she had a swoon which lasted so long that they thought her dead, but it was an ecstasy in which Our Lord told her that she would die the following

Friday, the day sacred to His Passion. When she came to herself Anna showed lively joy and told Mgr. Natali the good news.

After that she called Domenico to her on two occasions, consoling him and thanking him for the care he had taken of her. Then she saw her children in turn and told them to be faithful to their prayers, the saying of the family rosary, the love of Our Lady, and to remain on good terms with one another. Then all the children gathered round her bed, and the dying woman blessed them with tears in her eyes, for she thought of the morrow.

But the Master who had wished her to remain poor took this anxiety from her: "I will take them under My protection. Do not fear to leave them in poverty for the love of Me. The benefactors who are good to them will themselves be recompensed."

The maid Annunziata describes this agony-in-peace. "Her rosary in one hand, a picture of Jesus of Nazareth in the other, she only stopped praying to murmur: 'For the love of God'. If anybody asked her how she was, she would answer: 'I do not do badly, thank God'." She called Sophie to her lastly and alone, to confide the whole family to her, urging her to watch over the aged Domenico, over Mariuccia and her own children, and to have them always accompanied whenever they went out. "There will be yet much to suffer, poverty, persecutions, malicious tongues. But have no doubt: sooner or later Our Lord will console you." Sophie says: "As I could no longer keep back my sobs, she said it was useless to say more, and gave me her blessings." Then she was left by herself with God alone.

There was one more lesson for her to give, that of obedience unto death. "I always found her docile and submissive as a lamb," said Domenico. He did not ponder the tragic realism of his comparison. She obeyed unto the slaughter.

The doctors' science, as sure of itself then as it is to-day, recommended for that broken body violent revulsives. Our Lord warned her that the doctors would kill her, but if the treatment was insisted upon she would have to obey, and her obedience would be crowned. The doctors and Domenico did insist, and she resigned herself into their hands, and the poultices, laid on with a prodigal hand, were the final blow.

On the Wednesday she received the Viaticum. A Trinitarian father gave her absolution and the plenary indulgence in the hour of death, and she entered into a long period of silence.

A quaint custom demanded that, in order not to disturb a person in his agony by noisy manifestations of grief, the family should withdraw as death approached. Anna herself invited hers to go and rest. Before leaving, the confidential priest asked her how she was. She murmured: "Mortal agonies." It was at this moment that she raised her hand and lightly touched Mgr. Natali on the chest, thus curing him of a congestion, and bade him go and take his rest.

§

In the evening of the Thursday she received extreme unction, and the pains of her agony grew fiercer. The children and Domenico wept aloud, and so they were sent away and there remained none but strangers. The fathers of St. Camillus de Lellis also withdrew, for they did not think the end was just yet. The curate went to another room to say his breviary. Towards four in the morning Mgr. Natali, awakened by an interior voice, went to her in haste.

The sick woman was breathing with the death-rattle. The curate was summoned. He recited the prayers for the dying, and gave a last absolution. A great sigh was heard like a cry of deliverance: Anna-Maria Taigi had entered into her rest.

Domenico tells of the end with admirable simplicity: "I was in the next room and I heard her reciting the prayers with the priest. Those who were with her told me she died in peace."

It was half-past-four in the morning of Friday, 9th June 1837. Anna was sixty-eight years old. She was then living at number eight in the road called after the Holy Apostles, in the parish of Santa Maria, in Via Lata, facing that church.

Mgr. Natali, after weeping his fill, opened her purse and found four crowns inside.* It was all they had to cover the cost of the funeral (which had gone up to two hundred crowns) and to support the whole family. But God was watching. Cardinal Pedicini sent fifty crowns; from Milan and Turin other alms came. Even during the plague of cholera which followed her death the necessary money kept coming in as Anna had foretold.

Once she had breathed her last, Cardinal Pedicini, the vice-chancellor, wrote to the cardinal-vicar,

---

* The price of a poor man's coffin.

Mgr. Rafaële Natali left undone absolutely nothing that should be done. After a cast had been taken of the face the body was enclosed in a leaden coffin. The cast served for the making of a wax bust which has been reproduced in pictures. "Those who knew Anna-Maria," says Father Calixtus, claim that none of the portraits was a perfect likeness. Later on in a similar vein, he makes a remark that leaves us thoughtful: "Dom Rafaële used to make the statement that this bust of Anna-Maria suddenly took on an expression of happiness in the form of a gracious smile whenever anything happened favourable to the Church." L'Univers of 15th March, 1871, carried this announcement: "Mgr. Rafaële Natali has just died, surrounded by Anna-Maria's family in whose midst he had lived. He was a nonagenarian and kept his faculties only to speak of her whose confidant he had been. He asked to be buried by her side in the church of San Chrysogono, but the law, which enjoins that all burials shall take place outside the city, in the cemetery of St. Lawrence, forbade the realisation of this request".

Odescalchi, asking him that honourable burial should be given to the woman in whom, during upwards of thirty years, he had admired "the extraordinary gifts and the astonishing light with which God had dowered her, of a quality equal to those of the greatest saints."

But the obsequies did not have all the lustre he desired. Our Lord had promised Anna that the cholera would spare Rome until her death. She had scarcely breathed her last when the scourge broke out amidst scenes of indescribable panic. The death of the Beata at first passed unnoticed, but piety recovered quickly and the body was left exposed for two days for the veneration of the faithful in the church of Santa Maria, in Via Lata. On the Sunday evening a devout cortège conducted it to the new cemetery, in the Campo Verano, where, conformably to the instructions of Gregory XVI, it was enclosed in a leaden sepulchre, with seals affixed, near the chapel. Mgr. Natali had caused a mask of the face to be taken before the body was placed in the coffin.

After a few days, in spite of the cholera, the procession of pilgrims began. Ordinary folk, bishops, cardinals, elbowed one another near the humble tombstone. Cardinal Odescalchi forthwith instructed Mgr. Natali to collect all the documents, from which Mgr. Luquet, postulator of the cause, published the first biography. It had an immediate success, and was translated into several languages.

The fame of her sanctity increased day by day. Mgr. Natali and Domenico did not know to whom to reply first. "Many people," says the latter, "who had known her plied me with all sorts of questions as to how she died. Some asked one question, some asked another. Some spoke of the special gifts she had received from God; others of the graces they had received through her intercession while she was yet alive. Everybody spoke well of her, praised her and described her as full of merits and virtues. As for me, I always thought highly of her and I declare that Our Lord took this, His good servant, away from me, because I was not worthy of her."

Cardinal Pedicini, while drawing up his voluminous memoirs of her, went often to pray at her tomb. Cardinal Micara, the Capuchin, doyen of the Sacred College, and Prefect of the Congregation of Rites, always carried a picture of her about his person. The Venerable Bernard Clausi, of the Minim Order of Franciscans, who often asked for her prayers, said to all who came his way: "If she is not in heaven, there is no room there for anybody."

The Blessed Gaspará del Bufalo, founder of the Missionaries of the Precious Blood, taken thoroughly aback by the death of the Beata, moaned: "When Our Lord recalls to Himself souls so dear as she it is a sign He is going to chastise us."

The Venerable Vincent Pallotti called Anna "his secretary, his plenipotentiary, charged with all the interests of his congregation in the presence of the Most Holy Trinity".

The Blessed Mary Euphrasia Pelletier, foundress of the Good Shepherd Congregation, confided to her the thorny questions she had to deal with in Rome.

Mgr. Flaget, Bishop of Louisville, who was to die in the odour of sanctity, had visited the Beata during her last illness and sang her praises throughout the United States.

The number of miracles increased and the people deplored the fact that the body of the Beata rested so far from Rome. By order of the cardinal-vicar it was brought to the church of Our Lady of Peace. The coffin, sealed for eighteen years, was re-opened,

and the body was found as fresh as if it had been
buried the day before. In spite of instructions for
secrecy, and although the middle of the night was
chosen as the moment of removal, a vast crowd came
to acclaim "The Saint of Rome and its Palladium".

§

Pius IX surrounded the servant of God with great
veneration. On the eve of the battle of Mentana,
pictures representing him beside Anna-Maria praying for the triumph of the Church, were spread far
and wide. Learning that she had expressed a wish to
be buried in the church of the Trinitarians, he had
the body brought on 18th August, 1865, to the
basilica of San Chrysogono. Three years later the
coffin was again opened, and though the clothes of
the Beata had decayed, her body was still intact. The
sisters of St. Joseph took off the poor clothing and
replaced it by new. For eight days the body was
exposed for the veneration of the faithful; the whole
neighbourhood of Trastevere seemed on the move,
and troops were necessary to ensure order. The
body, enclosed in a double coffin of lead and of
cypress, was near the chapel of the Blessed Sacrament in a memorial tomb, and, later on, in the chapel
to the left, under the altar within a large glass
shrine which allowed it to be seen in the habit of a
Trinitarian Tertiary. The hands were joined in front
of the breast. The face, giving an impression of
infinite serenity, was covered in a light wax mask
beneath the white coif.

Meanwhile the Process took its course. After the
official enquiry entrusted to Mgr. Natali, the
juridical enquiry was begun in 1852. Thirty witnesses upon oath were heard—cardinals, bishops,
nobles, servants, two daughters of the Beata and

finally, leaning on his stick, with hunched shoulders, an old man of ninety-two years, the man who, after God, had the most to do with making Anna-Maria a saint—Domenico. In 1863 Pius IX introduced the Cause of Beatification; on 4th March, 1906, Pius X declared the heroicity of her virtures. On 30th May, 1920, Benedict XV ranked Anna-Maria Taigi, mother of a family, amongst the Blessed. A little while later he made her the special protectress of mothers of families and the patroness of the Women's Catholic Union.

Among the miracles offered for scrutiny he approved the two that follow.

In 1869 a Roman lady of the Trastevere, Maria del Pinto, a Trinitarian Tertiary, like Anna, was suffering from chronic inflammation of the womb itself, and of the membrane of its inner surface, and was reduced thereby to the condition of a skeleton. Being given up by the doctors, she was urged to make a triduum to obtain her cure through Anna's intercession. She said in her own account of the matter: "I did not wish to be cured, for I preferred to suffer. Consequently I made a novena to the Holy Ghost to find out if it was God's will that I should make the triduum. During the course of the novena I seemed to see Our Lady Immaculate, shining with light, receiving a petition from the hands of a gracious old lady who was kneeling in front of her. 'Beg for your cure, My daughter,' said the Blessed Virgin; 'you shall be perfectly cured of this disease. There will be plenty of other opportunities for you to suffer.'"

The triduum was made under obedience. There was a fresh apparition of the Blessed Virgin and Anna-Maria. The latter had a handkerchief in her hand "as if to wipe away the tears that I shed in abundance because of the intensity of the pain. The Blessed Virgin said to me, 'Behold your deliverer.' At that moment I felt a wrenching that made me cry out loud. People came to my assistance, but I was cured. I arose without difficulty to make a pilgrimage of thanks at the church of San Chrysogono."

But it was France that furnished the first miracle that was retained for the Beatification. It was sworn to by a French doctor of Lyons, Dr. Edouard Carrier. Here is the story.

In 1867, at the boarding-school of the Dames of the Assumption, at Saint-Foy, a girl by the name of Mélanie Sevin, while playing in the courtyard of the school, caught her foot between two paving-stones and fell, sustaining a twisted ankle with wrenching of the muscles. Dr. Carrier marked in his journal day by day the process of the injury. The foot became deformed and withered; a bony formation developed and projected from the fracture, fever followed. The child suffered so much that her appliance was removed. The good sisters searched for a relic and found nothing but a picture of Anna-Maria. This was placed upon the affected parts of the foot and leg. Instantaneously the four sisters who were looking after the child saw the foot straighten itself, the twisted nerves regain position, the excrescence disappear! An invisible seamstress stitch by stitch had woven a new garment. The child cried out: "I am cured." Dr. Carrier arrived and found every trace of the injury gone and drew his conclusion. "It is a miracle."

France gave to the Beata her first postulator,* her

* Mgr. Luquet, Bishop of Hesebon. The author is French, and rightly zealous for France, but as he himself says in other words, the saints are much more interested in the fact that the garment of the Church is seamless, than that it is a coat of many national colours. Anna-Maria belongs to all nationalities, and England was not slow in the past to take her to herself, for as early as 1864

first biographer, and Anna's gratitude gave France the first miracle. These are proud titles for France, but they are, above all, very special motives for trustful devotion to the Beata.

§

May, 1920, saw St. Peter's in Rome often filled with enthusiastic crowds. Benedict XV, for the first time since his elevation to the papacy, was about to give honour to certain heroes of the Christian life. In this group of elect souls France counted three of her children: 9th May, beatification of Louise de Marillac; 13th May, canonisation of Saint Margaret Mary; 16th May, canonisation of St. Joan of Arc.

On 30th May, the Feast of the Most Holy Trinity, Benedict XV brought this glorious series to a close by declaring "blessed" "Anna-Maria Taigi, wife and mother".* Cardinal Pompili, in an eloquent message, invited all the people of Rome to acclaim this humble woman of the people, the glory of "this Rome of ours". The heart of Rome accepted the invitation. The immense Basilica was filled with a mighty crowd of people, but, above all, of humble ones, poor working people who had come to acclaim their sister and their model in the heroism of hidden lives.

Benedict XV, in approving the miracles of the Beata, had already spoken in praise of this heroism

Mgr. Luquet's life was translated, and the bishop himself, postulator of the cause, enriched the translation with a letter in which he commended the efforts of Mrs. Laura de Lisle and made her the treasurer for England of all moneys offered for the expenses of the cause. May England become zealous again for the Beata that "blessed" may soon be changed into "saint" (*Translator's note*).

* The French word "Mere de famille", "mother of a family" has not an English ring, while the word "Matron" too readily connotes hospitals! God grant that in the Breviary the Church may one day have not merely a section for "non-Virgins", but for "Wives-and-Mothers" (*Translator's note*).

and he did so a second time: "It is a question of a humble wife and mother, an angel of consolation to her parents, a model of school-girls and young women of the working classes, a mother of children who knew how to unite labour with recollection, a mother of children upon whom weighed the care of her old parents, the care, too, of a husband who was not always good-tempered, and the education of a large family. It is a question of a mother of children, who, without neglecting any duty whatever, yet found time to visit the sick and to make herself all things to all men."

On the evening of 30th May, 1920, after the crowd had had plenty of time to acclaim the glorious woman of Rome, whose picture shone radiantly in the Basilica of the Prince of the Apostles, Benedict XV came alone to prostrate himself silently and humbly before the relics of Anna Taigi, the wife of Domenico, the porter.

In broad Trastevere an immense crowd of pilgrims filed past the altar containing the relics of the Beata: more than ever in her lifetime Anna-Maria was "the Palladium of Rome".

During Lent I often went to pray in the suburban church; the "red" quarter was not far away, but in spite of that (or because of it) there was never any lack of good people in front of that little chapel where the aged "mamma" in her sleep, her serene face (yes, serene, though furrowed with wrinkles that tell the story of so many sufferings) turned towards her suppliants, seems to give ear to their petitions. These are her suppliants—housewives returning from market with their baskets in hand, workmen and women-workers in their working dress.

On Holy Thursday I was half misled. The "sepulchre" where the Blessed Sacrament kept watch* was erected in the transept where the Beata's body lies, and the glass shrine within which she rests underneath the altar, had been covered by a violet veil. The eyes of the pilgrims sought her in vain behind the balustrade, but she was there in the first rank of the adorers. Invisible and yet in honour, the fairest flower of the field of corn. For, possibly in memory of those apparitions in which sacramental Jesus,† coming to life as it were, said to her, "I am the flower of the fields", the Trinitarian fathers and the devout women of the neighbourhood had transformed the chapel into the likeness of a field of corn. The symbolism was very moving. Was not the poor woman a magnificent flower that opened out in the broad cornfield of the ordinary people of the world?

But the saints belong to all men. Rivalries of race or social position they hold in horror, and more often than not it is people of their own social position and their own family who most cruelly crucify them. Italy, land of martyrs, and Rome, Mother of the Churches, have made us the gift of the Beata. Have we estimated the gift at its value? *No*. Very few in France know this great woman of Rome. She appeals to the imagination less than Joan of Arc, for what we look at most is the epic heroine, forgetting the Calvary of two years that made of her a saint and a redemptress. Anna's Calvary lasted forty-eight years; you might say that for half a century God bruised this womanly heart whose mission embraced the whole Church. She suffered for all and suffered *by* all, and first of all by those

---

* The author may have meant this, or it may be a slip for "was being watched" (*Translator's note*).

† Alas! "Jesus-Hostie" is untranslatable unless we force ourselves to accept the French most tender idiom "Jesus-Host". The Italian is equally beautiful 'Gesu Sacramentato", "Sacramented Jesus". The *personal* touch of a lively Faith. (*Translator's note*.)

from whom it seemed she might expect consolation. A small number of chosen souls recognised the precious pearl; the majority trampled her underfoot. But that was not sufficient for her. She was her own executioner, refusing gifts from those who were under obligation to her, heaping favours upon her detractors, consoling and tranquillizing the agony of the Bonapartes, at whose hands she and humanity had suffered so much.

It was a great lesson for which humanity stood badly in need. There is no other peace for peoples, or families, or individuals but "the peace of Christ in the Kingdom of Christ crucified".

Such was one of the messages of the Beata; it was not the only one. The mind of mankind is still more diseased than is the body social. Now the lesson brought by the Beata to a society in full apostasy was primarily in the intellectual order. Has this been sufficiently noted? The moral to be drawn for the lowly, the poor, for wives and mothers of children has been emphasised by everybody. There remains another moral not so easily drawn, and yet of capital importance.

VI

THE MESSAGE OF THE BLESSED ANNA-MARIA TAIGI TO THE TWENTIETH CENTURY – THE FACT OF THE SUPERNATURAL – THE DIGNITY OF THE HUMBLE

THE mission of this great woman of Rome was to provide a counter-weight to the crimes of a society which had become like a place infested with dangerous and evil characters; it was also to provide a testimony to intellect in revolt. Her first mission ended with the death of the expiatress; the second began with it. The message of the Beata to the twentieth century is to prove by the argument of facts that God and the supernatural exist. This testimony scarcely reached those for whom it was destined in Anna's lifetime; indeed it could not reach them without the saint leaving the obscurity in which it was her duty to live.

Philosophers and men of letters did not so much as know of her existence, and Napoleon to whom she was in triumphant opposition did not know her name. But death gave the seer her entry into history, and her place therein will become larger as time goes on. Hers is a great contemporary testimony that gives us news of the other world. The Europe of the Revolution and of the Empire did not listen, for it lacked a sense of silence. It would appear that we have at last acquired a sense of silence. I have said as much elsewhere,* and refrain from enlarging upon the matter here.

Yesterday, on the evening of the elections and the triumph of the Popular Front, one of the great soldiers of the last war said: "We are at one of these three dates—1789, 1791 or 1793; we shall know to-morrow which."

§

So be it, but a new element has intervened since the first 1789. Among better-disposed people at least there has been an awakening of soul that is respectful towards mystic realities. Bergson is an echo as well as a forerunner when he writes: "The complete mysticism is that of the great Christian mystics. From their accumulated vitality there has issued an

---

* "*Jesus et l'Art Contemporaine—Face au Paganisme*" Edition Spes.

extraordinarily forceful and daring power of conception and realisation." Referring to the fantasies of Charcot, he says: "There is an exceptional form of health based upon solid foundations that is easily recognised. It manifests itself in a taste for action, a faculty of adapting itself and re-adapting itself to changing circumstances—firmness joined to pliancy, prophetic insight into what is possible and what is impossible, a spirit of simplicity that triumphs over complexity; in a word a superior form of common sense. Is this not precisely what we find in the case of the mystics we have been considering? And would they not serve as the definition itself of robust intellectuality?"*

These words give the answer to certain die-hard prejudices. It was little good realising the bankruptcy of Charcot's theories, if our intelligence had been so long poisoned by a would-be medical literature, that an involuntary reflex induced us to make pathological cases of mystic states, even when the very facts laid bare a moral and intellectual healthiness. Of course, the opposite reaction is possible. A fool will think himself to be Plato, but will anything flash forth from him that suggests Plato? Every gesture of the fool reveals the underling, every gesture of the true mystic the hero.

Bergson continues: "It is an unbounded soaring of the soul, an exaltation that is yet calm, a science inborn. From this exaltation the mystic draws no pride, but, on the contrary, his humility is deep, equal to his charity. Through God and by God he loves all humanity with love divine." The tree is known by its fruits. The great mystics are not outside humanity, they dominate it. They are the heroic

* Henri Bergson, of the French Acadamy's *Les Deux Sources de la Morale et de la Religion*. Paris, Alcan. pp. 243, 244, 251.

forerunners whose task is "to transform humanity at the roots; they begin by giving an example".*

Believers knew all this, but it was not without its value that these truths should have been re-stated by a philosopher who did not receive the gift of Faith. The tone of M. Louis Bertrand is different. In his introduction to the life of *Saint Teresa*† he bids the doctors leave his heroine alone. It is quite enough that "their equals had all but killed her", as in fact a number of them together did kill Anna-Maria. "It is," he writes, "one of the most absurd and at the same time afflicting sights to see the clumsy hands of certain people touching the souls of the saints."‡ "Certain doctors have covered themselves with ridicule by wandering in these lands where there is nothing for them to see."

In cultured circles Louis Bertrand's *Sainte Thérèse*, and a thousand works of the same kind, written by laymen who testify truly to their own epoch, have been granted the success due to work of a high standard, and that surely shows how far we have travelled. We are as far from the superficial scepticism of Voltaire and Rénan as from the physics of the Middle Ages. If with Father de Grandmaison the believer proclaims: "These great experiences of the mystics stand recorded by those who underwent them, and are like the documents brought back by the explorers of the inaccessible lands," the unbeliever of good-will can, at least, confess with William James: "It is a question of whether mystic states may not be windows opening upon a new world . . . a world new and fascinating

---

* Ibid. 256.

† Artheme Fayard, 1927.

‡ Similar expressions are found in *Man the Unknown*, by the celebrated Dr. Carrel. Did he not dare to write in the days of Freud: "There are as many truths in Ruysbrock the Admirable as in Claude Bernard!"

beyond all the spectacular events of history."*

The life of the Blessed Anna-Maria is just that—a message from the invisible world, a contemporary answer to what we now (in this centenary of her death)† know better to be the one and only problem than her contemporaries in those disturbed times in which she lived.

In a novel of his George Duhamel has a scene wherein are two friends, Edouard Loisel and Salavin. Salavin is the eternal pilgrim in quest of the ideal friendship. Once more he is disappointed and makes his farewell to his friend. His friend not understanding, questions him:

'What do you miss?" Salavin lowers his eyes and answers:

"Things which you cannot give me."

"What are they?"

"Peace, joy, an immortal soul, God."

The "servitude", but also the greatness of the contemporary mind is this discontent which is "all the keener at this precise moment of ours, in that the ancient security of our civilisation seems to be threatened by every kind of barbaric excess".‡

But who shall give the answer to the Salavins of our time? Sacred orators? Yes, but there are so many groups claiming obedience and the search for truth is for many a misleading labour. And then argument leaves unexplored so many areas of the soul!

There remains the witness of the saints. They are good for the people and good for thinkers: for the people that have eyes to see, and for thinkers who can assert with better reason than others that "the mystics have gone much deeper down into things than our cleverest dramatists and novelists."

---

* Louis Bertrand, ibid.

† The book was written in expectation of 1937. Anna-Maria died in 1837.

‡ Louis Bertrand, ibid.

Consider the life of Blessed Anna-Maria. See a "bit of a" woman who, faced with the denials of triumphant Voltairianism, dared to utter these unheard of words: "Not only do I believe in God because of the Christian Revelation, but I believe in Him because I have seen Him. I have seen Him every day for half a century."

Others, of course, before her have dared to say, not indeed a thing so audacious, but, at any rate, one not very dissimilar, but she is nearer our time. Like Teresa "what astonishes us in her is not so much her bold and prodigious intuitions, but her level-headed wisdom, her submission to rule and distrust of herself." Like the noble Teresa born of Cepeda and Ahumada, Anna presents us with an extraordinarily human figure. But the daughter of Luigi Gianetti owes nothing to her forbears. The theory of environment and heredity (supposing there is anything in it) would to some extent explain Teresa. From her early years she was among her own folk in a school of nobility, magnanimity and sanctity, but there was nothing of all this in the daughter of Gianetti, the chemist, and the wife of Domenico, the porter: everything was set for her to be entirely ordinary. The masterpiece of the Invisible Artist appears only the more clearly for that.

Teresa had a literary and ascetic culture; she was a disciple of the mystical doctor, St. John of the Cross; Anna Taigi knew only what God taught her. He was her sole instructor, and she was the humble piece of parchment upon which the Invisible Hand wrote a prodigious poem of sacrificial charity. This poem was written in a century when, to use Taine's expression, there was re-born "crocodile religion" with "the cult of the guillotine", wherein the imperial armies in Germany, Italy and Spain played the Vandal a second time. "One cannot tell," wrote an officer who stood an aghast spectator of the sack of Cordova, "with which we are loaded the more, with spoil or with curses."* And it was at this juncture of history that God wrote the life of this woman who was dying of the inability to die for each single one of her brethren.

There is yet another message of the Beata to the twentieth century. God raised her up in that class of the ordinary people to which Jesus, Mary and Joseph belonged. Now, as J. Maritain† writes: "The capital event of the modern world is the achievement by the masses of a place in history, and the fact that they constitute a dominating factor everywhere by the part they play. Many are either scandalised or appalled by this. The result is that others feel a profound resentment because of the humiliation and offence to human dignity, for it is an offence to human dignity that so many Christians can ignore what reserves of true humanity, of kindness, and of heroism, embedded in daily work and in poverty, the artisan and peasant classes stand for in history."

The life of Anna-Maria Taigi is a divine answer to this aspect of the social problem. This life is woven into the designs of Providence. It is a commentary, not of a revolutionary kind, but all instinct with the divine charity, on the verse of Scripture:

Deposuit potentes de sede, et exaltavit humiles.

He hath put down the mighty from their seat and hath exalted the humble.

Rome, Feast of St. Louis of the French.
Easter, 1936.

---

* *Maurice de Fascher*, by F. de Fascher, Plon.
† *Letter on Independence.*

APPENDIX

Below is given in full the text of the prayer referred to in the text (p. 142), in the original French.

Prostrate at Thy most holy feet, great Queen of Heaven, I venerate Thee with the profoundest homage and confess Thee to be the Daughter of the Divine Father, the Mother of the Divine Word, the Spouse of the Holy Ghost. Thou art the treasurer and the almoner of Their Mercies. Thy most Pure Heart overflowing with gentle and tender love for Sinners is the reason why I call Thee Mother of Divine Pity. Wherefore, Mother most loving, I, in affliction and anguish, present myself before Thee with great confidence, and beg Thee to make me taste the truth of the love wherewith Thou lovest me, and to grant me the grace I ask of Thee, if it be conformable to the will of God, and the good of my soul. Ah! turn, I beg, Thy most pure eyes towards me and towards those in particular who have recommended themselves to my prayers. Behold the cruel warfare which the devil, the world and the flesh wage against our souls, and see how many of those souls perish. Remember, Mother Most Tender, that we are all Thy children, bought by the most precious Blood of Thine Only-Begotten Son. Deign with all importunity to ask the Most Holy Trinity to grant me the grace ever to have the upper hand of the demon, the world, and of all my perverse passions—that grace wherewith the just become more holy, sinners are converted, heresies destroyed, the heathen enlightened, the Jews changed in heart.

Request this grace, Mother Most Loving, by the

Infinite Goodness of God, by the merits of Thy
Most Holy Son, by the milk wherewith Thou didst
feed Him, by the good offices Thou didst render
Him, by the love with which Thou didst love Him,
by the tears which Thou didst shed, by the sorrow
Thou didst suffer in His most holy Passion. Obtain
for us the great boon that all the world may form
one only people and one Church to give glory,
honour and gratitude to the Most Holy Trinity, and
to Thee who art the Mediatrix. May this grace be
conceded to me by the Power of the Father, the
Wisdom of the Son, and the Virtue of the Holy
Ghost.

Here ends the prayer, as given by Cardinal
Salotti.

Edward Healy Thompson in his *Venerable Anna-
Maria Taigi* (Burns & Oates, 1873), gives the
following further words, but on what authority the
present writer cannot say:

"Mother, behold the extreme peril of Thy children;
      Mother, who canst do all things, have pity on
      us.
Virgin Most Powerful, pray for us. (Three Hail
      Mary's.)
Eternal Father, increase evermore in the hearts of
      the faithful devotion to Mary, Thy Daughter.
Eternal Son, increase evermore in the hearts of the
      faithful devotion to Mary, Thy Mother.
Eternal Spirit, increase evermore in the hearts of the
      faithful devotion to Mary, Thy Spouse.
Glory be to the Father . . ."

If you have enjoyed this book, consider making your next selection from among the following . . .

Prices guaranteed through December 31, 1992.

Prices guaranteed through December 31, 1992.

Prices guaranteed through December 31, 1992.

The Curé D'Ars. Abbé Francis Trochu..............18.50
Humility of Heart. Fr. Cajetan da Bergamo........... 6.00
Love, Peace and Joy. St. Gertrude/Prévot............. 5.00
Père Lamy. Biver....................................10.00
Passion of Jesus & Its Hidden Meaning. Groenings.....12.00
Mother of God & Her Glorious Feasts. Fr. O'Laverty... 9.00
Song of Songs—A Mystical Exposition. Fr. Arintero...18.00
Love and Service of God, Infinite Love. de la Touche...10.00
Life & Work of Mother Louise Marg. Claret de la Touche10.00
Martyrs of the Coliseum. O'Reilly...................15.00
Rhine Flows into the Tiber. Fr. Wiltgen.............12.00
What Catholics Believe. Fr. Lawrence Lovasik........ 4.00
Who Is Teresa Neumann? Fr. Charles Carty........... 1.25
Summa of the Christian Life. 3 Vols. Granada........36.00
St. Francis of Paola. Simi and Segreti.............. 6.00
The Rosary in Action. John Johnson................. 8.00
St. Dominic. Sr. Mary Jean Dorcy................... 8.00
Is It a Saint's Name? Fr. William Dunne............. 1.50
St. Martin de Porres. Giuliana Cavallini............10.00
Douay-Rheims New Testament. Paperbound...........12.00
St. Catherine of Siena. Alice Curtayne.............11.00
Blessed Virgin Mary. Liguori....................... 4.50
Chats with Converts. Fr. M. D. Forrest............. 8.00
The Stigmata and Modern Science. Fr. Charles Carty... 1.00
St. Gertrude the Great............................. 1.25
Thirty Favorite Novenas............................ .75
Brief Life of Christ. Fr. Rumble................... 1.50
Catechism of Mental Prayer. Msgr. Simler........... 1.50
On Freemasonry. Pope Leo XIII..................... 1.00
Thoughts of the Curé D'Ars. St. John Vianney........ 1.50
Incredible Creed of Jehovah Witnesses. Fr. Rumble...... 1.00
St. Pius V—His Life, Times, Miracles. Anderson....... 4.00
St. Dominic's Family. Sr. Mary Jean Dorcy...........20.00
St. Rose of Lima. Sr. Alphonsus....................12.00
Latin Grammar. Scanlon & Scanlon..................12.50
Second Latin. Scanlon & Scanlon...................11.00
St. Joseph of Copertino. Pastrovicchi.............. 4.50
Three Ways of the Spiritual Life. Garrigou-Lagrange.... 4.00
Mystical Evolution. 2 Vols. Fr. Arintero, O.P.,..........30.00
My God, I Love Thee. (100 cards)................... 5.00
St. Catherine Labouré of the Mirac. Medal. Fr. Dirvin..11.00
Manual of Practical Devotion to St. Joseph. Patrignani..12.50
Eucharistic Miracles. Joan Carroll Cruz.............13.00
The Active Catholic. Fr. Palau..................... 6.00

Prices guaranteed through December 31, 1992.

At your bookdealer or direct from the publisher.

Prices guaranteed through December 31, 1992.